Through Random Doors We Wandered

Women Writing the South

Through Random Doors
We Wandered
Women Writing the South

by

Clara Juncker

University Press of Southern Denmark

2002

© The author and University Press of Southern Denmark 2002
Printed by Narayana Press
ISBN 87-7838-711-6
Cover design by Klaus Bjerager, DesignCo
Cover Illustration: Polfoto
Published with support from:
Forskningsstyrelsen, Danish Research Agency

University Press of Southern Denmark
Campusvej 55
DK-5230 Odense M
Phone: +45 6615 7999
Fax: +45 6615 8126
E-mail: Press@forlag.sdu.dk
Internet: www.universitypress.dk

Distribution in the United States and Canada:
International Specialized Book Services
5804 NE Hassalo Street
Portland, OR 97213-3644, USA
Phone: +1-800-944-6190

Denne afhandling er den 18. december 2001
af Syddansk Universitets humanistiske fakultetsråd
antaget til forsvar for den filosofiske doktorgrad.

Flemming G. Andersen
dekan

Forsvaret finder sted fredag den 14. juni 2002
på Syddansk Universitet i Odense.

Through random doors we wandered
into passages disguised as paradise
and out again, discarding,
embracing hope anew, discarding again:
exits and entrances to many houses.

From *Exits and Entrances* (1978)
by Naomi Long Madgett

For Maria, Eva and Anna

Table of Contents

ACKNOWLEDGMENTS 9

INTRODUCTION 11-27

CHAPTER ONE
  Southen Sojourn:
  Frances Anne Kemble 28-51

CHAPTER TWO
  Confederate Bodies:
  The Journal of Ella Gertrude Clanton Thomas 52-67

CHAPTER THREE
  Negotiating Southern Territories:
  Kate Stone's *Brokenburn* 68-89

CHAPTER FOUR
  Writing Herstory:
  Mary Chesnut's Civil War 90-101

CHAPTER FIVE
  Behind Confederate Lines:
  Sarah Morgan Dawson 102-118

CHAPTER SIX
  "Over the Water":
  Frances Butler Leigh's
  Ten Years on a Georgia Plantation Since The War 120-136

CHAPTER SEVEN
  Battle of Brains:
  Andrew Sheffield, a Southern Madwoman 137-163

CHAPTER EIGHT
  Festival of the Dead:
  The Stories of Grace King 164-186

CHAPTER NINE
Pirates' Treasures:
Mamie Garvin Fields's Carolina Memoir 188-211

CHAPTER TEN
Woman(ist) as Artist:
Alice Walker's *The Temple of My Familiar* 212-226

CHAPTER ELEVEN
Bodies in Motion:
Maya Angelou's *Wouldn't Take Nothing for
My Journey Now* 228-247

CHAPTER TWELVE
Southern Dreams:
Ruth Moose's Fiction 248-260

CONCLUSION 261-266

BIBLIOGRAPHY.. 267-278

Acknowledgments

I am grateful to Lars Ole Sauerberg for his early belief in this project and for seeing it through, and to Jan Nordby Gretlund for helping it along and for his conscientious attention to details. Also thanks to the publishers at University Press of Southern Denmark, Thomas Kaarsted and Martin Westergaard, for their professionalism, and to the friends and colleagues who read sections of the manuscript: Inger Juncker, Russell Duncan, Justin Edwards, Anders Hougaard, Carl Pedersen, Anette Jacobsen, Torben Huus Larsen, Anette Nibe, Helle Porsdam, and Thomas E. Bjerre. I appreciate as well permissions from the publishers who have printed earlier versions of my work: A portion of the chapter on Fanny Kemble was previously published in *Rewriting the South: History and Fiction*, ed. Lothar Hönnighausen *et al.* (Tübingen: A. Francke Verlag, 1993); earlier versions of the chapters on Mary Chesnut and Sarah Morgan Dawson appeared in *Southern Studies: An Interdisciplinary Journal of the South* 26.1 (Spring 1987) and *The Southern Literary Quarterly* 30.1 (Fall 1991), respectively. Sections of the chapter on Grace King came out in different forms in *The Southern Literary Journal* 20.1 (Fall 1987) and 26.3 (Spring 1988), and the chapter on Alice Walker, in *American Studies in Scandinavia* 24.1 (1992). Much gratitude also to the people in my private life who helped me during the writing and publication process, not least my daughters Maria, Eva and Anna, who themselves arrived through random doors. This book is for them.

INTRODUCTION

The women who came to this volume entered it expectantly, randomly. Fanny Kemble rowed up to the dock and secured her boat without assistance. Gertrude Thomas found the pantry door, from where she discreetly eyed the desserts. Mary Chesnut rushed her carriage to the front entrance, just behind Kate Stone. Sarah Morgan calmly descended a mule wagon and greeted Frances Butler Leigh, Fanny Kemble's daughter, despite the ravings of Andrew Sheffield, on furlough from the former Alabama Insane Asylum. Grace King escaped to the balcony, where she joined Mamie Garvin Fields lecturing Alice Walker on flower arrangements. Maya Angelou hid in the back with a glass of sherry, while Ruth Moose called in everybody for a group photograph. As the hostess, I worried about Mary Chesnut leaving for lack of gentleman admirers, and about introducing and seating everybody properly.

The British-born actress Frances Anne Kemble would not have needed an introduction in her own time. In April 1834 the celebrated Fanny Kemble had bid the stage farewell and married one of her most ardent admirers, a member of the wealthy Butler family of Philadelphia, whose fortune derived in part from a profitable slave property on the Altamaha River. Two years later, Pierce Mease Butler assumed control of the family plantations, and the former Shakespeare actress found herself the wife of one of Georgia's largest slaveholders.[1] In the years that followed, Kemble passionately devoted herself to the subject of slavery. Prior to her journey to Georgia from Philadelphia with her husband, two baby daughters, and a nurse, Kemble had put down her antislavery convictions in

---

1. See Malcolm Bell, Jr., *Major Butler's Legacy: Five Generations of a Slaveholding Family* (Athens: U of Georgia P, 1987).

the journal segment "Thoughts on Slavery." Despite such preparations, Kemble's actual experience as a plantation mistress, recorded in *Journal of a Residence on a Georgian Plantation in 1838-39*, unsettled not just her marriage but also herself. When in 1863 she published the series of letters from Georgia on her encounter with the institution of slavery, she had for many years been divorced from her husband and without custody of her daughters. With the publication of the *Journal*, however, the "darling of the stage" became instead an abolitionist heroine on both sides of the Atlantic.[2]

"Southern women are I believe at heart abolisionists [sic]," wrote Ella Gertrude Clanton Thomas in her journal in 1859. Born in Augusta, Georgia, in 1834, the year of Kemble's marriage, Thomas recorded her development from privileged southern belle in the antebellum era to impoverished breadwinner during Reconstruction in the approximately 450,000 words that make up her original diary manuscript, edited by Virginia Ingraham Burr into *The Secret Eye: The Journal of Ella Gertrude Clanton Thomas, 1848-1889*. One of seven surviving children to Turner Clanton and his wife Mary, among the richest planter families in the state, Ella Gertrude belonged to the elite section of southern women who had access to higher education. She graduated from Wesleyan in 1851, married James Jefferson Thomas in 1852 and gave birth to ten children, seven surviving beyond the age of five. A drop-out medical student, Jefferson Thomas showed signs of financial incompetence early in the marriage and would, after a stint as a Confederate soldier, live to squander Gertrude Thomas's wealth and deteriorate physically and emotionally during early Reconstruction.

As Nell Irvin Painter writes in her introduction to *The Secret Eye*, "downward mobility sums up Gertrude Thomas's postwar experience."[3] The former southern lady became the family provider by writing, teaching and taking in boarders. She also joined a a number

---

2. See the introduction by Charles E. Wynes to Francis Butler Leigh, *Ten Years on a Georgia Plantation Since the War* (1883; Savannah: Beehive, 1992), p. vii.
3. Nell Irvin Painter, "Introduction," *The Secret Eye: The Journal of Ella Gertrude Clanton Thomas, 1848-1889*, ed. Virginia Ingraham Burr (Chapel Hill: U of North Carolina P, 1990), p. 12. I am indebted to Painter for the biographical details on Gertrude Thomas.

Introduction

of women's groups and served, for example, as Secretary and Vice President of the Augusta chapter of the WCTU. Financially destitute, she and Jefferson Thomas joined their son Julian, now a medical doctor, in Atlanta in 1893. In 1899, Gertrude Thomas was elected President of the Georgia Woman Suffrage Association and attended suffrage conventions across the continent. At the time of her death in 1907, she had, as Painter writes, "become a full-fledged feminist whose stature was recognized throughout her state and region."[4]

As a bright, educated woman living in the patriarchal South, the author of *Brokenburn: The Journal of Kate Stone, 1861-1868* walked like Gertrude Thomas the slippery lines between femininity and feminism. As the fifty-nine-year-old Kate Stone Holmes in 1900 was preparing the introduction to the Civil War journal she had written four decades earlier, her antebellum youth nonetheless takes on a fairly rosy hue:

> In looking over the yellowing pages and faded writing of my old diary written in the troubled years from 1861 to 1865, how the old life comes back, the gay, busy life of the plantation at Brokenburn with Mamma, a beautiful, brilliant woman of thirty-seven at the head of it all.[5]

Before "the troubled years" set in, the Stones' Brokenburn existence apparently inspired only happiness and satisfaction, at least in those inhabiting the Big House. Despite the early death of their

---

4. Painter, p. 19. Following established practices within feminist (literary) theory, I use in what follows the term "feminist" for persons, male or female, who seek to revise or overthrow inequalities in personal and social relations between men and women. Again following other scholars in the field, I use the terms "female" for biological difference and "feminine" for linguistic, social or other non-biological constructions of gender difference. "Gender," I might add, designates social constructions of biological difference. For terminology, central issues and various strategies within feminist theory, see, for ex., Robyn R. Warhol and Diane Price Herndl, ed., *Feminisms: An Anthology of Literary Theory and Criticism* (rev. ed. Houndmills, UK: Macmillan, 1997)
5. John Q. Anderson, ed. *Brokenburn: The Journal of Kate Stone, 1861-1868* (Baton Rouge: LSU P, 1955), p. 3.

father, the eight Stone children were growing up upon the capable Amanda Stone's handsome property of northeastern Louisiana land. Before enlisting in the Confederate army in 1861, Kate's twenty-year-old brother William R. Stone ran the 1200-acre plantation, while the nineteen-year-old Kate, a recent graduate of Dr. Elliott's Academy in Nashville, lived the leisurely life of a southern belle. This "easy and bright" existence ended abruptly also for Kate Stone as the war approached northeast Louisiana in 1862 and Federal gunboats materialized only a few miles up the Mississippi. On March 22, 1863, Federal soldiers entered Brokenburn; Kate and a sister were held at gun-point by an armed slave some days later, and the fleeing Stones lost all luggage in the swamp on their way to Monroe.

In the second part of *Brokenburn*, Kate lives with her reduced family in Lamar County and Tyler, Texas, where she meets Lt. Henry Bry Holmes, whom she would marry in December, 1869. Two of the four children she bore lived to adulthood. Though the question Kate Stone poses at the end of her journal – "shall I ever care to write again?" – must be answered in the negative, she participated for decades in community life in Tallulah, where both her children resided. She founded the Madison Infantry Chapter of the United Daughters of the Confederacy, co-organized the Madison Parish Book Club and helped set up a Confederate memorial on the courthouse square in Tallulah, where she died on December 28, 1907, a Confederate lady to the end.

Included with Kate Stone in Edmund Wilson's chapter "Three Confederate Ladies" in *Patriotic Gore: Studies in the Literature of the American Civil War* (1962), Mary Boykin Chesnut has finally received the attention she so craved. C. Vann Woodward's voluminous *Mary Chesnut's Civil War* (1981) and Elizabeth Muhlenfeld's *Mary Chesnut: A Biography* (1981) depict a vivacious, frustrated and intelligent southern lady, who met and manouevred most Confederate luminaries as the wife of planter politician James Chesnut, Jr. On November 10, 1860, Chesnut, Jr. gave up his seat in the U.S. Senate to return to his native South Carolina, help draft the secession ordinance and attend the first Confederate Congress in Montgomery.[6]

---

6. See C. Vann Woodward's biography of Mary Chesnut in his introduction to *Mary Chesnut's Civil War* (New Haven: Yale UP, 1981), p. xxxviii.

Introduction

For Mary Chesnut, the war meant an escape from the boredom she experienced at Mulberry, the family plantation in Camden, and, in Vann Woodward's words, "fulfillment for some of the yearnings that life with her cool and aristocratic husband had somehow denied her."[7] In the opening pages of her diary, Mary Chesnut lies awake in a hotel in Charleston listening to Colonel Barton, Mayor of Savannah, entertaining his male companions, as well as the guest upstairs, with fire-eating southern eloquence. "The events [are] crowding in so that it takes one's breath away to think about it all," she wrote excitedly in February, 1861. Mary Chesnut recorded gay times in Richmond that year at the Spotswood and Arlington hotels, the headquarters for private and political intrigues, or in Columbia, across the street from Varina and Jefferson Davis from November 1862. Some eight hundred pages after she began her journal, Chesnut returned with other survivors through desolate landscapes to Camden, "hopeless" and "penniless." In her last entry, dated July 26, 1865, she notes: "I do not write often now – not for want of something to say, but from a loathing of all I see and hear. Why dwell upon it?"[8]

Nonetheless, Mary Chesnut began in 1873, at the age of fifty, a writing career in the library at Sarsfield, the Chesnuts' new house in Camden, despite reduced circumstances, a series of family deaths, a growing influx of dependents, and her own depressions and health problems. She put together drafts of three novels and started various projects, including a biography of her husband. She never finished the daunting task of editing her diaries for publication, and, after her husband's and mother's deaths in 1885, she lost everything but her humor. "Earthquakes for all & Angina Pectoris for me," she wrote in 1886, the year of a major Columbia quake and her own death from a heart attack.[9]

Edmund Wilson's third Confederate lady, Sarah Morgan of Baton Rouge, Louisiana, recorded like Kate Stone the war from a

---

7. Vann Woodward, "Introduction," p. xxxviii.
8. Vann Woodward, *Mary Chesnut's Civil War*, p. 834.
9. My account here is indebted to Vann Woodward's introduction and to Elizabeth Muhlenfeld's biography.

younger woman's perspective. Almost twenty when she began her diary in early 1862, Sarah Morgan had the previous year lost both her brother Harry in a New Orleans duel and her prominent father, Thomas Gibbes Morgan, who before his death in the Morgan home on Church Street had served as district judge and district attorney in Baton Rouge.[10] Three other brothers had joined the Confederate army, while Sarah Morgan remained at home with her mother and her sister Miriam and saw Union forces take control of their city. When Confederates in the summer of 1862 attacked Baton Rouge, the Morgan women fled and eventually, in 1863, reached New Orleans after reluctantly taking the required Oath of Allegiance. On June 15, 1865, the last entry in her diary, Sarah Morgan reports on the pistol shot fired at Lincoln that brings down the Confederacy, if not the young diarist's determination and pride: "I only pray never to be otherwise than what I am at this instant – a Rebel in heart and soul, and that all my life I may remember the cruel wrongs we have suffered."[11]

Prior to marrying the Charleston editor of the *News and Courier,* Frank Dawson, in 1874, Sarah Morgan contributed to the paper a series of pieces on women's issues that leads Charles East, the editor of *Sarah Morgan's Civil War Diary,* to conclude that "despite her strongly voiced antipathy to the women's righters and their cries for the right to vote," Sarah Morgan was "one of the nineteenth-century feminists."[12] When her husband was shot to death in March of 1889 and his murderer acquitted, Sarah had to raise their two children alone. She eventually became the somber figure Grace King encountered on a North Carolina mountaintop, walking with her son Warrington Dawson: "She knew no one, no one spoke to her; the men raised their hats, she bowed graciously and passed on, pale, silent.... She had been sent to the mountains in search of health and did not seem to care if she lost or found it." Grace King later visited her new acquaintance in France, where she had joined

---

10. See "Introduction," in *The Civil War Diary of Sarah Morgan,* ed. Charles East (Athens: U of Georgia P, 1991), p. xvi.
11. East, p. 611.
12. East, "Introduction," p. xxxvii.

Introduction

her son in 1899, possibly, as King felt, "to leave a country that had become loathsome to her."[13] Sarah Morgan Dawson died in Paris in May 1909, four years before the first edition of her journal was published as *A Confederate Girl's Diary*, with an introduction by Warrington Dawson.

Despite her famous mother, Frances Butler Leigh lived and died in relative obscurity. She was Fanny Kemble's "other daughter," the youngest of the two little girls Kemble reluctantly left with their father, Pierce Butler, in 1845. The impulsive marriage between the charming, hardheaded Shakespearean actress and the spoiled slaveowner ended in divorce in 1849, with custody of Sarah and Frances granted to their father. Sarah grew up to share her mother's northern sympathies and to give birth to Owen Wister, author of *The Virginian* (1902) and *Lady Baltimore* (1906), while Frances became a staunch Confederate, surely her father's child. An infant when her parents spent the winter of 1838-39 on the Georgia plantation her mother described, Frances returned with Pierce Butler to St. Simon's and Butler Islands, off the Georgia coast, in 1866, to assist her father in reclaiming the family plantations and to manage the former Butler slaves. After the war, a majority of the slave population had returned to the islands, though Pierce Butler had auctioned off 436 men, women and children in March, 1859, to pay off his gambling debts.

A devoted daughter, Frances chronicles the first year in Georgia with her father, his death from malaria in 1867, and the subsequent seasons she herself reigned as island queen in *Ten Years on a Georgia Plantation Since the War* (1883). Much to her mother's dismay, Frances struggled for a decade to make profitable the Butler family holdings, first alone, later assisted by her British-born husband, Rev. James Wentworth Leigh, who turned out to be a talented rice planter, his background notwithstanding. Leigh's desire to return to a "future appropriate to a well-born and widely liked Church of England clergyman"[14] prompted his wife to relocate, though, she

---

13. East, "Introduction," p. xl.
14. J. C. Furnas, *Fanny Kemble: Leading Lady of the Nineteenth-Century Stage*. New York: Dial, 1982.

told Henry James in England, she nursed a life-long homesickness for the Georgia islands.

Unlike Mrs. Leigh and the three Confederate ladies Edmund Wilson discusses, Andrew Moore Sheffield was at best a delinquent one. As John S. Hughes notes in his introduction to the roughly ninety letters collected in *The Letters of a Victorian Madwoman* (1993), she "was a woman apart from her peers. Having borne a man's name for all her forty-one years, she never married, never managed to conform to standards of ladylike behavior, and never succeeded in pleasing the men of her prominent family."[15] In July 1890, her male relatives decided that her presumed insanity required her prompt commitment to the Alabama Insane Hospital, after 1892 renamed Bryce Hospital.

At the time of her admission to the asylum, the eccentric Andrew Sheffield sat jailed for arson in Guntersville, Alabama. Addicted to chloral hydrate, she had begun a stormy, presumably abusive, affair with the doctor who supplied the drug and had attempted to burn down the house of a neighbor with whom the doctor quarrelled. Conveniently escaping the stigma of Sheffield's trial and conviction, her nephew and the Marshall County sheriff traveled by train with her to Tuscaloosa and committed her to the hospital she would never again leave. In 1920, patient # 3910 died as a ward of the state of Alabama and was buried on Bryce Hospital grounds. If nothing else, she managed to outlive the men who committed her, as well as her main correspondent, Dr. James T. Searcy, Superintendent at Bryce 1892-1919, and several of the Alabama governors she wrote to intervene on her behalf. But Sheffield's letters had no effect, except for personal therapy. She sums up her problem with male authority figures in a letter dated shortly before Searcy's retirement: "I can't and never could eat *humble* pie – and more, if I could eat it, I could not digest it."[16]

While Andrew Moore Sheffield lived and died with a masculine name and an aggressive personality, Grace Elizabeth King became

---

15. John S. Hughes, *The Letters of a Victorian Madwoman* (Columbia: South Carolina P, 1993), p. 1.
16. Hughes, *Letters*, p. 234.

Introduction

a genteel writer in a feminine environment. King notes in an introduction about her native New Orleans that "[her] difference from other cities is one of her charms." She continues: "Her people, in imagination, love to picture her in the handsome old age of a grande dame of the old regime; sitting in her high back antique chair, dressed in flowing black satin, garnished at neck and wrist with real lace...."[17] King's description suggests as well her own personality and literary production. As the Grande Dame of Louisiana letters, she wrote, with appropriately feminine frills, about her exotic birthplace and its Creole population, both in historical works and in fiction.

Born in 1852 into a New Orleans family scrambling to uphold its antebellum gentility during Reconstruction, King became a writer as late as in 1885, when the Cotton Centennial Exposition brought distinguished outsiders to her city. Julia Ward Howe inspired a notion of an active, even activist life outside the domestic sphere, and Richard Watson Gilder challenged King to correct the depiction of New Orleans by George Washington Cable. Literary critics have thus traditionally seen King as a minor local colorist, whose stories of New Orleans Creoles sought to defend her native city from Cable's criticism of its racial arrangements. Robert Bush, Anne Goodwyn Jones and Helen Taylor have nonetheless positioned her work in wider contexts. "Her career," writes Bush in 1977, "was an announcement that women of the South could successfully compete with men in the intellectual world."[18] Even King's obscurity became her strength. "I have often thought how stupid and commonplace to write novels about what happens to people; what does not happen to them is far more interesting and exciting," she writes in "Destiny" (1898) about women much like herself.[19]

Mamie Garvin Fields was as attached to Charleston as Grace King to New Orleans. Born in 1888, and respected in South Carolina for a life devoted to religious and civic activism, she was named the

---

17. S. Charwood Burton, *Pen Sketches of New Orleans*. N.p.: N.p., n.d.
18. Robert Bush, "Grace King: The Emergence of a Southern Intellectual Woman." *The Southern Review* 13 (Spring 1977), p. 272.
19. Grace King, "Destiny." *Harper's* 90 (March 1898), pp. [541]-48.

state's Senior Citizen of the Year in 1971. Her autobiography *Lemon Swamp and Other Places: A Carolina Memoir* (1983), which she narrates to her granddaughter, depicts African American life in Charleston over many decades, until Mamie Fields becomes State President of the Federation of Colored Women's Clubs in 1948. She presents the Jim Crow South of her childhood and youth, her college days at Claflin, her one-room school in "A Place Behind God's Back," her beauty parlor devoted to the Poro System, and her wide-ranging community work. She recalls her great-uncle J. B. Middleton, a prominent minister, and Mary McLeod Bethune, who influenced Fields's career and life significantly. In a central chapter, "Lemon Swamp," she recollects her grandfather's farm or "plantation," where the Garvins of African descent lived in what used to be their master's house and cultivated what used to be his fields. With its lush vegetation and wild alligators, Lemon Swamp brings back, like the autobiography itself, "another world."[20]

While Mamie Garvin Fields gave up her dreams of becoming a missionary in Africa and instead became a schoolteacher in other culturally remote locations, Alice Walker explores in her travels as well as in her fiction and prose the continent of Africa and "other" worlds. She began life in Georgia, where she was initiated into a southern and African American "womanist" tradition of creativity, described in her collection of essays *In Search of Our Mothers' Gardens* (1983). Often set in the South, her poetry and short fiction zoom in on her primary focus, the lives of African American and African women, central to her most famous novel, *The Color Purple* (1982), which won the Pulitzer Prize. Residing now in San Francisco, Walker has in subsequent works – *The Temple of My Familiar* (1989) among them – expanded her Pan-African vision to include a multitude of centuries, continents and racial categories, and, in the process, relinquished traditional notions of author-biography and author-ity to the characters she joins. Not lending itself to linear plot summary, *The Temple* whirls from South America to Victorian England, contemporary San Francisco, pre-historic Africa and back,

---

20. Mamie Garvin Fields, with Karen Fields, *Lemon Swamp and Other Places: A Carolina Memoir* (New York: Free Press, 1983), p. 68.

through the multiple voices and themes that make up what Walker labels "a romance of the last 500,000 years."[21]

Maya Angelou too is everywhere: on a video commemorating James Baldwin, in Nathan McCall's autobiography, at Bill Clinton's inauguration, on the latest Oprah Winfrey show. Her work as a professor, a performer and a poet aside, she has recorded her innumerable activities and careers in autobiographical works from the 1970 classic *I Know Why the Caged Bird Sings* through sequels such as *Gather Together in My Name* (1974) and *The Heart of a Woman* (1981). In contrast to the linear progression of these more traditional autobiographies, *Wouldn't Take Nothing for My Journey Now* (1993) collects "some lessons in living ... learned over many years," as Angelou puts it in her acknowledgements. The slim volume offers her thoughts on everything: taking time for oneself, death and survival, sherry and style, being a woman, which, in Angelou's view, is "hard work. Not without joy and even ecstasy, but still relentless, unending work."[22]

Ruth Moose, a native of North Carolina, would probably agree. As the blurb to her first collection of stories, *The Wreath Ribbon Quilt* (1987), reads, "Ruth Moose's stories are about how it is to be a woman – how hard and how joyful. Her literary territory is domestic, where are housed the most familiar and ordinary of details." Also in *Dreaming in Color* (1989) Moose has explored southern women's lives from Avon ladies to housewife artists to shotgun brides, often through feminist and autobiographical filters. Her writings include as well two collections of poetry and a novel in manuscript, "Going to Graceland." Moose has received a PEN award for Short Story and grants from the North Carolina Arts Council and the National Endowment for the Humanities. She teaches Creative Writing at the University of North Carolina and displays in her work a life-long habit of listening to and recording southern women's conversations. Her own life experiences

---

21. See the back cover of the paperback edition of *The Temple of My Familiar* (New York: Pocket, 1990).
22. Maya Angelou, *Wouldn't Take Nothing for My Journey Now* (1993; New York: Bantam, 1994), p. 6.

merge with those of her women characters also in other settings, for example in "Even the Bees in Denmark," a story in *Dreaming in Color* written after Moose and her artist husband visited Copenhagen and Odense in the 1980s.

All the women assembled here have written about the South. Following the principle of inclusion in *The Literature of the American South* (1998), I might label them southern women writers. The "signature" of southern writing involves, as we know, the past in the present, the emphasis on place, the tragic vision, the fascination with the peculiar or the grotesque, and more.[23] The women writers in this volume recognize that the South is a good story, but wish to complicate the master narratives by the female, even feminist tradition they collectively represent. They aim to uncover the story of southern femininity from a positional alterity.

From Kemble to Moose, the women writers came by this volume to open up and investigate genderic and social margins and new representational spaces. In "Calliope and Clio: The Style and Substance of Recent Historical Writing on the South" (1996) Joseph Reidy argues that historians (and writers and literary critics) of the nineteenth- and twentieth-century South face a recurring list of binary oppositions, which simplify a complex reality: "victors and vanquished, villains and victims, rich folk and poor folk, men and women, whites and blacks."[24] The women here question these binaries, make them shimmer – even disappear. Little accustomed and therefore little inclined to "'construct meaning' on a grand scale," Germaine Brée argues, women are better positioned "to see beyond the constraints of our conceptional representations, beyond our dichotomies and abstractions ... and to look to 'the multiplicity of the real.'"[25]

What constitutes "the real," or the real South, remains nonetheless problematic. The post-Reconstruction economy marked the

---

23. William L. Andrews *et al.*, ed. *The Literature of the American South* (New York: W. W. Norton, 1998), pp. xvii.
24. Joseph P. Reidy, "Calliope and Clio: The Style and Substance of Recent Historical Writing on the South," *The Southern Review* 32.2 (April 1996), p. 388.
25. Germaine Brée, "Autogynography," *Southern Review* 22 (Spring 1986), p. 227.

Introduction

region, as W. J. Cash notes in *The Mind of the South* (1941), as "not quite a nation within a nation, but the next thing to it."[26] Other historians have located a regional distinctiveness in southern race relations, or, linking white supremacy and white male supremacy, in southern gender relations.[27] In the 1960s and 70s the debate focused on the "Americanization of Dixie" and the Snowbelt/Sunbelt dichotomy. More recently, regional changes, which Numan Bartley maps in *The New South, 1945-1980* (1995), have triggered, in his phrase, "a reverse tendency to extol southern culture and to regret the Yankee invasion."[28] Indeed, Peter Applebome argues in *Dixie Rising: How the South Is Shaping American Values, Politics, and Culture* (1996) that the South is everywhere (though everywhere, as we know, is not the South). Perhaps, as David Smiley suggests, the central theme of southern historiography is the quest for a central theme.[29]

The search for the South originates, perhaps, in a crisis in nationalism, which, in Roberto Maria Dainetto's view, propels criticism to "a different social space from the nation."[30] In fact, Sarah Morgan might whisper to Maya Angelou about a "'spatialization'

---

26. W. J. Cash, *The Mind of the South*, qtd. in Bartley, "Social Change," p. 7.
27. See, for example, Mechal Sobel, *The World They Made Together: Black and White Values in Eighteenth-Century Virginia* (Princeton: Princeton U P, 1987); Julia Kirk Blackwelder, "Ladies, Belles, Working Women, and Civil Rights," in Paul D. Escott and David R. Goldfield, ed., *The New South for Southerners* (Chapel Hill: U of North Carolina P, 1991), esp. pp. 98 and 105, and Stephanie McCurry, "The Two Faces of Republicanism: Gender and Proslavery Politics in Antebellum South Carolina," *The Journal of American History* 79 (March 1992), esp. pp. 1246, 1254-57. I am indebted to Numan Bartley's "Social Change and Sectional Identity," *The Journal of Southern History* 61.1 (February 1995), pp. [3]-16 for several references in this paragraph.
28. Numan V. Bartley, *The New South, 1945-1980* (Baton Rouge: LSU P, 1995). I am quoting Bartley, "Social Change," p. 16.
29. Peter Applebome, *Dixie Rising: How the South Is Shaping American Values, Politics, and Culture.* New York: Random House, 1996; David Smiley, "The Quest for the Central Theme in Southern History," *South Atlantic Quarterly* 71 (Summer 1972), pp. 307-25.
30. Roberto Maria Dainotto, "'All the Regions Do Smilingly Revolt': The Literature of Place and Region," *Critical Inquiry* 22 (Spring 1996), p. 487.

of marginality," a space untouched by the "totalizing unity of nationalism," where the difference and identities these women represent would thrive. The South, then, becomes an imagined community, "a spatial region of restoration and rehabilitation," where the past, as Faulkner knew, is no longer the past. Region, in short, represents "spatialization of time." As Dainetto explains, "what separates us from our past is, at most, a geographical distance. Nothing is lost in time."[31] Perhaps we should ask with Baudrillard, "Will the real American South please stand up?"

Fanny Kemble reluctantly stood on the antebellum stage to play the southern lady, but the Civil War intensified the drama of southern gender arrangements. In *Civil Wars* (1991), George C. Rable discusses women's "often deeply ambivalent roles as social actors" during wartimes.[32] His emphasis on ambivalence revises the oversimplified accounts of southern life that Joseph Reidy mentions. The editors of *Civil War Women* (1988) stress, moreover, "the celebration of *activeness*" in stories about the war by Louisa May Alcott, Kate Chopin, Grace King, and others.[33] War, Margaret Randolph Higonnet argues, is the ultimate "*gendering* activity, one that ritually marks the gender of all members of society, whether or not they are combatants."[34] LeeAnn Whites identifies in "The Civil War as a Crisis in Gender" the "gendered face" of the conflict, which triggered an increased reciprocity in gender relations and brought increased intellectual freedom for (white) women.[35] It transformed

---

31. Dainotto, pp. 487, 497. Michael Kreyling discusses the South as simulacrum in *Inventing Southern Literature* (Jackson: UP of Mississippi, 1998). Patricia Yaeger problematizes inclusion criteria for southern literature in *Dirt and Desire: Reconstructing Southern Women's Writing, 1930-1990* (Chicago: U of Chicago P, 2000).
32. George C. Rable, *Civil Wars: Women and the Crisis of Southern Nationalism* (Urbana: U of Illinois P, 1991), p. x.
33. Frank McSherry, Jr., Charles G. Waugh and Martin Greenberg, *Civil War Women* (New York: Touchstone, 1990), p. 8.
34. Margaret Randolph Higonnet, *et al.*, ed. *Behind the Wars: Gender and the Two World Wars* (New Haven: Yale U P, 1987), p. 4.
35. LeeAnn Whites, "The Civil War as a Crisis in Gender," in *Divided Houses: Gender and the Civil War*, ed. Catherine Clinton and Nina Silber (New York: Oxford U P, 1992), pp. 3-21.

ladies otherwise ineligible for or indisposed towards writing into eye-witnesses of historical changes that disrupted their lives and prompted their journals. It also cleared the way for the African American women's writings that followed.

Their inherent appeal aside, the self-narratives of this volume have appeared at a time when formal autobiography, journals, letters and autobiographical fiction occupy a central position in the critical debate on the status of the subject, the nature of self-representation and, in Sidonie Smith's phrase, "the textualization of the signature."[36] As traditional notions of selfhood disperse, at least among literary and cultural critics, the "mimetic hypothesis" at the core of autobiographical (critical) discourse is abandoned.[37] William C. Spengemann notes that "the connections between autobiography and what it appears to describe have become increasingly problematical, and the difference between autobiography and other written forms correspondingly indistinct, until there no longer seems to be anything that either is or is not autobiography."[38] Alice Walker thus inserts herself into the life stories of her characters, just as her characters narrate their individual experiences over decades or centuries to one another. Poststructuralist dismantlings of selfhood, author/ity, and extra-textual truth and meaning push the formerly marginal genres of self-narration into the center of literary production and critical inquiry. The attention to women's autobiography, new access to southern women's texts through (re)publications and the Internet, and scholarship on gender in southern literature notwithstanding, the women in this volume have received little or no attention from literary scholars. Some of them, like Kate Stone and Andrew Sheffield, remain downright obscure, while writers such as Alice Walker and Maya Angelou are

---

36. Sidonie Smith, "Self, Subject, and Resistance: Marginalities and Twentieth-Century Autobiographical Practice," *Tulsa Studies in Women's Literature* 9 (Spring 1990), p. 7.
37. See Earl Miner, "Literary Diaries and the Boundaries of Literature," *Yearbook of Comparative and General Literature* 21 (1972), p. 48.
38. William C. Spengemann, *The Forms of Autobiography: Episodes in the History of a Literary Genre* (New Haven: Yale U P, 1980), p. 188.

celebrated for works other than those discussed here, and infrequently in southern contexts.

Long off-center in relation to literary establishments, the South engendered writings within "intimate" genres not immediately linked to publication processes. Eudora Welty locates the region's predilection for autobiography (or autobiographical fiction) in southerners' desire to "place everybody"; she also points to stable, tightly knit kinship and community structures. Asked in 1988 "what else in southerners might encourage them to write about themselves," Welty answers: "It's entertaining when it's done well. It helps you get a narrative sense of community when there are so many stories through the generations – something that connects people together."[39] Her words hold true, literally, for Mamie Garvin Fields, and for the connections across generational and racial boundaries this volume highlights.

Though all the writers included here seem drawn to the genre of self-narration, to find a language for the story of southern femininity remains their communal project. As Joseph Reidy concludes about southern historiography, "those who resist the simple oppositions have difficulty, of course, in formulating a vocabulary, much less a program, to address the multiple and interconnected layers of reality."[40] The Civil War tragedies certainly resulted in loss of language in the wake of loss of life. Drew Gilpin Faust observes that "appeals to the incapacities of language were commonplace; battlefield slaughter was impossible to describe, much less to understand."[41] Moreover, Confederate gender ideology left women, in Julia Le Grand's phrase, with "no language, but a cry," with subversion as the means of self-articulation.[42] Nonetheless, throughout

---

39. Sally Wolff, "Some Talk About Autobiography: An Interview with Eudora Welty," *Southern Reader* 2 (Summer 1990), p. 58.
40. Reidy, p. 389.
41. Drew Gilpin Faust, "'A Riddle of Death': Mortality and Meaning in the American Civil War," 34th Annual Fortenbaugh Memorial Lecture, Gettysburg College, 1995, p. 18.
42. Qtd. in Drew Gilpin Faust, "Altars of Sacrifice: Confederate Women and the Narratives of War," *The Journal of American History* 76 (March 1990), p. 1228.

Introduction

the nineteenth and twentieth centuries, (southern) women writers have continuously searched for a language outside the systems of gender and race that threaten to erase their signatures. If, as Daphne Athas argues in "Why There Are No Southern Writers," southernness is primarily "detectable in style," southern women writers have inscribed their femininity primarily rhetorically and stylistically, in modes of representation waiting to be explored.[43] The wandering voices of Maya Angelou's prose, or Ruth Moose's, suggest that writing women enter into language, and into literature, through random doors.

---

43. Daphne Athas, "Why There Are No Southern Writers," in *Women Writers of the Contemporary South*, ed. Peggy Prenshaw (Jackson: U P of Mississippi, 1984), p. 306.

Frances Anne Kemble

CHAPTER ONE

Southern Sojourn: Frances Anne Kemble

Frances Anne Kemble's *Journal of a Residence on a Georgian Plantation in 1838-39* recounts in epistolary form the experiences of a young British actress, who during a tour of America in 1832-34 met and married Pierce Mease Butler of Philadelphia, the heir to a plantation in Georgia with upwards of six hundred slaves. Kemble's account of a segment of her married life, which would end in separation, divorce in 1849, and custody of the couple's two daughters awarded to their father, has traditionally been read as a record of antebellum southern life, of the clash of two traditions, and of a Christian temperament's recoiling from the institution of slavery.[1] While *Journal of a Residence* is all of this, and more, it constitutes, above all, an example of feminine historiography and autobiography. The result of numerous revisions of rough notes and letters, Kemble's published work illuminates the ways in which the recorder's position as woman inflects the textual and interpretative strategies of what Elizabeth Bruss labels the autobiographical act.[2] Kemble's *Journal* reveals a recorder struggling to imagine an identity in the isolation of her exotic surroundings and in the context of what Sidonie Smith in *The Poetics of Women's*

---

1. John A. Scott, "Introduction," in Frances Anne Kemble, *Journal of a Residence on a Georgian Plantation in 1838-39* (1863), ed. John A. Scott (Athens: U of Georgia P, 1984), pp. [ix]-lxi. Page references to Kemble's journal entries will appear parenthetically in the text.
2. Elizabeth W. Bruss, *Autobiographical Acts: The Changing Situation of a Literary Genre* (Baltimore: Johns Hopkins U P, 1976).

Autobiography calls "communal figures of selfhood."[3] Such intertexts shaping Kemble's self-narrative include most importantly the myth of the southern lady. Kemble searched through conventional southern fictions for postures and positions from which to speak and write (against). The result is a resisting southern lady existing simultaneously within and without the cultural discourses of her day.

Fanny Kemble's *Journal* undoubtedly helped its British-born author navigate the alien and exotic South of the antebellum planter class, and its slaves, in enabling her to understand and control her experience through writing. At the same time, however, the *Journal* allowed the Shakespearean actress turned plantation mistress to shape and assert a new identity out of the crisis brought about by unfamiliar roles and surroundings that threatened to marginalize and silence her effectively. Kemble's *Journal* additionally sought to legitimize the inner reality of imagination and creativity, in her case sharply clashing with the reality of the slaveholding society around her. In short, Kemble's textual exploration of the antebellum South demonstrates the ways in which she negotiates the discursive authority to read and write (about) southern history.

The discontinuity and competing foci of women's autobiography, and, perhaps, of autobiographical practice in general,[4] manifests itself in Kemble's work in sudden shifts of attention, as when the author turns from the dismal stories of her many slave visitors to the bayou surrounding them all, and back. Kemble further breaks up her *Journal* into the Butler Island section, lasting from December 1838 to mid-February 1839, and the St. Simon's Island section covering the last part of February through April 19, 1839. To name just a few of her techniques and genres, Kemble courts narrative disjunction by mixing travel accounts, character sketches, essay fragments, dialogue, and self-commentary. She conciously exploits the accepted and/or expected explosion of

---

3. Sidonie Smith, *A Poetics of Women's Autobiography: Marginality and the Fictions of Self-Representation* (Bloomington: Indiana U P, 1987), p. 45.
4. Estelle J. Jelinek, *The Tradition of Woman's Autobiography: From Antiquity to the Present* (Boston: Twayne, 1986), p. 48; Bruss, p. 164; Sidonie Smith, *Poetics*, p. 17.

narrative linearity for her own purposes of argumentation by including, for example, lists of slaves, their medical history and complaints: "*Fanny* has had six children; all dead but one. She came to beg to have her work in the field lightened. *Nanny* has had three children; two of them are dead..." (229). Through mere enumeration and repetition, she creates a catalogue of atrocities more persuasive than her own bitterest tears or words.[5]

Still another source of narrative disruption comes from within. The effaced voice of Kemble's marital dissatisfaction betrays in structural shifts and silences, as well as in metaphorical and dramatic choices, an alternative, more private story. While this partially suppressed tale of marital grief and disappointment is entwined with the plot of slavery and the Christian conscience, it subverts and occasionally overflows the story Kemble intended to tell. Apparently, this story of betrayal and disenchantment was one she could not write and possibly would not read. It was Pierce Butler who initiated the couple's divorce proceedings; throughout the 1840s Kemble strove to keep her home and marriage intact.[6]

In moments of great intensity, Kemble further ruptures conventions of unity and linearity and writes confusion and emotionality into her syntax. She mentions, for example, "a long and painful conversation with mr. [Butler] upon the subject of the flogging which had been inflicted on the wretched Teresa." The sentences that follow establish in form (through parallelism) and content the agony and distress that the relationship of slaves, mistress, and master occasion. Immediately after this contemplation of especially Mr. Butler's share in "this horrible system," Kemble's language affords a view of the author's indignation and passion:

> But after all, what can he [Mr. Butler] do? how can he help it all? Moreover, born and bred in America, how should he care or wish to help it? and, of course, he does not; and I am

---

5. Cp. Catherine Clinton, *The Plantation Mistress: Woman's World in the Old South* (New York: Pantheon, 1982), p. 224.
6. John A. Scott, "Introduction," p. xlv.

in despair that he does not: *et voilà*, it is a happy and hopeful plight for us both. (159)[7]

With the short, ruptured sentences frequently ending in question marks, the contrasts and contradictions, the mixture of languages, and the shift from sincerity to irony, Kemble expresses grammatically her disappointment in finding herself a woman whose intervention on behalf of her slaves seems "worse than useless" (159).

Nonetheless, like Simone de Beauvoir who emphasizes the truth value of her memoirs and compares autobiography to a policeman's report, and the majority of nineteenth-century female autobiographers, Kemble insists upon "the carefulness of [her] observation, and the accuracy of [her] report" (11).[8] This thrust for honesty and credibility inspires Kemble's choice of form, of the dailiness and immersion characteristic of the diary,[9] which could offer, in Kemble's phrase, "minuteness of detail, and fidelity in the account of my daily doings" (53). Yet Kemble chose to record her life and observations in Georgia not in a traditional journal but in thirty-one undated letters addressed to "Dear Elizabeth" and never mailed. Mrs. Elizabeth Dwight Sedgwick of Lenox, Massachussetts, was a close friend of Kemble's, a member of a prominent group of New Englanders counting Dr. William Ellery Channing and Catharina Maria Sedgwick, and a reputed educator

---

7. Fanny Kemble's description of Mr. Butler evokes Daniel R. Hundley's portrayal of the Southern Gentleman in *Social Relations in Our Southern States* (1860), ed. William J. Cooper, Jr. (Baton Rouge: LSU P, 1979), p. 63: "[T]he Southern gentleman has never been, and is not now, influenced by the popular and world-wide denunciation of the 'peculiar institution.' For he is a man every inch, bold, self-reliant, conscientious; knowing his own convictions of duty, and daring to heed them."
8. Deidre Bair, "'My life… This Curious Object': Simone de Beauvoir on Autobiography," in *The Female Autograph*, ed. Domna Stanton (New York: New York Literary Forum, 1984), pp. 241, 242; Jelinek, *Tradition*, p. 78.
9. Suzanne Juhasz, "Towards a Theory of Form in Feminist Autobiography: Kate Millet's *Flying* and *Sita*; Maxine Hong Kingston's *The Woman Warrior*," in *Women's Autobiography: Essays in Criticism*, ed. Estelle J. Jelinek (Bloomington: Indiana U P, 1980), p. 224.

from her founding of an elementary school in 1828 till her death in 1864. If these letters were not, as John A. Scott notes, "literally written *to* Elizabeth, they were written *for* her."[10] But while Kemble perhaps intended to hold up a steady mirror of the real, her letters offer a glimpse into, if not an actual surrender to, flux.[11]

Kemble's epistolary form and her "passionate outpourings" to Elizabeth originated, no doubt, in the complex female world of intimacy and gender-segregation characteristic of nineteenth-century women.[12] Kemble's need to reveal to a trusted friend her thoughts and experiences presumably intensified with her isolation on Butler and St. Simon's Islands, and with her injection into a planter economy in which every woman was, indeed, an island.[13] The letter form moreover allowed Kemble to negotiate "the sin of writing."[14] By employing a feminine genre with the potential for disguised essay-writing, this temporarily southernized lady could practice self-expression without "unsexing" herself.[15] Kemble carefully refrained from the masculine self-assertion implicit in formal literary genres, as when endeavoring to describe a species of fish "which deserves more glory than I can bestow upon it. Had I been the ingenious man who wrote a poem upon fish, the white mullet of the Altamaha should have been at least my heroine's cousin" ([89]). In line with Catherine Stimpson's observation that Virginia Woolf's letters adapt the conventions of the good hostess,[16] Kemble's modesty and implicit flattery conform to the gracious, ladylike behavior her surroundings, not least her husband, expected. In fact, Kemble's authorial stance suggests the southern hostess eager to entertain a visitor: "I purpose, while I reside here,

---

10. John A. Scott, "Introduction," p. xlii.
11. Juhasz, p. 227.
12. John A. Scott, "Introduction," p. xlii; Caroll Smith-Rosenberg, *Disorderly Conduct: Visions of Gender in Victorian America* (New York: Alfred A. Knopf, 1985), pp. 53-76; Clinton, *Plantation*, p. 7.
13. Clinton, *Plantation*, p. 164.
14. Stanton, p. 15.
15. Catherine R. Stimpson, "The Female Sociograph: The Theater of Virginia Woolf's Letters," in Stanton, p. 197.
16. Stimpson, p. 194.

keeping a sort of journal, such as Monk Lewis wrote during his visit to his West India plantations," she writes to Elizabeth in January 1839, modestly adding: "I wish I had any prospect of rendering my diary as interesting and amusing to you as his was to me" ([53]).

Kemble's remark to her friend indicates her awareness of trespassing onto masculine territory. As Stanton puts it in *The Female Autograph*, "the speaking 'I' constituted the reading 'you' as the representation of society's view of women and thus as the personification of the writing interdiction."[17] Projecting onto her reader(s) the cultural expectations of significance and authority, Kemble strikes a precarious balance between "anticipated reader expectations" and "responsive authorial manoeuvres."[18] She remains, then, immersed in an exchange with the reading other, who becomes the sounding board for her efforts to identify and justify herself (writing). Kemble encodes, in other words, Elizabeth as the "amused critic of the eccentric female speaker,"[19] whose graphing of the auto implies a self-assertion incompatible with white femininity in the South.

By signing her *Journal* Frances Anne Kemble instead of Frances Anne Butler or, like other southern matrons, Mrs. Pierce Mease Butler, Kemble discards the proper name that would inscribe her into systems of southern patriarchy and slavery. Instead, she opts for the role of *femme impropre*, to which also her acting, her poetics, and eventually her divorce would qualify her. Yet Kemble's autograph is more accurately a sociograph. Due to the *Journal*'s female emphasis, it becomes, in a sense, not just *a* woman's story but Woman's story. It forms, in the words of Catherine Stimpson, "an autobiography of the self with others, a citizen/denizen of relationships."[20] The slave women of Butler and St. Simon's Islands fill the diary pages with words, pleas, and cries, thus mingling their voices with Kemble's and creating not just a text of femininity but a feminine text.

---

17. Stanton, p. 15.
18. Sidonie Smith, *Poetics*, p. 50.
19. Stanton, p. 15.
20. Stimpson, p. 193.

Kemble's representation of slave women's verbosity nonetheless shows her to be an uneasy usurper of language. The women of Mr. Butler's plantation holdings speak endlessly of pregnacies, nursing, back pains, miscarriages, rape and disease, and through their verbiage articulate an implied connection between women's bodies and women's speech, between loose morals and loose language. In the words of Ann Rosalind Jones, "a woman's accessibility to the social world beyond the household through speech was seen as ultimately connected to the scandalous openness of her body."[21] A chaste woman, so revered in the South, was apparently also a silent one, and women given to verbal outpourings were, so to speak, asking for trouble. Smith-Rosenberg reminds us that nineteenth-century male educators and clergymen "forbade overt anger and violence as unfeminine and vulgar and they did not reward curiosity, intrusiveness, exploratory behavior, in women."[22]

Within the patriarchal plantation society, the compassionate Kemble represents "false" power as opposed to Mr. Butler's "real."[23] "I am anxious to spare both myself and them the pain of vain appeals to me for redress and help, which, alas! it is too often utterly out of my power to give them," she records within the same entry. "It is useless, and, indeed, worse than useless, that they should see my impotent indignation and unavailing pity…" (133). At the same time, however, Kemble's moral outrage suited perfectly her slaveowning husband's needs. "As plantation mistresses were charged with the direct care of slaves," notes Catherine Clinton, "their behavior was critical to the bolstering of planter claims to humanitarianism."[24] This behavior corresponded as well to the nineteenth-century Cult of True Womanhood. Though virtues exalted in sex and health reformer William Alcott's *The Young Wife* – domesticity, obedience, submission – were hardly Kemble's

---

21. Ann Rosalind Jones, "Surprising Fame: Renaissance Gender Ideologies and Women's Lyric," in *The Poetics of Gender*, ed. Nancy K. Miller (New York: Columbia U P, 1986), p. 76.
22. Smith-Rosenberg, *Disorderly Conduct*, pp. 212-13.
23. Clinton, *Plantation*, p. 40.
24. Clinton, *Plantation*, pp. 14-15.

fortes, the passion and emotion of her pleas to her husband confirmed Victorian notions of female irrationality[25] and thus legitimized Mr. Butler's patriarchal power.

Kemble speculates how it might fare "with slaves on plantations where there is no crazy Englishwoman to weep, and entreat, and implore, and upbraid for them" (140), yet she must learn that her husband tolerates no such eccentricity in his wife. He forbids her pleas for alleviating the sufferings of his slaves and meets Kemble's verbal transgressions with stony silences. "I have since thought that the intemperate vehemence of my entreaties and expostulations perhaps deserved that he should leave me as he did without one single word of reply," Kemble notes (137), thus displaying what Patricia Meyer Spacks designates the "rhetoric of uncertainty" of autobiographers torn between the competing identities of woman and writer.[26] Indeed, Kemble did not publish her writings from Georgia until 1863, when political developments forced her into print. With her long silence, she voiced her awareness of the cost of notoriety in a society that would hold her in its fictions.

If only to save her marriage, Kemble felt partially compelled to "altruistic surrender," the denial of own desires and displacement of ambitions and abilities onto masculine figures.[27] To some extent, then, Kemble assumed the position as other and created for her readers the story of Mr. Butler. *Journal of a Residence* is not only an account of Mr. Butler's plantations, Mr. Butler's slaves, and Mr. Butler's wife; Mr. Butler co-authors, so to speak, the diary by making his appearance in authorial "we"s as well as by editorial revisions. He sarcastically undermines Fanny Kemble's position among "women of genius" by mocking her interest in "commonplace objects" (144). In a sense, he determines the plot of the *Journal* by choosing to grant or dismiss his wife's requests, thus sending her into jubilance or depression, or both.

---

25. Smith-Rosenberg, *Disorderly Conduct*, pp. 25, 196.
26. Patricia Meyer Spacks, "Selves in Hiding," in Jelinek, *Women's Autobiography*, p. 131.
27. Smith-Rosenberg, *Disorderly Conduct*, p. 213.

But despite Pierce Butler's authorial presence in the thirty-one letters that constitute Kemble's diary, he is not as observant a reader as his wife. In commenting on London, an accomplished slave who knows how to read, to teach, and to preach, Kemble notices, unlike her husband, the contrast between London's talents and his fate: "How can we keep this man in such a condition? How is such a cruel sin of injustice to be answered? Mr. [Butler], of course, sees and feels none of this as I do..." (150). Blinded by his seigneurial privilege, Mr. Butler ignores as well Kemble's increasing dissatisfaction with her husband, which she expresses in images of emasculation. When forcing pregnant slave women to return to the fields, he seems "positively degraded" in the eyes of his wife, who is aware that her sojourn in the South might reduce her respect for him: "for the details of slaveholding are so unmanly, letting alone every other consideration, that I know not how anyone with the spirit of a man can condescend to them" (114). While Mr. Butler accordingly occupies the center of the *Journal* and the world it describes, his authorial and editorial decisions unbalance the power he seeks to uphold. As a result, Kemble's *Journal* effectively dramatizes generic tension and problematizes the self/other dichotomy typical of linguistic hierarchies of signification and formal autobiographical discourse.[28] Fanny Kemble disappears from the scene between Mr. Butler and the slaves she cannot bear to watch, thus resigning herself to absence and impotence, but her script dismisses in turn her husband's masculinity and deletes him from the southern landscape. At the bottom of the page (114), Kemble is rowing on the river, her husband nowhere in sight.

Kemble achieves her literary authority as autobiographer by erasing her sexual self from the *Journal*. To write the empowered life story she desires, she must, as Smith argues, distance herself from "the cultural fictions of female passion" and "contaminated" female sexuality.[29] Denying the Victorian connection between woman's speech and sexual frivolity, she must write herself as a "good woman" by suppressing her eroticism. The celebrated and beautiful

---

28. Sidonie Smith, *Poetics*, p. 40.
29. Sidonie Smith, *Poetics*, p. 55.

Shakespearean actress, for whom this task cannot have been easy, accordingly seeks solitude whenever her position as writer and woman is under attack. "I have been out again on the river, rowing," she writes in January 1839. "I do not weary of these most exquisite watery woods, but you will of my mention of them, I fear," she continues on a note of authorial defensiveness that leads her to end the entry (114). Despite the relationship of literary authority and sexuality as presence and absence in her text, Kemble's lingering attraction to Pierce Butler threatens the precarious balance achieved in the *Journal.* "We rowed home through a world of stars," she records after a visit with her husband to a neighboring plantation, commenting on "the still blue sky," "the flashing swathes of phosphoric light" and "the smooth blue water." The sensuous and romantic mood of the evening leaves traces in Kemble's word choice, but remains otherwise unarticulated. "It was lovely," she concludes (324), relying on the blankness of her page to speak the unspeakable.

Kemble draws on her literary knowledge to strengthen her position, contrasting, for example, the "material beauty" of the southern spring with the "moral degradation" below the surface: "it gives one a sort of Melusina feeling of horror" (226). References to Shakespeare, Dante, Swift and other literary figures came naturally to the former actress, but they serve as well to validate her own writing project. At the same time, the literary fathers of the *Journal* reaffirm the notion of female subordination to male voices. As Smith concludes upon the female autobiographer, "to the extent that she establishes her chastity within the text, to the extent that she reaffirms through the text, as well as in the text, her subordination to all fathers, she is allowed the voice of authority."[30] Interestingly, Kemble ends her *Journal* with two appeals directed to the Editor of the London *Times* and to Charles Greville, an old acquaintance who "disapproved of her acting, her divorce, and her politics" (369, note 1). With this ending, Kemble openly acknowledges her sensitivity to masculine (dis)approval.

---

30. Sidonie Smith, *Poetics*, p. 55.

Drawing on other masters of fiction, Kemble's epistolary form is in itself a fiction in that the resisting Georgian lady early on envisioned a wider audience than her "Dear Elizabeth" would offer. In a letter to Harriet St. Leger from October, 1840, she notes: "I have sometimes been haunted with the idea that it was an imperative duty, knowing what I know, and having seen what I have seen, to do all that lies in my power to show the dangers and the evils of this frightful institution."[31] The public letter form enables Kemble to take a polemic stance on slavery and patriarchy by encoding her resistance within a form that itself articulates protest against restrictions. In Jane Marcus's words on Woolf, "her anger and hostility at the exclusiveness of male institutions are all the more effective because 'cabin'd and cribb'd' in limited and limiting letters."[32] Kemble's letters accordingly occupy a space between the private and the public, and between fact and fiction. They negotiate a perfect, if precarious, balance between exposure and concealment and at the same time, like their author, situate themselves in a sphere of liminality. This "wild zone" of women's texts, to use Elaine Showalter's terminology,[33] falls like Kemble's rural Georgia outside the dominant culture's boundaries in a spatial and ideological no-man's land, where anything might happen. Liminality, in other words, suggests structural transcendence and opens up vistas of emotional, social and historical alterity.[34] This breakdown of formal distinctions, as well as of previous codes of silence, obviously accellerated in the lives and writings of mid-nineteenth-century southern(ized) women. As debates over slavery propelled the nation towards a civil war, divisions between the personal and the political blurred, and ladies of various persuasions found themselves outside established forms and norms.

---

31. Frances Anne Kemble, *Records of a Girlhood* II (London: Richard Bentley and Son, 1878-79), p. 40.
32. Stimpson, p. 196.
33. Elaine Showalter, "Feminist Criticism in the Wilderness," *Critical Inquiry* 8 (Winter 1981), p. 200.
34. Patricia Sharpe, F. E. Mascia-Lees and C. B. Cohen, "White Women and Black Men: Differential Responses to Reading Black Women's Texts," *College English* 52.2 (February 1990), p. 146.

Like other autobiographers, diarists, and historians, Kemble blended the literal with the literary through several means of fictionalization. Her self-interpretation draws on the myth of the southern lady, a privileged cultural fiction that, in a sense, renders Kemble "readable" and allows her to rewrite the systems of interpretation defining her.[35] As Avon Fleishman argues in *Figures of Autobiography* (1983), "idealized" and "ideologized" literary figures constitute "the instruments with which autobiographers make themselves unique, by creative reenactment, revision, and reversal."[36]

Apart from the fiction of a coherent, recording "self," fractured through necessities of genre into the narrating "I" and the narrated "I," as well as into various "speaking postures,"[37] autobio/historiography becomes a fictive process through the narrative choices involved in telling a story. But Kemble relied in addition on literary devices that practically transform her journal into an epistolary novel, in which characters come and go, engaging in dialogue and monologue and, through their very presence, simultaneously fragmenting and constituting plot.

Like other writing women shrinking from self-assertion and self-display, Kemble declares her strength and power, as it were, in disguise.[38] Slaves and neighbors express through processes of externalization the author's own opinions. Mr. Couper, who occupies the neighboring plantation at Cannon's Point, thus voices Kemble's own misgivings about the former overseers at the Butler estate. "Of the two latter functionaries his account was terrible, and much what I had supposed any impartial account of them would be," begins a long passage on the cruelties and sexual exploits of Mr. King and his son (266f).

Irony and humor also allow the unruly plantation mistress to put forth her views behind a mask of detachment and, perhaps, of

---

35. Nancy Miller, "Emphasis Added: Plots and Plausibilities in Women's Fiction," *PMLA* 96 (January 1981), pp. 36-48.
36. Avon Fleishman, *Figures of Autobiography: The Language of Self-Writing in Victorian and Modern England* (Berkeley: U of California P, 1983), p. 33.
37. Sidonie Smith, *Poetics*, pp. 5, 47.
38. Spacks, "Selves in Hiding," pp. 113-14.

safety: the function of humor is, after all, "to challenge order but not to overthrow it."[39] In detailing the curfews and bell tollings of Charleston, Kemble notes that "these daily and nightly precautions are but trifling drawbacks upon the manifold blessings of slavery." Still, she adds, "I should prefer going to sleep without the apprehension of my servants' cutting my throat in my bed..." (39). A Scotchman's fondness for the term "our blackies" also calls for irony from someone who, as Kemble describes herself, has "some small prejudices in favor of freedom and justice yet to overcome before I can enter into the merits of this beneficent system, so productive of cheerfulness and contentment in those whom it condemns to perpetual degradation" (46). In the same ironic vein, she suggests that Iago in his first soliloquy substitute "I hate the Moor" with "'I hate the nigger,' given in proper Charleston or Savannah fashion" (121).

Most interesting is, however, Kemble's choice of metaphors, which reinforces her protest against slavery and patriarchy. The recurring underworld images of Kemble's *Journal* originate in her intertextual engagement with Dante's *Inferno* and allow her to present the slaveholding Georgia as an evil empire. The swamps are "slimy, poisonous-looking" (55), with rattling sedges matted with the "evil-looking" nightshade that shelters alligators and snakes. Over the bayou soar the "unsightly" turkey buzzards, whose "heavy flight," "awkward gait," and "devotion to every species of foul and detestable food" render them "almost abhorrent" to Kemble (59). Yet the forbidding aspects of southern nature pale in comparison with the sufferings of the region's damned:

> When I am most inclined to deplore the conditions of the poor slaves on these cotton and rice plantations, the far more intolerable existence and harder labor of those employed on the sugar estates occurs to me, sometimes producing the effect of a lower circle in Dante's 'Hell of Horrors,' opening beneath the one where he seems to have reached the climax of infernal punishment. (122)

---

39. Smith-Rosenberg, *Disorderly Conduct*, p. 107.

In the inferno of southern plantation life, Kemble suggests with images of dehumanization the collapse of human dignity, the departure of the Christian soul, or, perhaps, the fecund disorder of liminality. On her many walks, Kemble observes "the long-necked waterfowl by dozens" and finds that "it arouses the killing propensity in [her] most dreadfully," despite resistance: "for the life of me I cannot help wishing I had a fowling piece whenever I put up a covey of these creatures..." (58). Kemble's Georgia acts, in other words, as a "foil to the self" in illuminating and shaping its strengths, lacks, and desires.[40] Surrounded by bestiality and evil, Kemble finds herself invaded by "animal *humanity*" (58). The perforation of the human/animal distinction implies the lack of reason and restraint she finds characteristic of her adopted region and the victory of anti-structure. As a sort of feminized Davy Crockett, Kemble discovers the wild power of liminal disorder,[41] a power she, possibly unconsciously, associates with phallic signifiers.

Kemble's account of a local duel relies heavily on masculine images, which help her connect the institution of slavery with the brutality of southern patriarchy. Dr. Hazzard and Mr. Wylly have challenged one another to fight a duel with firearms. Whoever will kill the other is, as Kemble writes, "to have the privilege of *cutting off his head, and sticking it up on a pole...*" (292). By expressing her critique of southern mores in phallic imagery, she places the responsibility for southern horrors squarely on the shoulders of southern gentlemen: "they must be as idle, arrogant, ignorant, dissolute, and ferocious as that medieval chivalry to which they are fond of comparing themselves" (332). Also inscribed into this attack on southern planters is Kemble's disenchantment with her own slaveholding husband, whom she in vain entreats to take pity on his dependents. Only by writing him into her script may she, it seems, transgress the boundaries within which he was, in fact, her Master.

---

40. Marcus K. Billson and Sidonie A. Smith, "Lillian Hellman and the Strategy of the 'Other,'" in Jelinek, *Women's Autobiography*, p. 173.
41. Smith-Rosenberg, *Disorderly Conduct*, pp. 100-01.

In her account of southern insensitivity and inhumanity, Kemble additionally draws upon bodily metaphors. The maimed, disfigured, aching and suffering bodies of Mr. Butler's slaves stretch across innumerable *Journal* pages, as when Kemble visits the plantation infirmary and spares her reader no details:

> Among the patients in this room was a young girl, apparently from fourteen to fifteen, whose hands and feet were literally rotting away piecemeal from the effect of a horrible disease, to which the Negroes are subject here, and I believe in the West Indies, and when it attacks the joints of the toes and fingers, the pieces absolutely decay and come off, leaving the limb a maimed and horrible stump! (76)

Women's bodies crippled by childbirths and hard work form the "pitiable objects" that in Kemble's account signify the inhumanity of slavery and its destruction of life and dignity: "An old crone called Hannah," for example, "whose face and figure, seamed with wrinkles, and bowed and twisted with age and infirmity, really hardly retained the semblance of those of a human creature..." (227). The biological bodies Kemble describes become, in other words, symbolic representations of the social body that has created – and destroyed – them. The physical ills of Butler Island's slaves accordingly signify a diseased South intent on (self-)destruction.

Moreover, since "the body was a temple,"[42] the obvious disregard for maintaining the Lord's dwelling signaled to Kemble the ungodliness of southern plantation society. She constantly seeks out the immortal souls of the slaves' only too mortal frames, observing "this pathetic expression of countenance in them, a mixture of sadness and fear... a sense of incalculable past loss and injury, and a dread of incalculable future loss and injury" (133). Kemble's obsession with cleanliness, which compels her to have fatigued field hands sweep their hovels and to reward the cleaning of babies with small coins, serves as a metaphorical expression of

---

42. Clinton, *Plantation*, p. 98.

her disgust with an evil system openly displaying impiety through neglect of physical appearance. At the same time, of course, her gestures towards hygiene illustrate her powerlessness to bring about more fundamental changes in the lives of her charges.

Other metaphor clusters articulate Kemble's impatience with southern ladyhood and the patriarchal forces defining her. Her sense of isolation impels her to describe the plantation as "this *ultima Thule* of all civilizations" (115) and triggers as well images of entrapment and fear. The plantation house, for example, "consists of three small rooms, and three still smaller, which would be more appropriately designated as closets..." (63); her physical movement is hindered by narrow dikes, impenetrable thickets, and, as the season grows hotter, snakes. Kemble's encounter with one "enormous rattlesnake hanging dead on the bough of a tree" sends her back to her house "perfectly sick with horror" and intensifies her sense of southern imprisonment: "I wished very much to come back to the North immediately, where these are not the sort of blackberries that grow on every bush." Only the sound of the Atlantic Ocean and the freedom it represents can soothe her: "I thought no more of rattlesnakes – no more, for a short while, of slavery" (318).

Kemble makes her mark on the southern landscape with what Virginia Woolf first saw as a feminine sentence: "still more welcome were the golden garlands of the exquisite wild jasmine, hanging, drooping, trailing, clinging, climbing through the dreary forest, joining to warm the aromatic smell of the fir trees a delicious fragrance as of acres of heliotrope in bloom" (181). Not just the spatial metaphor of the last line creates for Kemble a room of her own; the present participles of the passage suggest a sense of activity and non-restraint. Through excess and waste, Kemble offers to her readers a poetic gift *a la* Bataille that establishes an economy of difference. Like "the exquisite wild jasmine" that encloses and penetrates "the dreary forest," Kemble's syntax inserts alterity and femininity into the discourse of mastery that bound her.

In fact, the narrative energy Kemble bestows upon the southern bayous, rivers, and vegetation indicates that southern nature functions in her journal as an uncolonized woman's zone, a language-scape allowing for feminine textuality and interpretations. Riding or rowing into the swamps surrounding Mr. Butler's plantations, Kemble experiences an awakening of self and senses, a state of mind reminiscent of the repressed and gagged "other," in French feminist theory associated with the unconscious:

> These beautiful shrubberies were resounding with the songs of mockingbirds. I sat there on my horse in a sort of dream of enchantment, looking, listening, and inhaling the delicious atmosphere of those flowers; and suddenly my eyes opened, as if I had been asleep, on some bright red bunches of spring leaves on one of the winter-stripped trees.... (226)

As this passage illustrates, Kemble discovers on the bayou a different language, which, in Julia Kristeva's phrase, "sets the being of the law ablaze in a peaceful, relaxing void."[43] In other words, Kemble imagines a feminine aesthetics valorizing components of difference erased from masculine sign systems: song, color, detail, dream, body. On another page, she notes a close "embroidery" of creeping moss and comments on a path "edged with an exquisite pattern of coral; it was like a thing in a fairy tale, and delighted me extremely" (224). Apart from the metaphors that combine domesticity and fantasy in feminine pleasure, the description of nature captures again the rapture of the observer in emphasizing *how* she observes as much as *what* she observes. Kemble's sketches of southern swamps accordingly aim at (re)creating the recording self.

Interestingly, the feminine artist at work is unable to name the plants and birds that constitute her material. Employing, perhaps, what Gilbert and Gubar call a "non-alphabetic 'maiden language,'"[44] she reads and writes the South on/off the border of masculine signification, thus imagining herself outside of master discourse. Indeed, the sensibility inscribed onto the landscape interprets and rejects the seductive evil of southern plantation society:

---

43. Julia Kristeva, *The Kristeva Reader*, ed. Toril Moi (New York: Columbia U P, 1986), p. 295.
44. Sandra M. Gilbert and Susan Gubar, "Ceremonies of the Alphabet: Female Grandmatologies and the Female Authorgraph," in Stanton, p. 38.

> Those bright leaves ... reminded me how soon I should leave this scene of material beauty and moral degradation, where the beauty itself is of an appropriate character to the human existence it surrounds: above all, loveliness, brightness, and fragrance; but below!... all swamp and poisonous stagnation, which the heat will presently make alive with venomous reptiles. (226)

Unlike William Bartram, another British-born explorer in the South, Kemble encounters a paradise invaded by snakes, emissaries of the phallic powers that threaten to undo her. Thus, Kemble's southern landscape becomes the battleground for masculine and feminine signatures, as the snakes she associates with social horrors violate the feminine aesthetics encoded in the wilderness. While Kemble's woman artist operates with physical and moral beauty, the snakes evoke destruction and death: "an enourmous cypress tree which had been burned, stood charred and blackened, and leaning toward the road so as to threaten a speedy fall across it, and on one of the limbs of this great charcoal giant hung a dead rattlesnake" (226-27). "The two together made a dreadful trophy," Kemble continues, "and a curious contrast to the lovely bowers of bloom I had just been contemplating with such delight" (227). The phallic inscriptions in her feminine text threaten her, yet the *Journal* stages a sort of feminine victory. Aided by slaves whom she pays for their labor, Kemble clears a road in the snake-sheltering thickets, thus forcing cracks in the linguistic and economic order that encloses her.

Occasionally, Kemble's revisions of southern scripts, masculine and feminine, takes the form of explicit criticism. After a visit from a neighbor, Mrs. Troup, who expatiates on the impossibility of securing good nurses, Kemble stresses that "the causes of this unworthiness and incapacity for a confidential servant's occupation were ignored, and the fact laid to the natural defects of the Negro race." Impatient with the racism of her guest, Kemble bursts out: "I am sick and weary of this cruel and ignorant folly" (177). Mrs. Spalding's conversation upon the same topic sends Kemble into a fit of disgust with southern ladyhood, recounted to Elizabeth, her supposedly more enlightened northern friend:

> If you are half as tired of the sameness and stupidity of the conversation of my Southern female neighbors as I am, I pity you; but not as much as I pity them for the stupid sameness of their most vapid existence, which would deaden any amount of intelligence, obliterate any amount of instruction, and render torpid and stagnant any amount of natural energy and vivacity. I would rather die – rather a thousand times – than live the lives of these Georgia planters' wives and daughters. (192)

While the syntactic and idiomatic intensity of the passage suggests Kemble's investment in deconstructing southern femininity, the dichotomies of the text indicate her revisionist plot. She associates southern ladies with emptiness, stagnation, and death, thus inscribing them as nobodies mirroring the Georgia planters upon whom they are symbolically, socially and linguistically dependent. In Kemble's rewriting of ideologized ladyhood, however, qualities such as intelligence, education and physicality are paramount.

Ultimately, Kemble's rebellion against southern gender scripts includes her decision to master her own body, thus, ironically, canceling her position as mistress. "Oh, if you could imagine how this title 'Missis,' addressed to me and to my children, shocks all my feelings," Kemble writes upon her arrival at Butler Island (60). Her refusal to enter southern racial hierarchies becomes apparent in a subsequent infirmary scene, when she begins to build a fire, to the horror of the slaves around her: "I hereupon had to explain to them my view of the purposes for which hands and arms were appended to our bodies" (71). To transcend the psychological and geographical limitations of her role, Kemble resorts, as we have seen, to rowing, a sport that besides "a delightful row of blisters" on each hand (72) allows her to establish her difference from other southern ladies. "It was the singular fact of seeing a white woman stretch her sinews in any toilsome exercise which astounded them," she notes about the field hands witnessing her exercise and pronounces herself a firm believer in "devilish hard work" (87-88). The Butler Island slaves hardly need this lesson in Victorian work ethic, but the white women of her circle are, in Kemble's view, an incompetent and lazy breed from which she happily distances herself:

> The ladies I have seen since I crossed the Southern line have all seemed to me extremely sickly in their appearance – delicate in the refined term, but unfortunately sickly in the truer one. They are languid in their deportment and speech, and seem to give themselves up, without an effort to counteract it, to the enervating effect of their warm climate. It is undoubtedly a most relaxing and unhealthy one, and therefore requires the more imperatively to be met by energetic and invigorating habits both of body and mind. Of these, however, the Southern ladies appear to have, at present, no very positive idea. (101-02)

Interestingly, however, Kemble's recasting of the activities befitting a white woman in the South matches the leisure and luxury of which her southern sisters appeared to her overly fond. She rows for hours without any duties taking priority, and, like other women of her class, occasionally seems blind to others' toil. She "has" a pine tree planted and, she writes, "had a brand thrown into a bed of tall yellow sedges..." (104).

Kemble chafes, however, at the educational and mental constrictions that the "ignorance" and "folly" of her sex in Georgia impose. Faced with the many tasks of a southern plantation mistress, she regrets her own feminine socialization: "How much I wished that, instead of music and dancing, and such stuff, I had learned something of sickness and health, of the conditions and liabilities of the human body..." (75). Out of a sense of guilt, she performs such tasks as medical supervision and sewing, a skill she acquired as a young girl in France, when "cutting out and making my dresses was among the more advanced branches of *the* female accomplishment to which I attained" (142). Nonetheless, Kemble's irony and her rustiness in terms of traditional feminine occupations again inscribes her inconsonance. Her sewing, she writes, "might almost be called an experiment" (142).

In contrast, her innumerable allusions to Dante, Swift, Shakespeare and other emblems of her educational sophistication function as exits from her role and her text by allowing her to escape the southern ladies who bore her and to converse with interesting men of her choice. These conversations frequently lead onto topics such as business and politics and to what Elaine Showalter labels transvestite fantasies. "If I were a Southern slaveholder, I should not feel altogether secure of Mr. Van Buren's present opinions or future conduct upon [slavery]" (97), Kemble writes in January 1839. Two months later, she contemplates breaking the law to teach a favorite slave to read: "If I were a man, I would do that and many a thing besides..." (271). The range of male possibilities and accomplishments astounds her, as she records upon reading the narrative of J. H. Couper's escape from the wrecked *Pulaski*: "What a fine thing it must be to be such a man!" (329). But her position as (transgressive) woman is never forgotten: "I am a *feme couverte* [sic], and my fines must be paid by my legal owner," she states after having indulged in dreams of "mischievous incendiary" (272).

Still, Kemble's revisions of southern plots have emphasized genderic difference and even suggested a power of powerlessness:

> To our children, our servants, our friends, our acquaintances – to each and all every day, and all day long, we [women] are distributing that which is best or worst in existence – influence: with every word, with every look, with every gesture, something is given or withheld of great importance it may be to the receiver, of inestimable importance to the giver. (295)

Perhaps the repetitions of the passage reveal an unarticulated distrust in woman's power, but Kemble's emphasis on words, looks, and gestures is nonetheless important: while physicality and education would distance her from southern ladyhood, her most significant talent – and rebellion – was linguistic and dramatic.

Kemble's literary and dramatic gifts afforded her the opportunity to become an early nineteenth-century New Woman. Though she found acting distasteful, her experience as economically independent helped her define herself, even among Georgia belles, as a feminist. "For the last four years of my life that preceded my marriage I literally coined money," she writes on January 21, 1839, "and never until this moment, I think, did I reflect on the great means of good, to myself and others, that I so gladly agreed to give up forever for a maintenance by the unpaid labor of slaves" (139). She populates her *Journal* primarily with female slaves, partly because she cannot ignore the suppression and dependency uniting mistress and slave women: "I had my cry out for them, for myself, for *us*" (223). Through her alliance with slaves rather than with planters, with African American women rather than European American men, Kemble sets up a nurturing community that, despite its suffering, becomes a source of strength.

The South itself, however, eventually does her in. "We shall soon be free again," she writes in March of 1839 in contemplating her approaching return to the North. In April she admits: "I am getting sick in spirit of my stay here, but I think the spring heat is beginning to affect me miserably, and I long for a cooler atmosphere" (299). Kemble's spiritual sickness at the close of her stay in Georgia parallels, it seems, the sickliness she found typical of southern ladies upon her arrival. And like the slave mothers brought North to freedom, only to return to bondage because of their children, Kemble found little freedom outside patriarchal folds and molds. The overseer's comment on slave women appears on the last page of the *Journal* and elicits from Kemble a laconic response: "Mr. K[ing] was an extremely wise man" (344). With this closing statement, Kemble says goodbye with a deference befitting a southern, if secretly eloquent, lady.

Whether recording her sufferings in Georgia or her longings for the North, Kemble projected in fact a self in hiding. What Francis R. Hart entitles "the paradox of continuity in discontinuity" will always, of course, involve the autobiographer in a masquerade of sorts, since a coherent identity invariably gives way, in the act of narration, to competing fictions of selfhood and various textual representations.[45] Kemble's claims to honesty and truth notwithstanding, her *Journal* reads in part as a dramatic script. Its actress-author stages the southern landscape to serve as props for the cast of heroes, villains and victims entering and exiting her morality play. She devotes pages of the *Journal* to dramatic dialogues

---

45. Sidonie Smith, *Poetics*, p. 47.

and monologues, and she herself plays all the parts available to a young white woman of rare dramatic gifts: devoted mother, (dis)obedient wife, New Woman, artist, southern lady, and more.[46] Possibly wishing Fanny Kemble herself to remain off stage, the author of the *Journal* designed the masks of her era's female figures and hid behind them all.

The letters demonstrate, however, that Kemble could and would not censor her moral outrage over slavery, which also fills her *Journal* pages with vehement, explicit attacks on the peculiar southern institution. Though she did succeed in withholding the ultimate exposure of her linguistic and generic looseness – publication – for several decades, she ultimately ventured from the margins of her culture towards its center in order to engage in Civil War encounters. Some southerners credit her journal with preventing England's recognition of the Confederacy, thus propelling the South towards defeat, while others argue that *Journal of a Residence* appeared too late to have any impact at all.[47] Kemble's intervention in the master plots of her time nonetheless entailed both courage and costs. In 1863 she had lost her husband, her children, and her home. The transgressive woman who had begun as an actress and continued as a writer managed, however, to subvert the symbolic order of patriarchy into which she was and had written. She assumed, in short, a different voice and imagined in the process a new role, a new script, and, perhaps, a different South.

---

46. Mary W. Blanchard discusses the Victorian American self, male and female, as "a persona of changing roles and multiple voices" in "Boundaries and the Victorian Body: Aesthetic Fashion in Gilded Age America," *American Historical Review* 100 (February 1995), p. 24.
47. John A. Scott, "Introduction, " pp. l-li.

Ella Gertrude Clanton Thomas

CHAPTER TWO

Confederate Bodies: The Journal of Ella Gertrude Clanton Thomas

In February 1869 Ella Gertrude Clanton Thomas was suffering from a sudden illness causing repeated chills as well as the breaking out of her body in scarlet blotches. Her planter husband insisted on doses of sarsaparilla, to which Dr. Eve, the family physician, added a heavy dose of morphine. Upon her recovery, Thomas described in her diary, in its published form entitled *The Secret Eye*, the effect of the medicine:

> I would lay [sic] perfectly quiet upon the bed, *knowing* that I was there and with my eyes shut I would see a succession of pictures as in a panoramic view, some of them lovely, others hideous.... Sometimes the frame is pushed back to enable the edges to meet, this being done and a few seconds allowed to look upon it, the picture would glide by to be succeeded by others.... Lovely unknown countenances would be presented to my view and as I looked upon them suddenly they push out their tongues and looking like demons would advance towards me. All this would take place while Mr. Thomas and the children would be sitting by the fire.[1]

This entry in a plantation mistress's journal dramatizes poignantly the complexity of bodily representation in the Confederate South

---

1. Ella Gertrude Clanton Thomas, *The Secret Eye: The Journal of Ella Gertrude Clanton Thomas, 1848-1889*, ed. Virginia Ingraham Burr (Chapel Hill: U of N Carolina P, 1990), p. 308. Future references to *The Secret Eye* will appear parenthetically in the text.

and beyond. Itself framed by perfect familial quiet – the resting body on the bed, the husband and children seated in warmth and comfort in the Big House – the passage pushes forth other frames and other bodies, whose beauty gives way to a threatening diabolism, outside the control of the recorder. Constantly shifting and fluctuating, the figures that occasionally break through their frames hint at the contemporary critical notion that the body is no simple, "natural" given but a cultural construct with historical and gender-related connotations. Helen Mitchie, for example, argues that "sexual politics intervene to produce gaps between the representation of the body and its 'realities.'" The female body, in particular, is "no simple case of *différance*, but a historically aggravated instance of the violent and marked separation of signifier and signified."[2] In the diary vignette, Mr. Thomas and Dr. Eve have reduced Mrs. Thomas to a *tableau mourant*, her mute body a signifier with no signified or, in Susan Gubar's phrase, "a blank page" available for male inscription and interpretation.[3] Thomas's male- and morphine-induced fantasies suggest as well, though, that the female body houses the potential to usurp or escape cultural frames and, in a sense, write up its own monstrous identity. Frames embody, as Mitchie demonstrates, various, frequently conflicting meanings: accusation, ways of keeping women in/out, protection, and a space from which to assert power.[4] Frames might accordingly, in Dolores Rosenblum's analysis, be a means of "killing into

---

2. Helen Mitchie, *The Flesh Made Word: Female Figures and Women's Bodies* (New York: Oxford U P, 1987), p. 8; cp. Christine Delphy, "Protofeminism and Antifeminism," *French Feminist Thought*, ed. Toril Moi (Oxford: Basil Blackwell, 1987), p. 92. See also Judith Butler, *Gender Trouble: Feminism and the Subversion of Identity* (New York: Routledge, 1990) and *Bodies That Matter: On the Discursive Limits of "Sex"* (New York: Routledge, 1993); Susan Bordo, *Unbearable Weight: Feminism, Western Culture, and the Body* (Berkeley: U of California P, 1993), and Elizabeth Grosz, *Volatile Bodies: Toward a Corporeal Feminism* (Bloomington: Indiana U P, 1994).
3. Susan Gubar, "'The Blank Page' and the Issues of Female Creativity," in *Feminist Criticism: Essays on Women, Literature and Theory*, ed. Elaine Showalter (New York: Pantheon, 1985), p. 292.
4. Mitchie, p. 8.

art" but also of grabbing attention and presenting the body.⁵ It is, after all, Thomas herself who describes the scene in her diary, thus framing her body – and the men framing her – in order to signify herself. Indeed, the representations of the body in this southern woman's self-narrative demonstrate simultaneously her embodiment of established cultural figures as well as her desire to create in and with her body a locus of feminine interpretation and textuality. The female body was, after all, a central figure in the contemporary discourse of southern identity and self-preservation. As Ann Firor Scott explains in *The Southern Lady*, the chastity, beauty and charm of the southern belle represented everything good and virtuous in southern life.⁶

As a nineteenth-century southern woman wishing to shape a textual body of her own, Thomas faced, like Fanny Kemble, the region's patriarchal equation of "woman, beauty, literature, and irrelevance."⁷ Fictional literary forms were, in other words, to be as decorative as Thomas's restful (but diseased) body, ideally devoid of a signified. In contrast, the diary existed in a zone of privacy and intimacy free of formal prescriptions, to which, no doubt, it owed much of its popularity in the South. Moreover, the decentered and inconclusive diary form suits perfectly a feminine "writing of the body," a mode of self-inscription tuned into the shapes of women's lives, identities, and desires. Within the fluidity of the diary, a focus on bodily representations allows as well, Gail T. Reimer notes in a discussion of Margaret Oliphant, an escape from the dualism of conventional autobiographical discourse: "With mind opposed to external life, body can be reclaimed as something neither opposed to mind nor analogous to external life." She continues: "Body thus becomes a distinctive category of

---

5. Dolores Rosenblum, "Christina Rosetti: The Inward Pose," in *Shakespeare's Sisters: Feminist Essays on Women Poets*, ed. Sandra M. Gilbert and Susan Gubar (Bloomington: Indiana U P, 1979), pp. 82-98.
6. Ann Firor Scott, *The Southern Lady: From Pedestal to Politics, 1830-1930* (Chicago: U of Chicago P, 1970).
7. Anne Goodwin Jones, *Tomorrow Is Another Day: The Woman Writer in the South, 1859-1936* (Baton Rouge: LSU P, 1981), p. 44.

experience which mediates internality and externality and therefore might prove particularly fertile ground from which to discern the meaning of a life."[8] It is, however, impossible to rescue an authentic or "literal" body from language. Despite the focus in the Thomas diary on the experience of a female body from adolescence on, the body itself appears, in Mitchie's words, "only as a series of tropes or rhetorical codes that distance it from the reader in the very act of its depiction."[9]

The "aesthetics of distance" that governs Thomas's bodily representations surfaces in an early diary entry, which demonstrates her erasure of self-as-body. Instead of describing the symptoms of illness that have caused her family to send for a doctor on Christmas Day, 1851, the young diarist presents herself through the doctor's eyes: "This morning Dr. Dugas called again. He found me in the sitting room lying on the sofa with a warm brick to my face" (94). To some extent, Thomas depends on the gaze of others to experience herself. A disappearance of this gaze means to the southern lady a loss of identity and social standing and causes her intense shame – as when, after her husband's bankruptcy in 1869, Thomas feels compelled to hide in her carriage down Broad Street in Augusta, Georgia, and to refrain from visiting her husband's failing store or attending a local party.

Confederate women's absence as bodies is also apparent in Thomas's descriptions of the college girls at Wesley Female College in Macon, Georgia, to which the affluent Turner Clanton in 1849 had sent his privileged daughter. Thomas lists, without physical descriptions, all the girls she is "very much attached to" (83). Even in describing the attractive Bell Fernandez, Thomas relies on phrases such as "style" and "wonderful beauty," thus veiling her classmate's body in abstraction (85). This freezing of physicality in language prepares the way for Thomas's equation of femininity, goodness, and passivity. Throughout the journal, she responds to

---

8. Gail Twersky Reimer, "Revisions of Labor in Margaret Oliphant's Autobiography," in *Life/Lines: Theorizing Women's Autobiography*, ed. Bella Brodzki and Celeste Schenck (Ithaca: Cornell U P, 1988), pp. 204-05.
9. Mitchie, p. 5.

her husband's disastrous financial schemes with all the silence and resignation she can muster. Quite often, however, she displaces bodily desires with metaphor. In looking back upon days of courtship, she identifies her husband as "the one who could tune my heart to perfect melody and wake within me wild echoes which would sound his name alone" (122).

Not only the substitution of music for desire but also the replacement of body with "heart" signal the culturally determined taboos of Victorian America. As Mitchie argues, the selection necessitated by the period's erasure of female sexuality often takes the form of synecdoche, in Thomas's diary with hair and clothes most frequently hinting at the shape and sensuality of the body. In 1848, the fourteen-year-old girl's preoccupation with hair and hairstyles suggests an awakening sexuality (74-75); in 1880, the mature Thomas conveys the free sexual appetites of two passing gypsy women with an emphasis on the "beautiful strong teeth" of the one and the thick, dishevelled hair of the other (399). Above all, however, it is with clothes that a southern lady conceals the female body, though not without suggestion of its contours. Though the editor of *The Secret Eye* admits to deleting "many entries dealing with clothes" (xi) from the original 450,000-word manuscript diaries, the remaining detailed descriptions of garments communicate simultaneously the presence and absence of the author's body: "Went to Breakfast wearing my chamelion silk and red green baraishe [sic] saque with pink neck ribbon, belt and cuffs" (86-87). Synecdoche helps Mr. Thomas and his gentleman friends convey their fascination with the attractive Anna Russell, again with hair and dress in focus: "She was wearing what Mr T discribed [sic] as a white silk and Buddy a white satin and Mr Dortic was sure cost 1,000 dollars. It was trimmed with flounces of lace and her hair was powdered" (303).

The commodification of the female body reverberating in this description reappears in Thomas's concern with her marriageable daughter Mary Belle's attire, which must reflect the elegance and wealth the family no longer possesses, in order to attract an affluent suitor (309). Aware of the exchange value of the body, Thomas continues the genteel tradition of socializing young women to become decorative objects to be collected and displayed by men who can afford them. The special skill of southern ladies, then, lies in their exquisite representation of themselves as artificial or artistic creations.[10] To look as well as one can, writes Thomas in 1868, "is to make the most of the material nature has provided and I will go farther and say that when nature is lacking art should be called into requisition" (302). The notion of the body as artifact might, of course, suggest a woman experiencing her own body as the only available medium for her art, deflecting her creativity from the production of art to the recreation of the body as art.[11] Thomas implies as much in her awed description of a masquerade ball: "I wish I were an artist that I could transfer to canvas the sight I beheld..." (362). She continues to express her admiration for the various costumes in the hall, but emphasizes that "what was strangest of all was the silence! Everyone was afraid of betraying themselves by their voice and nothing was said except in whispers" (362). The passage hints that the commodification of the body results in loss of speech and repression of desire. Constrained by the tyranny of the eye, the body is deprived of its other physical and more sensual properties.

To suggest the presence of the body is thus in the South, as elsewhere in the Victorian era, to ensure its absence with a coded rhetoric, or to freeze it into art. This insistence on bodily erasure seems particularly adamant in records of physical realities of nineteenth-century women's lives such as childbirth, death, and illness. Thomas, who brought ten children into the world, reacts to a few of her own pregnancies, as well as to a college friend's giving birth to a daughter "*five months and twenty days* after her marriage" (127) with silence or italics only, but refers to other of her pregnancies with set phrases or refrains highlighting the socially glorified ma-

---

10. In "Boundaries and the Victorian Body: Aesthetic Fashion in Gilded Age America," *American Historical Review* 100 (February 1995), p. 23, Mary W. Blanchard notes: "The idea of the female form as a medium for 'beauty' and the dictum that dress should reveal the inner soul of the wearer and 'create' identity were present in the world of conventional fashions as early as the 1830s."
11. Gubar, pp. 296-98.

ternal role: "I am again destined to be a mother" (130), "I have prospects of becoming a mother" (148). She is obviously tempted to confide to her private journal her experiences of childbirth, but checks herself with a dash and proceeds to displace her physicality into art with a Shakespeare quotation: "Thursday morning September the 23rd the baby was born. I was not in pain more than an hour but it is a fearful agony – 'How sharper than a serpent's tooth' must be 'an ungrateful child' to a mother" (164). She resorts to cliché to repress the grief she experiences at the early death of little Anna Lou and other children (158), her syntax nonetheless conveying the bodily and emotional chaos the loss of the infant causes its mother. References to illness are equally coded, primarily into respectable categories such as "severe indisposition" (93), feeling "quite unwell" (108), or upset "nervous organization." Indeed, Thomas seems quite aware of her psychosomatic response to unpleasant events, which cause, in her own apt phrase, "depression of the body" (212). Similar to Thomas's emphasis on motherhood, this spiritualization of the body suggests its presence in the process of its disappearance. It also displaces from mind to body the moodiness that in the mid-nineteenth century constituted a significant flaw in female dispositions, which supposedly ought to radiate insistent cheerfulness.[12]

Like angelic heroines of Victorian fiction, of which she was more than fond, Thomas signaled with her frail body femininity as well as gentility. And, as in Victorian novels, Thomas's diary censors references to the protagonist's eating. The era's conflation of women's hunger, sexuality and power discussed by Gilbert and Gubar in relation to the Fall myth[13] prevented representations of female appetites, which in *The Secret Eye* must be satisfied off-stage.

---

12. See Nancy Schnog, "Changing Emotions: Moods and the Nineteenth-Century American Woman Writer," in *Inventing the Psychological: Toward a Cultural History of Emotional Life in America*, ed. Joel Pfister and Nancy Schnog (New Haven: Yale U P, 1997), pp. 84-109.
13. In Sandra M. Gilbert and Susan Gubar, *The Madwoman in the Attic: The Woman Writer and the Nineteenth-Century Literary Imagination* (New Haven: Yale U P, 1979).

The foods that make it onto the diary's dinner tables are moreover of the "feminine" variant,[14] with an emphasis on fruit and cakes. Thomas's entry for New Year's Day 1857 significantly moves from a description of feminine foods to complaints of feminine delicacy:

> I had dinner for them, a very nice dinner with dessert of Boston pudding and oranges, figs, raisens [sic] almonds and preserves and brandy peaches. I also have a beautifully iced fruit cake, which I had cooked in town last week. I have had a slight though constant pain in my stomach and side today.... (152)

An episode six years later at a New Year's social, attended also by a wealthy young man new to Thomas's circle, highlights the metonymic chain connecting food, eroticism, and the Fall: "His name is Keenan but he is not a gentleman 'to the manor born' for when one of the girls requested him to hand her a piece of candy last night, he walked into the next room *picked it up in his fingers* and carried it to her – " (220). The offering of food with the hands apparently constituted "unsafe" behavior, in Mitchie's view "too close a reenactment of the moment of temptation in the garden" (19). Moreover, such behavior barred membership of the genteel class, which reserved the "aesthetics of deprivation" for itself.[15]

This aesthetics extended from the orality of eating or eroticism to speech, reading, and writing. Thomas advocates in her journal a sort of verbal anorexia but actually calls attention to her words and flesh as she engages in self-deletion. In July 1852, for example, she records a "little misunderstanding" between herself and Jefferson Thomas, her husband:

---

14. Mitchie, pp. 15-16.
15. Mitchie, pp. 19, 20. This may be as good a place as any to note that many southern women faced the prospect of starvation for themselves and their families as the war intensified. For some upper-class ladies, however, "reckless indulgence" became a way to resist "the ideology of sacrifice." One Richmond hostess reportedly spent thirty thousand dollars on feeding and entertaining her guests during the last winter of the war. See Drew Gilpin Faust, "Altars of Sacrifice: Confederate Women and the Narratives of War," *The Journal of American History* 76 (March 1990), pp. 1213, 1227.

> I made use of some remark jesting, and he looked up with such a look of stern[n]ess! It startled me! and for a moment my old feeling of pride o'ercame me and I felt the blood gush to my cheek. I had almost said too much. Thank heaven! I did refrain.... (109)

By keeping in check her emotional and bodily urge to speak out, Thomas restores the conjugal harmony, her flaming cheeks and exclamation marks nonetheless suggesting the cost of self-starvation. Similarly, she suffers with regards to novel reading from literary anorexia, which compels her to resist the seduction of fiction: "I have no novels to read. I wish that it were possible to refrain from reading one for six months or a year. I am confident I could study much better" (77). Following a discussion of George Sand's "prostitution of talent" and the "contamination" of her novels, Thomas elaborates on the necessity of literary abnegation: "For a woman especially what a charm there is in a new book – I am of the opinion that too much novel reading is injurious to a mind..." (156). A recurring motif in southern women's diaries, the renunciation of novels originates in the equation of fiction, femininity, fantasy and eroticism. Yet the repeated avowals of literary abstinence evoke, like anorexia, the awareness of desire. To indulge in fantasy is, like writing, to satisfy an almost bodily hunger: "It comes just as natural for me [to] write in this journal as it does for me to eat a meal" (77).

Thomas's correlation of body and words comes out most significantly with regard to what Nell Irvin Painter labels "the journal's great and painful secret."[16] "The temptation sometimes to write the feelings which agitate my heart is almost irresistible," Thomas notes in March 1852. "My thoughts! Write those! and yet – Is it because I fear to write them?" (100). The explosions of Thomas's syntax signal her hunger for articulation, starved, nonetheless, into covert references to "my skeletons" (305). Like the anorexic

---

16. Nell Irvin Painter, "Introduction: The Journal of Ella Gertrude Clanton Thomas: An Educated White Woman in the Eras of Slavery, War, and Reconstruction," in Thomas, p. 2.

body, these skeletons are in complicated ways associated with male desire, as a so-called "leakage" entry[17] implies:

> There are thoughts, doubts, suggestions which present themselves to my mind. If I could only talk of them....
> I find my thoughts recurring to the Catholic confessional (that great repository of secrets) with a longing checked by the idea that these priests are *men*. Again with a feeling of intense relief I think of Mary – Mother Mary! Christ's Mother! and shall I confess it, I almost find myself believing in the intercession of the saints. (226-27)

The presence of men here checks Thomas's craving for expression and hints at the gender-related nature of her secret. Moreover, as Mitchie notes, the fall into hunger, erotic or verbal, "is recuperable only by the figure of the Virgin Mary," who comes to represent both fasting and chastity.[18] What Thomas tries not to articulate might indeed, as Painter speculates, be related to Mr. Thomas's physical and moral transgressions. Though the author of the Introduction disagrees with the editor, Virginia Ingraham Burr, Painter argues that Jefferson Thomas was not just an alcoholic, but from 1855 to 1875, perhaps until 1880, had a marriage-like sexual relationship, and possibly offspring, with a slave woman.[19]

Whether or not their husbands frequented slave concubines, the African American body intervenes in the self-representations of southern white women. Since people of African descent provided slave labor, Thomas associates their color with physicality and circumvents Victorian representational taboos in describing the black body. On the first day of 1857, for example, she moves straight from a description of appropriately feminine foods – huckleberries, tomatoes, peas – indicating her own etherealness to an account of a recent slave uprising in Tennessee: "Numbers of

---

17. Painter, p. 58.
18. Mitchie, p. 21.
19. Painter, pp. 55-56.

Negroes were arrested. Some had their heads cut off. Others were hung some severely whipped" (153). The raw corporeity of Thomas's unemotional report tells its own story of southern race relations, yet the physicality of the African American female body serves as well a mediating function. Recording in her diary the expected confinements of Judy and Maria Jones, both slaves, Thomas abandons the euphemisms reserved for white women; like Kemble, she indicates, however, a sort of cross-racial sisterhood that does not exclusively originate in the commodification and value of the African American body: "I know that had I the sole management of a plantation, pregnant women would be highly favored. A woman myself, I can sympathise with my sex w[h]ether white or black" (149). Women of both races might, she suggests, bond against southern patriarchy and the system of profit and loss it represents.

The African American body nonetheless constitutes a disturbing erotic presence in the gender economy of white southerners. To neutralize this physicality, Thomas resorts to the strategies of representation assisting in bodily erasure. She hints at yet displaces the sexuality of Union General Kilpatrick's African American mistress by placing her "lolling indolently in a rocking chair" and by stressing her, in Thomas's view, outrageous access to white men's food: "A seat at the table was furnished her – " (253). In describing a hired girl of color in 1866, she mentions no bodily attributes except the signifier of difference: Martha's brown complexion. While clothing might help veil African American female sexuality, Thomas, like other southern ladies after the war, feels nothing short of rage at watching black bodies wrapped in emblems of white femininity: "Yesterday numbers of the negro women some of them quite black were promenading up the streets with black lace veil shading them from the embrowning rays of the sun under whose influence they had worked all their life..." (274). Bodily concealment, despite strategic advantages, was not to erase southern racial boundaries.

The abandonment of these boundaries in southern sexual relations nevertheless presented particular difficulties of representation. In treating the interracial sexual contacts of her circle, Thomas vacillates, as with her own secret, between speech and silence, presence and absence:

> Southern women are I believe all at heart abolisionists [sic] but there I expect I have made a very broad assertion but I *will stand* to the opinion that the institution of slavery degrades the white man more than the Negro and oh exerts a most deleterious effect upon our children – But this is the dark side of the picture, written with a Mrs Stowe's feeling – but when I look upon so many young creatures growing up belonging to Pa's estate as well as others – I wonder upon whom shall the accountability of their future state depend – (168-69)

The enslaved African American body contaminates white gender and generational relations, yet exists in the passage only linguistically.[20] Thomas inscribes its sexuality only with italics, dashes, interruptions, and openendedness, as a threatening non-presence. Part of her representational problems involves, of course, the sexual taboos of her time and region; another concerns her inability to establish, in terms of moral conduct, a different signification for slaves and masters. In May 1869, she notes about whites in her community that "the majority of us expect no more virtue from our Negro men and women than we do from our horses and cows." A few lines down, she continues: "Just here the idea occurs to me that if virtue be the test to distinguish a man from a beast, the claim of many Southern white men might be questionable to the claim of 'Man made in the image of his maker' but this is a digression" (313).

While the master and the slave both signify bestiality rather than virtue, the African American body was to Thomas, and to her white peers, a blank page, the signifier of white fears and desires. She expresses, for example, her educational politics in a discourse in which the insertion of the sexualized African American body represents her resentment of equality and the prospect of social and racial

---

20. LeeAnn Whites argues that Thomas's statement concerning southern women as abolitionists refers less to a common bond between all southern women, slaves included, than to a wish among planter-class women to have the same power as their men to set the standards of their culture. See "The Civil War as a Crisis in Gender," in *Divided Houses: Gender and the Civil War*, ed. Catherine Clinton and Nina Silber (New York: Oxford U P, 1992), p. 7.

chaos. Faced with a woman of color who wishes her daughter to have a school education, Thomas states: "Such things as this made me shudder when I look into the future and see white women and mulattoes prove rivals unconscious though the former may be – Education will but intensify the tropical, passionate nature of the coloured woman..." (329). As Thomas's careful reference to the "unconscious" nature of white women's (sexual) rivalry indicates, the white southern woman saw the marked African American body as other, onto which she projected the dark side of her repressed self.

To suggest the corporeity of white southern ladies accordingly constituted an affront, in that it linked them with slaves and prostitutes, thus depriving southern ladyhood of racial and social privileges. "Beast" Butler's Order No. 28 of May 15, 1862, in which he stated that any lady in New Orleans displaying contemptuous behavior towards a U. S. officer or soldier "shall be regarded and held liable to be treated as a woman of town plying her avocation" triggers in Thomas's diary a vitriolic rebuttal of the "vile loathsome" Union general (206), the "honour" of white southern women the signifier of Confederate resistance. If nothing else, then, southern women shared, regardless of color, the dubious privilege of surrendering their bodies to discourse, pages upon which their racial or social superiors could, in Mitchie's phrase, "write their narratives of her significance."[21]

As Butler's order hints, the Civil War nonetheless liberated not just the African American female body from previous bondage. Thomas's own writing had, in an 1855 entry suggesting Jefferson Thomas's marital infidelities, burst the codes of corporal representation, her "agitated form" and the "wild tumultuous throbbings of early womanhood" (128) the signs of a bodily presence usually better concealed. During the war, however, Confederate bodies literally invade Thomas's coded rhetoric with a demand to inscribe the full horror of their suffering. On a visit to the 3rd Georgia Hospital in July 1864, Thomas finds "a state of destitution such as I had read of but never imagined before." Her entry goes on: "laying [sic] on the floor upon beds hastily filled with straw were wounded men,

---

21. Mitchie, p. 61.

wounded in every manner. Some with their arms and legs cut off, others with flesh wounds, two men in a dying state..." (229). The freeing of the body from representational taboos extends to some degree to Thomas's own flesh, which at high points of the war escapes rhetorical frames. Upon Jefferson Thomas's departure for the front, for example, his wife meets him for a last goodbye and exclaims in her diary, before she manages to censor herself with a dash: "What a thrill of contentment passed through me to see him again and receive the familiar kiss – " (192). Finding herself with child again (her husband spent only a total of nine months at the front), she notes with considerable frankness: "During the first months of pregnancy I am always sadly depressed and the body acting upon the mind my whole nature is affected" (258). Due to the prospect of "Sherman's visit" in March 1865, her "nervous system received a shock which was terrible" (258), yet she attempts to abandon the delicacy of privileged ladyhood: "It will not do for me to acquire a habit of becoming faint for I will require all my energy to meet the exigencies of the times ahead of us" (264). After the war, Thomas steps into liberty along with her slaves by usurping her physical freedom to move about without a gentleman escort. As she confides to her diary upon taking her first independent trip to Macon: "I think and think boldly, I act – and act boldly" (280). This new audacity, combined with the increased housework for white women in early Reconstruction, results in more frequent, if guarded, references to food and eating, as when Thomas briefly manages to hire a competent cook in May, 1865: "That night and the next morning I ate two biscuits which she baked (an unusual thing for me to do). At dinner the next day she baked one of the best plum pies I ever tasted" (273). When the family's financial misfortunes compel Thomas to take up teaching and writing for publication, the formerly protected lady announces without the shame the phrase might have caused her a few years earlier: "I am a public woman now" (400).[22]

---

22. George C. Rable discusses the Thomas family's financial decline in *Civil Wars: Women and the Crisis of Southern Nationalism* (Urbana: U of Illinois P, 1991), pp. 243-44.

Confederate Bodies: The Journal of Ella Gertrude Clanton Thomas

The narrative of Thomas's bodily experiences becomes, in other words, the story of the social body to which she pledged allegiance. As Julia Kristeva hypothesizes about women's texts, "it is as if the effects giving rise to intersubjective relations and social projects ... were here reduced to the level of secretions and intestines, carefully disguised by the culture of the past...."[23] With and through her body, Thomas commented on issues such as gender, identity, race, religion, work, and more, while simultaneously exploring and exhorting Confederate fantasies and demons. Her body, in other words, holds the clues to the cultural, political, and moral questions of her time, its scarlet blotches and unmentionable pains the marks of the diseases causing the downfall and possible redemption of her region. With its oscillations between presence and absence, between exposure and concealment, however, this southern woman's body, literal and textual, remains elusive. As Virginia Woolf would conclude upon her own production, "telling the truth about my own experiences as a body, I do not think I solved. I doubt that any woman has solved it yet."[24]

---

23. Julia Kristeva, "Talking about *Polylogue*," in Moi, p. 112.
24. Virginia Woolf, "Professions for Women," in Mary Eagleton, *Feminist Literary Theory* (Oxford: Basil Blackwell, 1986), p. 53.

Kate Stone

CHAPTER THREE

Negotiating Southern Territories: Kate Stone's *Brokenburn*

In the opening lines of her diary entry for March 15, 1863, Kate Stone writes:

> For the last two days we have been in a quiver of anxiety looking for the Yankees every minute, sitting on the front gallery with our eyes strained in the direction they will come, going to bed late and getting up early so they will not find us asleep. Today as it is raining, they are apt to remain in camp....[1]

At the time she recorded this experience, Kate Stone was, like Gertrude Thomas in the early sections of *The Secret Eye*, "the much indulged young lady of the house" (3). The twenty-two-year-old Kate was the oldest daughter of the dauntless widow Amanda Stone, thirty-nine years old in 1863, whose household included as well Kate's five brothers and a young sister. With her much-mentioned strong business acumen, Amanda had established her family at Brokenburn, a large cotton plantation in northeast Louisiana, in the present Madison Parish, where she owned 1,260 acres of the fertile, black soil and about 150 slaves. She had brought down for her children a private tutor and planned a grand European tour for 1862.

---

1. John Q. Anderson, ed., *Brokenburn: The Journal of Kate Stone, 1861-1868* (1955, Baton Rouge: LSU P, 1972), p. 179. Future references to *Brokenburn* will in this chapter be given parenthetically in the text.

As the title of Kate's diary indicates, social and geographical location is crucial to the project of southern self-definition. Indeed, the Stones' typical antebellum life is set in what Marie Louise Pratt labels a "contact zone," a colonial frontier "where disparate cultures meet, clash and grapple with each other, often in highly asymmetrical relations of domination and subordination."[2] Literally and textually, Kate Stone's Brokenburn owes its existence to a series of negotiation strategies that attempt to reconcile or highlight the conflicting impulses and interests of the contact zone. As she records her careless, leisured days at Brokenburn, and the increasing anxiety and northern victories that lead to the family's flight and refugee life in Texas, she must negotiate between social and natural landscapes and, in describing her southern environment, take into consideration dichotomies such as inside/outside, order/disorder, Louisiana/Texas, and, as the war proceeds, life and death.

These negotiating moves surface, if only partially, in the lines from her 1863 entry quoted above. Kate's gaze, as she wonders about the arrival of the Yankees, locates her in a domestic landscape, from which she surveys the grounds of the family plantation. Yet the gallery where she sits with eyes strained is in itself the result of negotiation: neither inside nor outside, it allows the author an ambiguous position appropriate to the transformation in terms of fate and fortune waiting just beyond her vision. Despite her earnest attempt at seeing, Kate remains strangely blind to the landscape itself, more or less reduced to "the direction they will come." The narrative segment focuses on the social terrain: her changed sleeping and waking-up schedule and the Yankees themselves. The enemy soldiers seem crucial to her familial and regional self-definitions – a "they" to enable the "we"s and "our"s of the passage. What attention Kate pays to natural phenomena seems rooted in a sort of military aesthetics: the connection between the rain and the Yankees remaining in camp. The scene surveyed originates, however, in Kate's imagination. After all, the Yankees

---

2. Marie Louise Pratt, *Imperial Eyes: Travel Writing and Transculturation* (London: Routledge, 1992), p. 4.

are *not* coming, and the natural and textual landscape remains, despite her gesture towards feminine quivering and fear, within the author's control. For now, at least, she has successfully negotiated the precarious (im)balance of the contact zone characteristic of *Brokenburn* as a whole. Such negotiations may appear less clearly in what Sara Mills calls dominant readings of women's texts, emphasizing the autobiographical, the personal.[3] The fault-lines of Brokenburn's various landscapes reveal more fully the tensions of southern culture.

This distinction between author and landscape is, of course, an arbitrary one. As Robert Lawson-Peebles points out, we perceive the geography we are conditioned to perceive[4]; encountering nature, the beholder turns toward the self or projects onto nature private emotions and moods. This "country of the mind" phenomenon surfaces throughout Kate's diary. On August 25, 1861, for example, Kate mourns an early victim of the war. The following entry begins with a melancholy description of a gloomy, wet scenery: "Do I hear it raining again tonight? After three weeks of it and two bright days, it is too discouraging" (48). Upon having her favorite horse stolen by Yankees in 1863, Kate makes even more explicit the connection between mood and environment: "I think I will never see lilac blooms again without recalling this sad incident" (183). Because they function as relatively unmonitored textual cracks, Kate's descriptions of social/geographical landscapes distinctly chart zonal conflicts, not all related to Union issues.

To a degree, the domestic landscapes that dominate Kate's account of Civil War life constituted a freedom from social/racial negotiations and contracts. Her own room at Brokenburn, at least, serves as protection against visual interference. "I have moved back in my own cosy room again," she writes in June 1861. "I like it better than the large east room with its staring windows" (23). Her room functions, in fact, both as a feminine site and as a temporary

---

3. Sara Mills, *Discourses of Difference: An Analysis of Women's Travel Writing and Colonialism* (London: Routledge, 1991), p. 51.
4. Robert Lawson-Peebles, *Landscape and Written Expression in Revolutionary America* (Cambridge: Cambridge U P, 1988), p. 4.

retreat from role requirements: "I did not see them," she notes after a visit from the neighboring planter and his son, " – it was a business visit – and I had a rising on my face" (95). Kate repeatedly equates her home with protection, whether from strangers' eyes, mosquitoes, climate, or Yankees. The indoor world, indeed, is the seat of the self and of regional identity. Mr. Stenckrath, a new tutor, attempts to control the free articulation of (southern) identity at Brokenburn, but is immediately stopped. "As if we could help talking in our own home circle of the most important and stirring facts in the world to us," Kate explains (98).

Any invasion of home thus means an invasion of self. Outside slaves and Yankees threaten to intrude upon feminine domesticity, a threat resulting in fear of what cannot be negotiated or articulated. In March 1863, Kate jots down: "The life we are leading now is a miserable, frightened one – living in constant dread of great danger, not knowing what form it may take, and utterly helpless to protect ourselves" (185). A segment that implicitly associates the invasion of "home" with the invasion of the female body constitutes the silenced realization of these fears. A rhetoric of rape permeates Kate's description of armed soldiers rushing into the Big House, "breaking things open," a "big black wretch" eventually "bursting into our room" (195) and approaching Kate and her sister, phallic paraphernalia in hand: "He came right up to us standing on the hem of my dress while he looked me slowly over, gesticulating and snapping his pistol" (196). The reversed positions – the black man standing, the white girls crouching – as well as the inverted pattern of looking – the soldier's slow gaze, Kate's downcast eyes – suggest a new order. Kate's emphasis on violence and sexualization, the young belle the object of African American desire, equates this break in established cultural hierarchies and spaces with perversity. Amanda's immediate decision to leave this violated domestic territory represents an attempt to restore Kate's home – and, by implication, her body and selfhood – to normality.

In a world turned upside down, however, a restoration of the domestic landscape creates problems. Accordingly, Kate postpones the articulation of self in her journal till a new domesticity may be enacted. She will not describe the flight from Brokenburn, after all, until "anchored somewhere" (189). Resuming routines of visiting and sewing helps restore a sense of home in the absence of everything that once constituted home (204, 205), to rephrase William L. Andrews on Mary Rowlandson in *Journeys in New Worlds*,[5] but the physical frailty of one of the Stones' "homes" highlights the difficulty of the project: "The boards have shrunken until daylight shines through," Kate notes in August 1863 about a shelter in Lamar County, Texas. "Lightning flashes continuously, thunder is rolling overhead..." (234). At one point, Amanda and Kate's sense of home is reduced to a rocking chair (269) or, eventually, to memory, as at the end of the war they admire the Mickie house "in the old style" (301) on their way back to the flooded and collapsing Brokenburn.

Throughout Kate's journal, however, "home" – and the identity it implies – remains a rhetorical signal, more important, in fact, than life itself. "We should make a stand for our rights," Kate states at the break-out of war in 1861," – and a nation fighting for its own homes and liberty cannot be overwhelmed" (19). She describes the North/South conflict in family metaphors, as "host against host" and as "children of one common Mother, now stand[ing] opposing each other in deadliest hate" (36). Transferred to the domestic landscape, war nonetheless becomes aesthetics, as the female inhabitants of the home environment work on "the boys' rosettes, red and white with a blue button for the center" that all of their company will eventually wear (38).

Despite the frequent connotations of shelter and protection surrounding Kate Stone's domestic landscapes, "home" remains in *Brokenburn* an ambiguous location, which Kate also describes as a prison (of gender). Though in the absence of home she attempts to transform public space into private, she dreads the seclusion and isolation of southern womanhood cut off from unchaperoned mobility. As in Gertrude Thomas's diary, Kate's dissatisfaction with the enclosed landscapes that define her occasionally ruptures her plot and her prose: "Oh, this inactive life when there is such stir and excitement in the busy world outside. It is enough to run one

---

5. William L. Andrews, ed., *Journeys in New Worlds: Early American Women's Narratives* (Madison, Wis.: U of Wisconsin P, 1990), p. 21.

wild. Oh! to be in the heat and turmoil of it all, to live, to live, not stagnate here" (87). The domestic settings of Kate's diary consequently appear unstable, not just because of the war but also due to their suspension between protection and imprisonment as well as between femininity and feminism.

The author's double function as subject and object of the negotiation process necessitated by domestic conflicts surfaces in the various (self-)contradictions of the journal. Thus, returning in 1865 to the family plantation she has so desperately missed, Kate highlights isolation and imprisonment: "How still and lifeless everything seems.... Everything seems sadly out of time" (365). What Kate has discovered, of course, despite the circularity of her narrative, is that she cannot go home again, and that the order she will negotiate for Brokenburn in the 1900 preface will forever remain rhetorical.

The ambivalence occupying Kate's interior landscape fills also her account of the space that defines it: the exterior. On the one hand, the outside perfectly matches the protection offered by the inside – in passages emphasizing the hardship and discomfort of exposure. Though Kate and her companions venture out in a carriage, thus carrying with them a certain domesticity, the outside challenges their protected space: "Had rather a stirring time getting to the Bend, a rough road and had to get out in the rain for the mules to pull up the levee and out again for them to pull down it" (22). The party spends a dry day inside the Reading residence, but as they return, nature again plays the antagonist determined to cause inconvenience: "in the afternoon [we] walked back through mud and slush to regain the carriage on the other side of the mudhole" (22). The sense of exposure outside the domestic turf originates in climate, roads, insects, war and whatnot, but also in looks from strangers. As Kate notes in November 1863, "There are more pleasant things than toiling a mile through heavy sand, up hill and down dale – too dark to see the road beneath you or the sky above, sitting for an hour listening to an indifferent sermon, and being gazed at by a battery of hostile eyes" (252). That Kate can neither speak nor see in this outside indicates, of course, the loss of power and control she associates with public terrain.

Negotiating Southern Territories: Kate Stone's Brokenburn

On the other hand, the outside also brings freedom and excitement, the complement to Kate's recurring sense of imprisonment within domestic scenarios. "Late in the afternoon I went with Brother Coley and Ashburn to the blackberry patch, a glorious ride, a fresh breeze, splendid horse, and a sweeping pace, and the two frolicsome boys," she records in June, 1861 (23). Kate's adjectives communicate her excitement at having escaped the immobility and isolation of domesticity, as well as its feminine bonds and rules. Refugee life thus has its rewards. In what Kate calls "the dark corner of the Confederacy," somewhere in Texas, the family loses its way, but, as Kate writes, "it was cool and bright moonlight and really more pleasant than a stuffy dirty room..." (237).

Kate negotiates inside/outside tensions not just by frequenting a space of neither/nor – the gallery – but also by bringing the outside inside and vice versa. "On the mantle," she writes in April 1865, "is our first spring bouquet, wreathes of flowering almond, tufts of brilliant phlox, a handful of the coral honeysuckle loved by the boys, gold and purple pansies, as large as those in Louisiana, and sweetest of all, the cluster of purple and white lilac" (326). Kate's details and narrative energy help nature blossom inside the sitting room of "Bonnie Castle" in Tyler, Texas. In an opposite move, however, Kate's descriptions of exterior landscapes reveal her desire to transform outside space to inside. She mentions repeatedly "Nature's *carpeting* of soft, green grass" (112, emphasis added) and pushes her domesticating impulse even further in descriptions like the one that follows:

> The ride home through Oasis was just perfect. On one side was the tall *colonnades* of cypress and on the other the far reaching rows of waving corn, *emerald* in the sun. The horses were fleet and free as the wind that *fanned* us, and a smooth, hard road rang *like metal* under the hoofs of the horses. (116, emphasis added)

She speaks as well of "yellow coreopsis in full bloom and *gemmed* with countless little mounds of bright green, *like emeralds set in gold*" (225, my emphasis), the italicized words and phrases indicating her civilizing impulse in describing natural landscapes. Hiding in

Kate's prose, one might guess, is the fear, or hope, that negotiations between inside and outside – in short between civilization and nature – will break down, leaving herself and her family at the mercy of the contact zone, with its threat of unknown and unknowable social/geographical constellations.

Kate encodes these concerns upon the Louisiana terrain by dividing the outside up into zones. The gallery, as we have seen, represents a compromise between interior and exterior landscapes. The garden, moreover, serves as a domesticated zone, in which order and civilization reign, while the woods beyond suggest the opposite: disorder, even savagery, but also, not surprisingly, freedom. Mrs. Savage's garden, for example, comforts its owner in the face of scarlet fever on her place (and the African bodies carrying it). As Kate sees it in 1861, "her garden is lovely, such a variety of flowers all in bloom and in lovely order" (21). Kate's garden descriptions indicate her primary goal of presenting herself as feminine and sensitive.[6] In admiring plantation gardens, she reverts to a limited vocabulary of clichés that signal femininity and order, established linguistically through a comforting repetition of words and phrases. "Her garden is lovely now," she writes of Mrs. Savage's place again in 1862 (119). As Kate's clichés suggest, the garden functions less as observable terrain than as a setting enabling genteel social interaction. "Joe, Mr. Baker, and Mr. McNeely made themselves very agreeable," Kate notes in June 1862. "We had a charming time in the grand old garden" (120). Gardens serve, in short, as a safe backdrop for romance or as mere social signifiers. "The flowers are getting on beautifully," Kate records in June of 1861. "We will soon have a garden to be proud of. It will rival Mrs. Savage's and Mrs. Carson's" (27). Pattie Booth's home in Vicksburg thus meets with Kate's approval: "What a delightful home they have and the loveliest flower garden, nearly equals Mrs. Savage's" (104). In its garden variant, then, nature signifies civilized, feminine relations, its social signifieds just about blocking the garden itself from view. "Mrs. Carson gave Mamma plants of sweet olive,

---

6. Cp. Mills, p. 179.

Negotiating Southern Territories: Kate Stone's Brokenburn

magnolia fuscata and purple magnolia," Kate writes with unusual detail, but immediately moves on to an interpretation of the plants as social gesture: "She has been most kind and is very lovable" (61). Significantly, discourses of natural and social description overlap.

The woods offer freedom from social conventions, but consequently threaten with disorder and danger. Kate jubilantly records "delightful" rides through the woods, outings often referred to as "frolics" to suggest the overthrow of social restrictions. Kate's entry for October 4, 1861, typifies her many rides: "All enjoyed a most glorious dash through the rain this evening. Had gone up to thrash a pecan tree near Mr. Hardison's when the shower came up and we raced home" (57). Though the account lands Kate and company safely at home again, her wetness and speed might suggest a displaced sexuality. Indeed, nature occasionally seduces Kate and her friends off beaten tracks in Little Red Ridinghood fashion: "we were going only 'a piece' with [Jimmy]. But the roads, the weather – it misted on us all the way – and the fine condition of our horses tempted us on, and we went all the way, returning by Winn Forest …. Rode up at a sweeping gallop" (67).

The sexual terrain of the forest nonetheless inspires anxiety and fear, though Kate cannot articulate the erotic subtext. On August 24, 1861, for example, Kate returns "alone" from Vicksburg, the faithful and solicitous driver of her carriage having obviously lost his way: "we were about two hours after dark – and it was pitch dark – coming through the woods. I was horribly afraid…" (46). Though the wilderness thus implies both freedom and danger, Kate frequently opts to contemplate it from a position of safe domesticity: "All night long through the beating of the rain and the wailing wind, we could hear the screams of a poor mother whose little child was 'lost and gone in the forest wild' – a wee tot of two years who had wandered away in the morning hunting nuts" (306). Situated in the geographical and cultural ambiguity of the contact zone, such retreat remains, however, illusory.

The Louisiana swamp epitomizes most intensely the ambiguity, chaos, or even barbarism of the contact zone. For one thing, the river constantly threatens to break through the levees protecting plantation society, thus literally flooding the land/water opposition (15, 104). Moreover, the swamp air invades the minds and bodies residing on the bayou, infections that lead to what Kate refers to as "trouble" in the quarters and chills and fevers, even death, among slaves and owners alike – in short, to loss of control.[7] In the middle of the Tensas swamp during the first stage of the Stones' flight, Kate's verbs as well as their agents suggest that the family has entered an ambiguous, chaotic realm in which nature overpowers culture – a realm, in short, of process and change:

> We went on in company and were in the boats for seven hours in the beating rain and the sickening sun, sitting with our feet in the water. Not an inch of land was to be seen during the journey through the dense swamp and over the swift curling currents. The water was sometimes twenty feet deep, rushing and gurgling around the logs and trees.... [Aunt Laura] was terrified nearly to death and was alternately laughing and crying. (201)

Kate populates the tumultuous bayou not just with hysterical refugees tempted into a sort of insanity but also with dark creatures in various ways representing (human) regression,[8] the erosion of civilization into savagery. The distinction was at best fragile in Kate's plantation world, for, as she explains in the introduction, "on this new place, stretching back into a cypress swamp that extended miles away, the wolves were still at home" (6). On the pages of the diary itself, the swamp shelters runaway slaves, southern traitors and not least Yankees, all in Kate's thinking forces of anarchy and evil: "The Yankees are very daring, swimming the bayous, plunging through the mud of the unbroken swamp, often only two or three of them together. One company of good men could put a stop to all of this, but all of our men are across the Macon..." (174). Like the woods, the swamp threatens as well with its unrestrained if unarticulated eroticism.[9] In a vignette paralleling Kate's trip back home from Vicks-

---

7. David Miller, *Dark Eden: The Swamp in Nineteenth-Century American Literature* (Cambridge: Cambridge U P, 1990), p. 13.
8. Cp. Lawson-Peebles, p. 129.
9. Cp. Pratt, p. 90; David Miller, pp. 118ff.

burg, Lou and Mrs. Morris arrive at the Templetons' Louisiana estate "quite worn out from the fatigue and the fright of being in the dark swamp alone with nobody but their driver" (295).

In a significant entry written in the last years of the war, Kate nonetheless links her own identity to the swamp:

> I feel a real Louisianan once more – in the very heart of the swamp, suffocating with the heat, fighting mosquitoes, lazy and languid, little appetite, but luxuriating on fruit for breakfast, dinner, and supper and enjoying curds and cream. The swamp is my own dear land – most natural, most restful. (296)

To an extent, the Louisiana swamp that Kate in 1864 recreates through memory and writing constitutes a fantasy of antebellum leisure and privilege, yet her emotional attachment to the swamp resides as well in the chaotic otherness of the bayou environment. As David Miller explains in *Dark Eden: The Swamp in Nineteenth-Century American Literature*, the swamp "became a symbol for Southern civilization, whether positively or negatively conceived," and for alternative visions of American culture associated with women and matriarchy, with change, and, despite Kate's misgivings, with African Americans. The swamp accordingly represents "the underside of patriarchal culture," a heretical, "wayward" landscape of the body, femininity, sexuality, infection, subversion, irrationality and creativity.[10] Indeed, Kate's swamp fantasy proposes a feminine, non-efficient, pleasurable, and irrational existence, associated with the "un-American" South though also, as she must realize, with dominance. These ambiguities perfectly dramatize the psychological and cultural negotiations of the contact zone, whether represented through descriptions of the Louisiana swamp or the Texas prairie.

Like the bayous of Kate's home state, the Texas landscape functions as an antithesis to civilization, belonging to what David Miller classifies as "'desert' places," characterized by indifference or hostility towards human concerns and social structures.[11] Kate refers

---

10. David Miller, pp. 8, 9.
11. David Miller, p. 1.

to the inhospitable Texas environment as "this land of misery" (244) or even "such desert places of life" (245), an almost evil zone outside human control, with "thick growing vegetation" and "frequent snakes gliding across" (245) or "stretched across the road basking in the sun" (238). The Goddards' home somewhere in the Tyler vicinity is, as Kate sees it, "just the wildest most remote section of civilization," with "only the necessaries, none of the luxuries of life" (275). Literally, the Texas prairie constitutes a colonial frontier, where cultures clash and disorder reigns. Kate highlights, for example, the hostilities between the Louisiana refugees and the Texas natives:

> The more we see of the people, the less we like them, and every refugee we have seen feels the same way. They call us all *renegades* in Tyler. It is strange the prejudice that exists all through the state against refugees. We think it is envy, just pure envy. The refugees are nicer and more refined people than most of those they meet, and they see and resent the difference. (238)

The contact zone, Kate notes, endorses lawlessness and crime, thus demonstrating its barbarism:

> We hear no news now but accounts of murders done and suffered by the natives. Nothing seems more common or less condemned than assassination. There have been four or five men shot or hanged within a few miles of us within a week. No one that we have seen seems surprised or shocked, but take it as a matter of course that an obnoxious person should be put to death by some offended neighbor. (226-27)

In order to establish what she defines as order and control in the Texas contact zone, Kate resorts to the discursive strategies of Pratt's imperialists. She refers, as in the quotes above, to Texans as generic "natives" or "they," a generalizing move that delegates the people she observes to the position of undifferentiated otherness. Like imperial eyes before and after her, Kate reduces the Texas population to a subhuman status, brought about, no doubt, by the class division between the "refined" refugees and the "envious" natives. Upon going to a Texas barbecue, one Mr. Michelle insists upon Kate's party not eating: "'Why,' said he, 'should we dine with plebians [sic]?'" As Kate explains, "we went out, as Mamma said, 'to see the animals feed'" (292). In a similarly imperialist mode, Kate describes the Texas population as inhabiting a mythological, eternal present or hopelessly caught in the past. Kate's letter to Anna Dobbs is a case in point. "I am already as disgusted as I expected to be," Kate writes in an unconscious adherence to the "country of the mind" phenomenon already discussed. "It is a place where people are just learning that there is a war going on.... Hoops are just coming in with full fashion.... We are in the dark corner" (223, 224). Finally, like imperialist travellers, Kate emphasizes the natives' difference from herself, which almost, as Lawson-Peebles notes about the Lewis-Clark expedition, threatens to break down discourse itself.[12] Here is Kate recording a funeral service in Lamar County: "It was the oddest-looking crowd one could imagine, and the very funniest dressing we ever saw. My pen is powerless to describe it" (234). Her perspective remains nonetheless "normalizing," her "manners and customs portraits" of Texas natives once again part of imperialist discursive traditions.

Kate's "judging voice," however, slowly becomes an "experiencing voice," a transformation that, as other critics have observed,[13] reflects the traveller's tendency to readjust established values and beliefs. In commenting on one of Amanda's trips to secure favors and provisions, Kate states that "the turnout for the trip was essentially Texas" (257). By the end of the *Brokenburn* journal, the natives have actually become individuals. "I know most of the love affairs of Tyler now," Kate writes in 1865. "I hope Janie Roberts and Lt. Alexander will make a match" (320). Though Amanda's "Texas turnout" is "anything but stylish" (257) and Janie Roberts belongs to the "*crème de la crème*" of Tyler society, Kate once again identifies with the contact zone producing her, the negotiations and tensions of the zone constructing her Texas script.

---

12. Mills, p. 86; Lawson Peebles, pp. 214f.
13. Andrews, *Journeys*, p. 76.

Whether in Louisiana or Texas, Kate finds the social rather than the geographical encounters with her surroundings most stimulating. She populates her journal with relatives, tutors, neighbors, cousins, friends, visitors, admirers and soldiers in endless processions; her psychological studies frequently relegate the geographical ones to the margin of her consciousness, and her diary pages. The tall, handsome Col. Ferguson "is fired with most eager ambition and thirst for distinction," but "has an air of frankness and the most engaging freshness and naïveté in conversation I ever saw in a man" (102); Carrie Lowry is "a very talkative, nice girl with only one good feature in her face, splendid grey eyes" (152); Mrs. Morancy "is the typical young widow and very bright," but, Kate suspects, "sly" (215). Even when camping outdoors, Kate soon turns away from scenery and equipment to the acquaintances visited along the way (366). Through personification, Kate even adds nature to her cast of characters. On a perfect day in July 1861, nature is "in a laughing mood" (38); after the first death in the family in November, Kate notes that "'the Melancholy days have come' for our household but not for Dame Nature" (70).

Nature occupies in *Brokenburn* a space bordering upon representation. Kate uses the geographical landscape as a prop allowing narrative and social events to take place, but the terrain as such frequently recedes into invisibility. In October 1861, Kate thus records: "Dr. Lily waylaid us wandering through the garden and we chatted out there until dark. Dr. Devine is to be married next Thursday. Dr. Lily is going and will report on the bride's dress and bring us a piece of dream cake" (58). Even in describing outdoor excursions, the landscape exists only through absence. In Kate's words, "In the late afternoon I went riding with Ashburn. We returned by Tensas bridge and stopped at Mr. Curry's for the mail…" (32). While the bridge here anchors Kate's (narrative) movement, the woods and the river remain implied and fail to enter the writer's and reader's vision. If Kate attempts a representational move in terms of terrain, she translates terrestrial invisibility into a linguistic one, i.e. into cliché. In describing a journey home, she needs for dramatic purposes an unfriendly environment and comes up with these lines: "Night came on apace, wrapped in her sable mantle and unbrightened by a star, and we were still four miles from our own hearthstone..." (246). Apart from the personification that displaces the natural onto the personal, Kate relies on clichés that, indeed, just barely bring a signified into existence. The additional displacement of spatiality into temporality, the darkened environment moving into the text as Night herself, further conceals the natural landscape, which, literally and metaphorically, remains wrapped in the sable mantle.

This discomfort with landscape formulation results in Kate's recurring choice of mediation in describing the environment she encounters and the emotions it inspires. Always an anxious authoress, she hides, so to speak, behind the words of others when her diary project calls for spatial sensibility. She writes in 1861 of a "lovely spring day" that it is "fair as a poet's dream of May" (15) and subsequently brings in poets and dramatists to speak for her of emotional and geographical experiences. To articulate the sad domestic locale at Christmas, 1863, Kate quotes form Lord Tennyson's "The Princess" (268); to sum up all of 1863, she links a series of quotations such as "We have swallowed our tears like water" and "His hands hath [sic] been heavy upon us" (272). She repeatedly approaches physical landscapes through reading (20) or protected by quotation marks. "'It is raining and it is hailing, and it is cold stormy weather,'" she begins the entry for February 1, 1862 (86). Possibly to create an ironic distance to the turmoil surrounding her, Kate resorts to mediation in moments of increased intensity. With this gesture, however, she also discloses her lack of interest – or competence – in the language of terrestrial description. Her absent discourse, in short, matches her absent landscapes, perhaps because of (writing) women's endemic absence from both. But the war redefined traditional visions and voices, and somewhat reluctantly Kate turned her attention towards the changing landscapes around her.

As Louisiana became contested territory, Kate directed an increasing amount of narrative energy to her besieged environment. Though still veiled in clichés, the southern terrain enters the diarist's vision: "Fair Louisiana, with her fertile fields of cane and cotton, her many bayous and dark old forests, lies powerless at the feet of the enemy" (100). Furthermore, a death in the household inspires in Kate a sense of loss and pain that opens her eyes, and her diary pages, to the natural landscape:

> The ride in the cool morning air through the dark still woods, sweet with the breath of the wild grape blossoms ... was a thing to enjoy. We stopped to gather the first blackberries, cool and wet with dew. How often I think of Ashburn when the pleasures he so enjoyed a year ago are in the world again. (116)

Due to the necessity of flight, nature takes on new significance, and thus new visibility (198-99), just as the unfamiliar Texas terrain forces itself upon Kate, at least as a screen upon which she, like other westward travellers, might project her hope and hostility (224, 225).[14] As the Texas landscape takes over her vision, however, the lost Louisiana fills up her mind. Seen from exile, the Brokenburn land thus becomes fully articulated:

> How I long for a glimpse at Brokenburn these pleasant autumn days – radiant in flowers and crowned with fruit, the grassy yard and tall oaks, the clump of sassafras changing now to bright crimson, and the fragrant sweet gum showering down its leaves of gold, the flower garden sparkling across the grass, its many kinds of fall flowers gay in the mellow September sun, and the wide fields stretching away, white with cotton and vocal with the songs of the busy pickers. (245)

The atypically long sentence and the details lavished upon the Brokenburn scene suggest the intensity of Kate's nostalgia, just as her panoramic vision and the laboring slaves evoke the dominance lost and missed. Yet Brokenburn is precisely what she does not actually see, as she is well aware with her "How I long for a glimpse of Brokenburn ..." introduction. Her preference for the landscapes of the imagination excuses her, to a degree, from grappling with her Texas surroundings and, besides, restores to her the sight, the sounds, and the control she fancied.

---

14. Cp. Lawson-Peebles, p. 229.

Negotiating Southern Territories: Kate Stone's Brokenburn

The war itself, however, provided Kate Stone with a language of terrestrial description. Along with other besieged southerners, she developed a way of perceiving her surroundings in terms of military strategies and manoeuvres.[15] Her forte remains the hierarchical military landscape of distinction and promotion. "My Brother," as Kate calls her brother William R. Stone, returns on leave on January 1, 1863, "in perfect health" but "oh," as Kate begins a lengthy passage on military rules and customs, "the disappointment that he is still only a captain" (167). Kate's concern with brothers, cousins and friends in the Confederate army lends new significance also to the geographical landscapes of the South. Upon learning that the Yankees have put "all the Negro men" to work on a ditch to be cut "across the point opposite Vicksburg above DeSoto," Kate notes in her diary: "They hope to turn the river through there and to leave Vicksburg high and dry, ruining that town and enabling the gunboats to pass down the river without running the gauntlet of the batteries at Vicksburg" (125). Though Kate's military aesthetics intermittently enables her to describe locales with new concreteness and precision, even the military landscapes originate in Kate's imagination. As a civilian (woman), she cannot enter the world in which her countrymen fight for success and survival, yet the martial viewpoint she appropriates rearranges the components of her environment and infuses her descriptive strategies with new authority.

Besides, the rearrangements in Kate's immediate surroundings were hard to ignore and entered her diary pages as descriptions of a world turned upside down. As in Thomas's *The Secret Eye*, southern bodyscapes were changing. "I must still cling to my calfskin *chaussures*, homeknit stockings and brogans, something different from the lace-like clock stockings and French slippers of the olden times," Kate writes in 1863 (231). In addition to bodily disturbances, primitivity and disorder invade as well the domestic and social milieus: "The room we are in has necessary furniture but looks

---

15. Elizabeth Leonard notes in *Yankee Women: Gender Battles in the Civil War* (New York: Norton, 1994), p. xvii, that many Civil War women diarists began to record their experiences through military imagery.

so dusty and dirty. There are no clean things for the beds and few towels and bathing facilities" (193). Only (white) female bodies, moreover, occupy the interior landscapes: "We are in a helpless situation," Kate writes some twenty pages earlier, "three ladies and two little girls and not a white man or even a gun on the place..." (175). In a passage that focuses upon the break-down of domestic habits and rituals, Kate's language itself signifies the insecurities of the social landscape:

> A year ago would we have thought of receiving, or of a friend offering, clothes as a present? ... How else shall we cover our nakedness? We have lost all and as yet can buy nothing. A year ago would we have thought of going even to the house of a friend to spend some time without an invitation? (189)

Not only the many question marks and the breathlessness of Kate's prose communicate the turmoil in which she finds herself; explicit statements testify as well to the collapse of community rites and bonds: "Our old neighborhood is scattered to the four winds," Kate concludes her last entry for 1863.

Terrestrial transformations further accentuate the cultural and rhetorical upheavals of Kate's war diary. As the Yankees approach Vicksburg, the river breaks through the city levee and Kate's syntactic order. "Such excitement!" she bursts out (103). At times, she cannot tell martial from natural upheavals: "Some think the cannonading at Vicksburg brings on the rains. It is seldom we hear the cannon that it is not succeeded by showers or a downpour, and often it is difficult to distinguish between the burst of thunder and the roar of the guns" (184). Even the southern climate enacts Confederate chaos. "The atmosphere has been most peculiar for several days," Kate notes in July 1863. "The air is cool and damp. The earth, the air, the sky, all are a dull dead grey. The sun seems to emit neither heat nor light, gleaming with a dim red glare like a blood-red moon" (227). More concretely, even, the increasing absence of slave labor transforms the southern terrain: "The fields as far as we can see," Kate observes, "are sheets of green and gold, the weeds are growing unchecked, and the yellow-top makes a brave show" (179-80).

Kate's landscapes of turmoil themselves oscillate between order and disorder. By representing a world turned upside down, she holds on, as Lawson-Peebles notes about writers of the American Revolution, to established, if inverted, horizons of perception.[16] Indeed, by depicting the southern landscape of war as somehow unnatural, she reinforces rather than expands antebellum systems of belief. At the same time, however, the overturned environment constitutes a cultural in-between, a transitory space susceptible to alterity. The sensory shift from sight to sound, for example, evident in the quote on Vicksburg thunder and cannons, immerses Kate in chaotic difference. As Miller explains with Walter Ong in *Dark Eden*, "sound surrounds the self" and "relates to a more spontaneous and immediate mode of being than does sight, which lends itself more to abstraction and preservation of experience as knowledge." Sound, Miller concludes, "presents the prospect of both immersion and absorption into otherness."[17] Suspended between self and other, as a white southern woman and a refugee and a writer at that, Kate realized, no doubt, the desirability, the inevitability and, perhaps, the impossibility of negotiations in the contact zone.

As military and political events turned the southern environment topsy-turvey, Kate's negotiations turned, in fact, distinctly geopolitical. In 1861 she describes Dr. Carson's slave quarters so positively that her geography of slavery enters political turf (41). The following year, her map of Maryland outlines a clearly political landscape of war and patriotism:

> There is great disappointment over Maryland. It was thought there would be a great uprising of the people as soon as the Stars and Bars should wave across the Potomac, but nothing of the kind.... Well, let the Old Bay State go, if her people had rather be slaves in the Union than masters in the Confederacy. (146)

---

16. Compare the anonymous correspondent to the *Montgomery Daily Advertiser* in July, 1864, whom Drew Gilpin Faust quotes in *Mothers of Invention: Women of the Slaveholding South in the American Civil War* (Chapel Hill: U of North Carolina P, 1996), p. 4: "The surface of society, like a great ocean, is upheaved, and all the relations of life are disturbed and out of joint."
17. David Miller, pp. 176, 177.

Kate dismisses Maryland precisely because it lacks the political zest of her own surroundings. The indefinite agents of the passage leave the political decision-makers of the Confederacy rather vague opponents to the Maryland people, but Kate's master/slave metaphor plants the passage firmly enough in southern geopolitical ground. In 1864 she enlists even the worms eating up the Yankee cotton crops in the river delta as southern sympathizers working in an entirely politicized terrain: "Those are true 'Confederate worms,' working for the good of the Cause" (298). As she makes clear in "the darkest hour" at the close of the war, nature basically tried to win the war the Confederates were losing: "The army worms were our best allies. They made the enemy abandon the country when our soldiers were powerless to drive them off" (313). In describing the contested southern territory, Kate, in short, entered geopolitics in order to enact a Confederate victory.

With the striking down of such Confederate hubris, however, Kate's landscapes suggest a just and natural order violated, resulting in the fall of a region rich in hope and promise and a state of abnormality and injustice. In 1863, Kate pushes to the foreground of her southern terrain the graveyard, a landscape of death that contrasts with her antebellum home and garden sketches: "The moonlight falls clear and cold on the graves of three of those who made the mirth and happiness of our home only two short summers ago ..." (262). Other graveyard sites, here Mr. Prentice's, enter Kate's tragic script and help delineate the unnatural state of affairs in the South: "Such a desolate-looking graveyard. Such sombre trees and leaden skies and such unhospitable soil and clay" (266). In 1865, Kate widens her scope and portrays a landscape of death stretching across the Confederacy and eroding all established differences between North and South, freedom and death:

> If nothing else can force us to battle on for freedom, the thousands of grass-grown mounds heaped on the mountainside and in every valley of our country should teach us to emulate the heroes who lie beneath and make us clasp closer to our hearts the determination to be free or die. (334)

Negotiating Southern Territories: Kate Stone's Brokenburn

Linguistically and perceptionally, Kate here makes a last bid for Confederate mastery, but the graveyard itself betrays, rather than sparks, her optimism and signals the end of Confederate negotiations.

At the close of the war, nature signals as well the beginning of hope. Beyond the silent graves, "Nature smiles down on all this wretchedness," Kate writes in May of 1865, her entry on the perfume, blooms and soil of the star jasmine concluding "That arbour is a favorite retreat" (343). Nature, in short, offered escape from southern defeat and protected, so to speak, Confederate survivors from themselves. The seasonal movement gave comfort, the cyclical recurrences of weather and crops as reassuring as the circularity of Kate's own life and text: "The lovely spring days are so fair that they make one love life in spite of trouble" (335). In a world of disorder and death, nature itself became a stabilizing force, delineating, in a sense, a demilitarized area within or beyond the contact zone.

In her account of life upon Confederate frontiers, Kate Stone crossed from interior to exterior settings, from order to chaos, from Louisiana to Texas, and back. Though her social landscapes reveal the dense conflicts of the contact region, her natural landscapes, however elusive and mute(d), communicate most subtly the anxieties, the hopes, and the survival strategies of Kate and her community. As she vacillates between enclosure and mobility, between speech and silence, between hope and despair, and between private and public realms, her southern landscapes articulate the innumerable changes that transformed the lives of Confederate men and women forever. Four decades after the war, Kate Stone thus observes that the gaiety of her Brokenburn years and the prospect of each of the Stone children eventually becoming a landowner collapsed "when in the winter of 1861 commenced the great events that swept away this joyous future and set our feet in new and rugged paths." "And," she concludes, "forty years from then, we are still walking the same rough path, laden with heavy burdens" (11). Why other southerners might have felt unburdened by the war and its aftermath, and whereto the new and rugged path might lead, remained, like much southern territory, forever beyond Kate Stone's horizon.

Mary Chesnut

CHAPTER FOUR

Writing Herstory: Mary Chesnut's Civil War

"The grandest of heroic deeds are those which are performed within four walls & in domestic privacy. And because history records only the self-sacrifices of the male sex & because she dips her pen only in blood – therefore it is that in the eyes of the unseen world our annals appear doubtless far more beautiful & noble than in our own." Johann Paul Friedrich Richter (1763-1825), quoted by Mary Chesnut.

In recording her observations of the inner circles of the Confederacy from February 18, 1861, through July 26, 1865, Mary Boykin Chesnut was at the same time redefining the notion of history. As historian C. Vann Woodward points out in his introduction to *Mary Chesnut's Civil War*, the "diary" of this intriguing writer was not the innocent woman's pastime it initially appeared to be. Instead, her published book on the fall of the South was a carefully arranged rewriting of raw notes, edited twenty years after the war to present a woman's version of southern history.[1] Mary Chesnut's work is, in fact, a feminist document, written by an observant, ambitious veteran of the battlefields of Confederate drawingrooms.

Mary Chesnut's Civil War is, moreover, a statement on Woman-as-Artist. Edmund Wilson was among the first to recognize the literary nature of what was then known as *A Diary from Dixie*, calling it "in its

---

1. C. Vann Woodward, ed., *Mary Chesnut's Civil War* (New Haven: Yale U P, 1981), pp. xv-xxix. Further references to this work will be given parenthetically in the text, with the designation *MCCW*.

informal department, a masterpiece."[2] Yet the "informal" form of the journal is in itself a rebellion against male conceptions of genre and gender. Throughout the many hundred pages of her work, Mary Chesnut repeatedly refers to the acts of reading and writing, distancing herself from masculine symbolic codes and, in the process, creating a subtext of feminine linguistic revolution. Through a hybrid form, a constant revision of events, and the multiple voices of her entries, Mary Chesnut established a discourse of femininity, an inscription of difference and *différance*. Herself an expert reader of politics and politicians, Chesnut thus composed herself as Woman and as rebel, writing a new text on a Lost Cause.

Chesnut's use of the diary form was initially a necessity rather than a conscious choice. In the rough draft, written during the Civil War and published as *The Private Mary Chesnut* in 1984, she repeatedly refers to interruptions and distractions which prevented sustained concentration.[3] Even during her revisions in the 1880s, she writes on a scrap of paper: "I have been interrupted three times in trying to *accomplish* this sentence."[4] In both versions of her diary, she includes shopping lists, records of money spent, and notes of visits paid and received in an effort to inscribe her woman's situation into the text.

At the same time, the genre was a strategic weapon in Chesnut's revision of his/story. "History reveals men's deeds – their outward character but not themselves," she notes in the 1880s version. "There is a secret self that hath its own life 'rounded by a dream' – unpenetrated, unguessed" (*MCCW* 799). The diary form allowed Chesnut, like Kemble, to pen-etrate her adversaries, to move the

---

2. Edmund Wilson, *Patriotic Gore: Studies in the Literature of the American Civil War* (New York: Oxford U P, 1962), p. 279.
3. C. Vann Woodward and Elizabeth Muhlenfeld, ed., *The Private Mary Chesnut: The Unpublished Civil War Diaries* (New York: Oxford U P, 1984). References to *The Private Mary Chesnut* will be given parenthetically in the text, with the designation *PMC*.
4. Elizabeth Muhlenfeld, *Mary Chesnut: A Biography* (Baton Rouge: LSU P, 1981), p. 195. For the writing and publication history of Chesnut's journals, see C. Vann Woodward's introduction to *Mary Chesnut's Civil War*, and his and Elisabeth Muhlenfeld's introduction to *The Private Mary Chesnut*.

battle to virgin soil, and to rescue the inhabitants of this domestic territory for posterity – without any revealing stains on her own femininity.

By erasing the line between the private and the political, Chesnut herself escaped from silence and, to an extent, from selfhood. "My subjective days are over," she writes on March 11, 1861. "No more *silent* eating into my own heart, making my own misery, when without these morbid fantasies I could be so happy..." (*MCCW* 23). At the opening of the Civil War, Chesnut discarded her "subjectivity" (closely related to her life at Mulberry, the family plantation) in order to enter history – and, in the process, to rewrite both.

Chesnut consistently inscribed her disposal of a passive, muted self within her accounts of the political intrigues of the Confederacy. As the wife of James Chesnut, Jr., a seasoned politician and lawyer close to Jefferson Davis, she had ample opportunity to watch the political theatre at Confederate headquarters. Though her marriage to the cool, detached "JC" was by no means unproblematic, Chesnut submerges her feminine powerlessness in the marital "we" when recording political strategies and schemes.[5] "We are here in Montgomery to make a new Confederacy – a new government, constitution, &c&c," she writes on February 18, 1861 (*MCCW* 5). Later in the book, she exclaims, "Now if *we* are not reelected to the Senate!" (*MCCW* 173, my emphasis). Through her husband, she hoped to influence the fate of the community in which she ultimately immersed herself: the South. "Why did *we* not follow the flying foe across the Potomac," she asks, arguing that "*We* had about 15,000 effective men in all" (*MCCW* 121, my emphases).[6]

Chesnut's intimate association with masculine power resulted in the emergence of an explicitly ambitious, feminist self, which demanded individual recognition rather than collectivist immersion. "I

---

5. For a discussion of Mary Chesnut's marital relations, see Bell Irvin Wiley, *Confederate Women* (New York: Barnes & Noble, 1975), pp. 35-37.
6. Drew Gilpin Faust notes in *Mothers of Invention: Women of the Slaveholding South in the American Civil War* (Chapel Hill: U of North Carolina P, 1996) that "southern ladies struggled to make the Confederacy a common cause with their men, to find a place for themselves in a culture increasingly preoccupied with the quintessentially male concerns of politics and battle" (p. 10).

have worked like a beaver – or rather a mole – for my friends, and this is the first one who has thanked me – seeing shrewdly my fingers in the pie," she comments on a letter from a grateful office-seeker (*MCCW* 83). "I wish Mr. Davis would send *me* to Paris," she writes in contemplating her husband's prospects for a French ambassadorship. Ultimately, she protests, like Kate Stone and Sarah Morgan, her prohibitive biology: "Oh, that I was a man!" (*MCCW* 142, 224). In an era of action and excitement, Chesnut chafed at her prison of gender: "I think *these* times make all women feel their humiliation in the affairs of the world. With *men* it is on to the field – 'glory, honour, praise, &c, power.' Women can only stay at home – – " (*PMC* 145). Within her own four walls, however, Chesnut usurped considerable political influence. By writing and conversing with political friends and enemies, she frequently settled JC's affairs, sometimes with his approval. Her November 19, 1861, entry reads: "Wrote sixteen pages in answer to the president's letter anent the Beauregard ante-Manassas plan of battle" (*MCCW* 238-39). Her explicit reference to "we outsiders" in the following sentence is possibly tongue-in-cheek.

Whether she slipped notes of warning to political allies, wrote her husband's letters, or discussed Confederate strategies with privates and generals, Chesnut's weapon was language. Barred from frontiers of direct action, she created with her diaries a linguistic combat zone, where, as general, she manoeuvred her troops. "I belong to the reserve corps," she declares at a social gathering (*MCCW* 621), but from her observer's position, she filled her pages with political analyses and military strategies, always siding with Jefferson Davis and her own husband against their adversaries. Though she carefully camouflaged her commentary as woman's folly ("what nonsense I write here" [*MCCW* 23]), she was conscious of writing history. About one of her (literary) heroes, the poet Paul Haynes, she writes to posterity: "Make a note of it. It is illness which keeps our poets from the wars" (*MCCW* 420).

While Chesnut defended the Southern poet because she admired his writings, she attacked the generals and the politicians because she distrusted their readings. To Chesnut, the men of her circle were oblivious to the signs inscribed in the dense text of Confederate society. JC is as blind to political opportunities as he is to drawingroom intrigues. Edward Boykin and other gentlemen compliment Mary Chesnut on her sunny disposition, only to mark themselves as poor readers: "Much they know of me – or my power to hide trouble – much trouble" (*MCCW* 29). With metaphor clusters of sight and blindness, centered around, for example, James Chesnut, Sr. and his ailing wife, Chesnut denounced the (gender) politics of the Old South. In a patriarchal society that encouraged feminine blindness to masculine incompetence and vice, women ironically emerged as expert readers.

Chesnut herself is a brilliant example. Not only does she read her husband, a man who can "control every expression of his emotion, who can play stoic or an Indian chief" (*MCCW* 356) like a book, she talks of him as one: "I am glad to see that JC's name, as they say of rare books, has not entirely gotten out of *print*" (*PMC* 162). Chesnut saw Confederate society as a storybook, written by and writing herself. Her sharp I/eye reads grieving widow's faces, military intrigues, and personal weaknesses with equal astuteness, a talent for observation repeatedly inscribed in her journals: "Saw Lamar very feeble on *crutches*.... Saw a vivandière today who played the *piano*.... Saw a bride of sixty & her husband *thirty five*. Saw *hundred & fifteen* sick soldiers yesterday – the saddest sight these poor eyes have ever encountered" (*PMC* 96). "A faithful watcher have I been from my youth upward – of men and manners," she explains to her own readers. "Society has been for me only an enlarged field for character study" (*MCCW* 690). Only the African American faces surrounding her she cannot decipher. Though her slaves read her slightest thoughts and wishes, they themselves are, from Chesnut's perspective, texts unwritten and thus unreadable: "These sphinxes give no sign" (*MCCW* 641, cp. 223).

Quite literally, Mary Chesnut was also a voracious reader. "How much I owe of the pleasure of my life to these much reviled writers of fiction," she states in her journal (*MCCW* 10), a fact to which her innumerable literary references testify. With the enemy a few miles from Richmond, and cannon fire thundering in her ears, she lost herself in Eliot's *Romola*; only a few days earlier, she had been reading a biography of Girolamo Savonarola with equal abandon: "I am absorbed in it, up to the ears, body and soul given up..." (*MCCW* 501). While reading provided Chesnut with the intellectual stimulation she required, fiction became as well a reading of the body, a physical pleasure to which also Gertrude Thomas confessed. Not always, however, were these southern women willing to open themselves to the text. Reading *Uncle Tom's Cabin*, or the correspondence between General Robert Toombs and Colonel Maxcy Gregg, Chesnut resisted textual seduction: "I did not think Toombs could be such a goose" (*PMC* 151). Often, she responded with feminist criticism to masculine canon(n)s: "Read Milton," she records under May 17, 1862. "See the speech of Adam and Eve in a new light. Women will not stay at home – will go out to see and be seen, even it be by the Devil himself" (*MCCW* 341).

Chesnut's discriminating readings of letters, newspapers, novels, and histories served well her own social and political purposes. Not only did the literature inspire her own character readings, it allowed her to cross gender boundaries to traditionally masculine zones. With books such as Cooper's naval history (1839), Help's *Friends in Council* (1847) and Dundonald's *The Autobiography of a Seaman* (1860-61), Chesnut vicariously entered a dynamic male world and returned with ammunition for her own battles. As she began to realize that her cause was lost, reading became primarily an escape. "I like pleasant, kindly stories now," she writes in the March, 1864 entry. "We are so harrowed by real life" (*MCCW* 581).

Chesnut's preoccupation with language nonetheless persisted despite the tragedies and losses of an increasingly meaningless war. Throughout her diaries, she draws comfort from language, as when she shares her disappointment with Confederate retreat with others: "we unfortunate women *talked*" (*PMC* 92). Besides, she finds in her own conversational and narrative victories a constant source of pride and joy. She demonstrates a linguistic playfulness with puns, jokes, and imitations: Mrs. Page Page has turned over a new leaf; Mr. Key cannot unlock Seward's heart. Despite Chesnut's hostility towards Lincoln, she applauds his neologisms, of which she particularly favors "interruptious" (*MCCW* 93). Even on a bad day, she has the energy to mock her unhappy niece's bad spelling: "I am miserable, too, today – with one *s* and one *l*" (*MCCW* 166). With an unusual linguistic awareness, she recorded details of spelling and diction along with thoughts on language and power.

Most interesting is perhaps Chesnut's reflections on language and gender. Men "talk so well, and we listen until almost they fool us," she writes after a visit from Jefferson Davis and his aides (*MCCW* 652). But Chesnut herself is hardly seduced. She notices the different topics of conversation between the men and the women of her acquaintance (*MCCW* 187) and proceeds to satirize the verbal bravado of a group of young officers. "J.C. takes words literally," she notes on one occasion, having earlier explained the multiple meanings invested in "That" among her female friends (*MCCW* 569, 519). In Chesnut's estimate, feminine linguistic instruments were the better tuned. "Mrs. Childs has the sweetest Southern voice – absolute music," she writes in an early entry (*MCCW* 21). Yet she holds no illusions as to the value of such instruments in a patriarchal economy: "The base submission of our tone must be music in our masters' ears" (*MCCW* 735).

Chesnut was well aware that her writings might jar masculine ears or offend masculine I's. Despite her artistic sensibility, she repeatedly revealed in her texts the anxiety of authorship typical, as we have seen, of nineteenth-century women writers. "I hope I may not be too conceited & spoil J. Chesnut's affairs by writing in such a hurry letters for him," she records in her original diary in October 1861 (*PMC* 183). "I think this journal will be disadvantageous for me..." (*PMC* 34), she further speculates, later to conclude: "Much good the reading & writing have done me" (*PMC* 45). Chesnut resolved the tension between self-expression and self-censorship by representing her writing as an involuntary act. "The scribbling mania is strong upon me," she admits concerning her desire to write a newspaper story. She strengthens her case by pleading a sort of mental illness: "have an insane idea in my brain to write a *tale* for Dr. Gibbes's weekly literary paper" (*PMC* 169). Even in the relative safety of her own diary, Chesnut distrusted her talent for written expression, unconsciously judging herself by traditionally masculine rhetorical standards: "I wrote a critique for the papers yesterday.... It read very flat. My sentences were too long & too intricate – & the ideas spun out. I could not compress & condense & intensify as I can do talking" (*PMC* 185).

Chesnut protected herself by locking away her journal and, of course, by choosing the seemingly innocent diary form in the first place. Moreover, she discarded what Wolfgang Iser labels "consistency-building," a cognitive mode of stabilizing ambiguities and discouraging revision, for a more flexible "wandering viewpoint."[7] By courting the indeterminacy of her texts through revisions and reorganizations, Chesnut avoided masculine codification and, at the same time, engaged her audience in the dynamic readings she herself preferred. Her many, ultimately unfinished, revisions of her diaries suggest perhaps most clearly her notions of writing and reading as processes. Often, she literally writes over erasures, or she adds afterthoughts, re-visions and rewritings in parentheses and margins. Unabashedly, she changes her mind on issues, or contradicts earlier recorded facts and fictions: "I write what I hear, not what I know," she explains to two puzzled (imagined?) readers. "I think what I say – *at the time*. But I am reckless – almost shameless about changing my mind" (*MCCW* 740). By including her own rereadings of old letters and journals, Chesnut constantly revised and reinvented herself.

The revisionary perspective Chesnut adopted throughout her journals combined with a non-linear notion of time to yield a record of herstory. Though Chesnut dated her entries, she did not do so consistently, or she treated exactness in this department with considerable nonchalance. In the 1880s version, the dates are mere conventions of the diary form, and Chesnut liberally shifted or regrouped entries for stylistic effect. In her original war diary, she writes, "I spend the time now like a spider spinning my own entrails" (*PMC* 34), her metaphor of writing suggesting circularity rather than linearity. In the writing process, past and present merge into subjective (woman's) time, as when Chesnut writing remembers similar moments in the past: "I cannot write in this book without thinking of the happy days when I sat & read & heard the scratching of my darling Mary Stevens' pen as she scribbled her love nonsense in a red book like this" (*PMC* 12).

Mary Stevens writing in Mary Chesnut's sentence suggests the multiple voices and perspectives of the latter's historical record.

---

7. Wolfgang Iser, *The Act of Reading: A Theory of Aesthetic Response* (Baltimore: Johns Hopkins U P, 1978), p. 126; cp. Maria Salvatori, "Reading and Writing a Text: Correlations Between Reading and Writing Patterns," *College English* 45 (1983), p. 661.

Writing Herstory: Mary Chesnut's Civil War

Chesnut herself appears in various personae and disguises. Literally, her brutally honest, private voice of the 1860s blends with the more cautious, public voice of the 1880s in the published version of *Mary Chesnut's Civil War*, but even these selves dissolve into less codifiable, coexisting entities: old/young/melancholy/jolly/aunt/wife/feminist/moralist/reader/writer. Moreover, like Fanny Kemble, Chesnut frequently projects her own personality traits onto characters of her revised journal (ex. "the irrepressible Isabella"), or she presents her own opinions through conversations between choruses of women. She further resists codification through irony, through an open-ended discourse of rhetorical questions, and through shifts from English to French and back again. The presence of inserted letters, quotations from her reading, recorded opinions of others, and comments from readers of the journal itself contribute to the communal discourse of Chesnut's text. Buck, a young Confederate belle, "rewrites" events in which she figures prominently by criticizing Chesnut's representations and interpretations, and Chesnut herself carefully cultivates (the appearance of) communality: "My journal ... lies wide open on my desk in the corner of my drawing room. Everybody reads it who chooses" (*MCCW* 676).

While Chesnut did not literally encourage the communal reading experience she describes, she nonetheless engaged her own writings in intertextual discourse. With biblical images of corruption and evil, Chesnut evokes the first invasion of Paradise; as the fall of the South becomes a reality, she adds references to *Paradise Lost* and *Exodus*. At the end of her journal, she draws on ancient Greece to describe the tragedy which consumes her: she becomes the wailing Cassandra, while an irritating, Yankee-loving niece turns into Hecate. Discarding a more Bloomian gesture of aggressive misprision, Chesnut thus invited mythological and literary precursors into her texts and ultimately composed a herstorical work of multiple signatures.

In the process, Chesnut composed herself. By wandering in the text from one viewpoint to the next, she engaged in a dynamic process of meaning-making, thus writing herself as writer.[8] She mapped in her

---

8. Salvatori, p. 664.

interaction with textual meanings a negative terrain of *différance*, composed of gaps between her own and other perspectives. By criticizing Yankees she created herself as southerner; in similar movements, she defined herself as, among other things, non-provincial, non-Chesnut, non-incompetent (politician), and non-innocent. True to her time and region, she also composed herself as non-black, but in an opposite and surprising move, she identifies herself with bondage: "There is no slave, after all, like a wife" (*MCCW* 59).[9] With impassioned expositions of plantation immorality, inspired undoubtedly by her father-in-law's slave progeny, she wrote herself as non-man. In Kristevan fashion, Chesnut thus defined Woman negatively, as an unrepresentable entity "at odds with what already exists."[10]

Chesnut signified this otherness with an excessive use of italics and dashes which, combined with an almost literal writing of the body, create a discourse of femininity. Often, she inscribes emotion literally, as when criticizing JC's decision not to join the military: "Hope it may be for the best – but I do not *feel* that to be the case – far from it!" (*PMC* 130). Like Gertrude Thomas and Sarah Morgan, she expresses discomfort or dissent through body signs. She leaves an offending discussion between General Walker and Mr. Barnwell with a good deal of commotion, on purpose dropping her fan and handkerchief "to divert them from their madness or folly" (*MCCW* 152). On other occasions, she "speaks" her responses with depressions, headaches, fainting fits and shivers. After Lee's surrender, Chesnut expresses her despair with a full-fledged hysterical attack, a bodily writing already suggested in her image of the spider spinning its own entrails.

These physical signs of Chesnut's discourse suggest most importantly her distrust of conventional symbolic systems. The gaps, the erasures, and the silences of *Mary Chesnut's Civil War* signal that, ulti-

---

9. For an analysis of the overlapping discourses of marriage and slavery in the antebellum South, and among Garrisonian abolitionists, see Stephanie McCurry, "The Two Faces of Republicanism: Gender and Proslavery Politics in Antebellum South Carolina," *The Journal of American History* 79 (March 1992), pp. 1245-64.
10. Julia Kristeva, "Woman Can Never Be Defined," in *New French Feminisms*, ed. Elaine Marks and Isabelle de Courtivron (New York: Schocken, 1981), p. 137.

mately, its author could not or would not represent her woman's experience in language. In addition to the many sentences that end in ellipses and nothingness, literal blanks in the text speak the unspoken in Chesnut's life. Words are erased, pages cut and torn out, and only through omissions does the reader surmise Varina Davis's pregnancy, Mary Chesnut's opium (ab)use, and her occasional marital disharmonies. Old Mr. Chesnut's sexual inconsistencies are hidden in biblical references to Rachel and her brood, and Chesnut's own desires are frequently expressed through quotations and silences. "She understands me without words" (*MCCW* 654), she writes about her sister Kate, perhaps suggesting the increasing impatience with language that characterizes Chesnut's journals.

The overwhelming reality of the Civil War outdistanced linguistic expression. "Fiction is so flat, comparatively" (*MCCW* 359), Chesnut writes in June 1862. "Why write when I have nothing to chronicle but disasters?" (*MCCW* 333). As the end of the Old South drew near, Chesnut sensed the limitations, and the inauthenticity, of (masculine?) discourse: "And I thought ... that I knew what men could do – swelling, repeating lying rumors, falsifying the half-time, exaggerating, depreciating, bragging!" Only the "quiet gentlemen" of the South are trustworthy: "They die – and make no sign" (*MCCW* 603). At the close of her journal, Chesnut prefers silence. "No words of mine can tell how unhappy I am," she records in the final entry of *Mary Chesnut's Civil War*, which ends in stuttering and in "blindness": "And – and the weight that hangs upon our eyelids – is of lead" (*MCCW* 836, 837).

The first person plural of the last sentence, and the indisputable achievement of Chesnut's eight hundred plus pages, nonetheless speak of an enduring (southern) community and of an emerging feminine voice. Despite and because of its anxieties, its gaps, and its chaos, *Mary Chesnut's Civil War* documents a period of instability and change that provoked a rereading of patriarchal hierarchies and a rewriting of American history. "*Mary Chesnut* is heavy as a telephone book – and reads like one," a student once complained; yet in its very sprawl and fragmentation, the work holds together a vanishing community. With her incessant observations, manipulations, compositions and revisions, situated in a political world of femininity, Chesnut read and wrote her story and survived, against all odds, the loss of language and of life.

Sarah Morgan Dawson

CHAPTER FIVE

Behind Confederate Lines: Sarah Morgan Dawson

Readers of Civil War diarists such as Ella Gertrude Clanton Thomas, Kate Stone, Mary Chesnut, and others have come to expect a certain narrative morphology from Confederates of the female persuasion: the packing and unpacking of favorite silk dresses, the Yankees' coming, the nightly flights, shifting places of refuge, shortage of food and plenty of chivalry, (dis)loyal slaves, and the devastating bulletins of loss and death. Sarah Morgan (Dawson) is no exception. The girl of the title her first editor chose, *A Confederate Girl's Diary,* began her journal in Baton Rouge in 1862 to escape the boredom of a quiet Sunday afternoon and chronicled a period of American history almost too "massively symbolic in its inexhaustible and sybilline significance," or, as Robert Penn Warren corrects himself, "significance*s*."[1] Yet Sarah was not just the dutiful daughter of the Confederacy. Despite the flag of stars and bars she pinned to her bosom to spite the Yankees landing at Baton Rouge, she too traversed in her diary the boundaries and loyalties that held together the world of southern womanhood. Throughout the turmoils of the Civil War, Sarah retained a fierce pride in her class, her race, and her state; but, like Thomas, Stone and Chesnut, she oscillated in her writings between respectability and rebellion. This oscillation produces the multiple displacements of her journal – from observer to observed, from reader to writer, from masculine to feminine, and from North to South – and creates, so to speak, a "writerly other" that defers meaning, truth and

---

1. Robert Penn Warren, *The Legacy of the Civil War. Meditations on the Centennial* (New York: Random House, 1961), p. 80.

closure. As Alice Jardine explains with Derrida, "Writing is the 'general space' that disrupts all presence and absence and therefore all metaphysical notions of limits (as well as the possibility of transgressing any one of those limits)."[2] Sarah Morgan thus emerges from the pages of her diary as a newly-born woman and a budding Louisiana de/reconstructionist.

The "Foreword" and "Introduction" that preface the 1960 edition of *A Confederate Girl's Diary* represent the boundaries of Sarah's existence. The editor, James I. Robertson, Jr., emphasizes the leavening effect of the Civil War narratives by women on both sides, whose "observations and experiences give to the war touches of human interest and warmth...."[3] The female diarists with whom the Confederacy was "blessed" thus epitomize the nurturing feminine ideal, also evoked in Robertson's dedication to his wife, "who tolerated neglect and held in check two Rebels as rambunctious as Taylor's Louisianans" (Rob xxv). Robertson presents Sarah to her readers as a younger version of idealized southern femininity, a golden-haired belle of twenty, with a "snow-white" complexion and "an hour-glass figure" (Rob xv). Praising Sarah's self-control and balanced judgment, he notes that her dignified conduct "gained her much more male attention than coquettishness would have achieved." Her diary, he concludes, is "feminine, fresh and frank" (Rob xxiii). The original introduction, written by Sarah's son Warrington Dawson for the posthumous publication of her Louisiana diary in 1913 and reprinted in Robertson's volume, predictably stresses the author's maternal virtues – common sense, forgiveness, and martyrdom. A new representative of the family patriarchy, he assumes the voice of authority in praising Sarah's correct word choice and unblotted manuscript pages (Rob xxx). Though both editors assure us that they have merely transcribed the author's original words, they matter-of-factly state that

---

2. Alice Jardine, *Gynesis: Configurations of Woman and Modernity* (Ithaca: Cornell U P, 1985), p. 184.
3. James I. Robertson, Jr., "Foreword," in Sarah Morgan Dawson, *A Confederate Girl's Diary*, ed. James I. Robertson (Bloomington: Indiana U P, 1960), p. xi. Future references to this edition of Sarah Morgan Dawson's diary will be given parenthetically in the text, preceded by the abbreviation "Rob."

they have omitted passages on "irrelevant topics" (Rob xxiii; xxxi). With a new edition, *The Civil War Diary of Sarah Morgan*, published by University of Georgia Press in 1991, Charles East has fortunately put forth Sarah's journal without cuttings and misreadings.[4] Sarah's words thus finally reach her audience without the masculine filters that strained her life.

Sarah was, in a sense, imprisoned by history. Her story, that of the Civil War, was being written elsewhere – at Manassas, in Washington, and in Richmond. The recurring incidents of feminine war journals – cotton burning, Yankee raids, etc. – demonstrate above all the writers' confinement to a male-authored plot. The dawn of Independence Day 1862 ironically finds Sarah in the bath-house, while her sister through the weather-boarding tells her of Stonewall Jackson's and McClellan's positions. "This is said to be the sixth battle he [Jackson] has fought in twenty days, and they say he has won them all," Sarah writes in her diary, the passive construction and the impersonal "they" testifying to her distance from action and power (151). "Still no authentic reports of the late battles in Virginia" (260), she complains the following September. In February 1863, she finally appeals to what she chooses to call Destiny: "Where do you take us? During these two trying years, I have learned to feel myself a mere puppet in the hands of a Something that takes me here to-day, to-morrow there, always unexpectedly, and generally very unwillingly..." (430-31). An actor rather than an author of history, Sarah is enclosed in a script she cannot control.

Read in this context, the bath-house becomes emblematic of the spatial sensibility typical of feminine fictions and of women's history.[5] Sarah Morgan's diary focuses on space, whether exterior, interior or, as Alice Jardine puts it in *Gynesis*, "hidden behind what we used to call Time."[6] Barred from systems of causality, Sarah is fundamentally indifferent to the reasons behind her predicaments, to the linear cause-effect patterns of traditional history. Thus

---

4. Charles East, ed. *The Civil War Diary of Sarah Morgan* (Athens: U of Georgia P, 1991). References to East's edition will be given parenthetically in the text, without a preceding abbreviation.
5. For a discussion of space and femininity, see Jardine, pp. 33-34, 88-90
6. Jardine, p. 82.

she consistently loses track of time, heroic efforts to the contrary notwithstanding. "I am in danger of forgetting the days of the week, as well as those of the month," she writes a couple of days after the bath-house incident. "Friday I am sure was the Fourth, because I heard the national salute fired. I must remember that to find my days by" (156-57). In September, she exclaims, "I had hardly realized spring, when now I find it is autumn" (246).

Nonetheless, Sarah's sense of space appears highly developed, often manifesting itself in images of enclosure and suffocation. In the family mansion: "I am afraid this close confinement will prove too much for me; my long walks are cut off, on account of the soldiers" (136). In Baton Rouge: "Penned in on one little square mile, here we await our fate like sheep in the slaughter-pen" (144-45). In a boarding-house in Clinton: "The house really has a suffocating effect on me, there is such a close look about it" (244). While Sarah's topographical emphasis usually originates in her feminine (historical) perspective, her spatial imagination occasionally suggests a longing for safety – the security of the womb: "I would dare anything, to be at home again. I know that the Yankees have left us little besides the bare house; but I would be grateful for the mere shelter of the roof" (246).

Sarah's yearning for her white-columned home on Church Street in Baton Rouge indicates her complicity in (re)constructing the walls separating the Morgans and similar prominent families from everybody else. Edmund Wilson notes in "Three Confederate Ladies," a chapter of *Patriotic Gore*, the amazing recurrence of family names in southern war documents: Sarah Morgan in Baton Rouge and Mary Chesnut in Richmond share relatives and friends. Their social world, consisting of what Wilson calls "that fraction of the ruling class that is at all public-spirited and well-educated," is thus "extremely limited."[7] Sarah obviously relishes the exclusiveness of her family circle. As the devoted daughter of Judge Thomas Gibbes Morgan, recently deceased when Sarah begins her journal, she carries "an aristocratic sense that has detached itself from planter solidarity."[8]

---

7. Edmund Wilson, *Patriotic Gore: Studies in the Literature of the American Civil War* (New York: Oxford U P, 1962), p. 278.
8. Wilson, p. 269.

Behind Confederate Lines: Sarah Morgan Dawson

The "everybody else" expelled from the Morgan universe includes above all the lower classes, slaves, and – to an extent – Yankees. In discussing her milkman, who has commented on the young lady's pride, Sarah declares, "I did not care for what he or any of that class could say; I was surprised to find that they thought at all!" (320). She winces at the sight of "some little clerk in his holiday attire" (182) and particularly dislikes "low white women," too given to gossiping and to intermingling with soldiers, African Americans, and "rabble" (517): "'Loud' women, what a contempt I have for you! How I despise your vulgarity!" (122). Sarah praises her servants' loyalty and the pleasant sound of their voices blessing their kind mistress (138), but like the young Kate Stone, she notices only the absence of her slaves: "What a day I have had! Here mother and I are alone, not a servant on the lot.... I actually swept two whole rooms!" (103). The non-identity granted African Americans surfaces as well in Sarah's juxtaposition of "cattle, mules and negroes" (440) and in the slaves' textual fragmentation into "black faces" and "shining teeth" (330). Faced with Lincoln's Emancipation Declaration, Sarah resists, like Gertrude Thomas and innumerable others, the role reversal feared by members of the ruling class and race: "I would rather have all I own burned, than in the possession of the negroes. Fancy my magenta organdie on a dark beauty! Bah!" (215). The Yankees are, of course, to blame for such threats to well-established southern order. "Yankees can't prosper unless they are pillaging honest people" (440), writes the young rebel, who "would not forego the title for any other earthly one" (410).

The codes of race and class to which Sarah willingly adhered nonetheless trapped her in the role of southern lady. In her efforts to play the part, she frowns appropriately at a "swearing guerrilla" (91); "reduced" to entering the occupied Baton Rouge in a mule cart, she gives her "whole attention to getting out respectably" (102). Anticipating a Yankee attack, she notes with feminine vanity: "My chief desire was to wash my face before running, if they were actually shelling us again" (136). At every forced flight, she records in great detail the items of clothing lost and saved: "I find myself obliged to leave one of my new muslins I had just finished ... the body of my lovely lilac, and my beauteous white mull. But then, I have saved eight half-made linen chemises!" (168). Sarah exhibits a good deal of self-irony and humor, however, in relating her struggle to descend the mule wagon like a queen, or in describing the "disgrace" of herself and her sister Miriam in helping a seemingly wounded Yankee soldier, who, it turns out, is merely drunk. Sarah's irony, as well as her consciousness of wearing a mask, indicate a distance from prescribed feminine roles. "Here I must confess to the most consummate piece of acting," she writes in describing her success in keeping an admirer from embarking upon a whiskey spree (369). Between the signifiers of femininity (lace, downcast eyes, barely audible sighs) and the signified "self", Sarah (un)consciously inserts a gap of unrepresentable resistance.

This slippage occurs predictably in Sarah's (non)approach to her own sexuality. According to the code, a southern lady was, of course, to remain as pure as Sarah's snow-white complexion, sexual appetites being confined to women of darker hues. Having internalized this prescriptive asexuality, Sarah vows to stab the first soldier who tries to kiss her: "Come to my bosom O my discarded carving knife.... I will find you a sheath in the body of the first man who attempts to Butlerize – or brutalize ... me" (77). In falling out of her buggy and injuring her lower spine, Sarah worries whether her feet might be exposed and with lady-like reticence cannot mention to her rescuers an injury so close to her "extremity" (336). In happier moments, Sarah nonetheless demonstrates an unmistakable, if unconscious, attraction to the soldiers swarming around her. In watching a Yankee drill, she notes, "One conceited, red-headed lieutenant smiled at us in the most fascinating way" (108); on being introduced to the "very handsome" Captain Bradford, Sarah compares him to "a moss-covered stone wall, a slumbering volcano, a – – what you please, so it suggests anything unexpected and dangerous to stumble over" (328). Hidden in the blank is, we might guess, the dangerous sexuality to which Sarah found herself responding. Courted by a Mr. Halsey some months later, Sarah resolves the sexual tension brought about by his visit by staying in her room but sending him a bouquet of flowers with her compliments. The bouquet itself is a writing of contradictions: a bunch of snowdrops tied with three of Sarah's gold-red hairs. With this gesture, Sarah successfully manages (not) to acknowledge her erotic inclinations and thus stays within feminine folds.

Sarah's six-month confinement following her injury may in itself be a bodily articulation of tension,[9] a way of erasing the boundaries between the dutiful and the rebellious daughter. As Elaine Showalter hypothesizes in *The Female Malady*, hysteria or "the daughter's disease" might be a mode of dissent for women without satisfying social, mental or expressive outlets.[10] Indeed, as in *Mary Chesnut's Civil War*, a subtext of nervous strain runs counter to the diarist's much-advertised calm and reserve. "This suspense is not calculated to soothe one's nerves" (139), Sarah writes when awaiting the arrival of Yankees in Baton Rouge; she further announces that the shout of "'Picayune Butler's coming, coming' has upset my nervous system" (140). On July 3, 1862, she jots down, "Another day of sickening suspense" (149). After her accident, the connection between mind and body becomes quite explicit: "The uncertainty is really affecting my spine and causing me to grow alarmingly thin…" (452). Through her inability to move, Sarah is literalizing feminine passivity, thus speaking with her body what cannot be spoken. Significantly, the mere thought of a change of scene gives her the strength to attempt to walk; an impending enemy attack causes her to *jump* out of bed (436). After her removal to New Orleans, she jubilantly writes, "I am getting well!" (488). Sarah's hysterical illness is, in other words, "a discourse of femininity addressed to patriarchal thought."[11] By confining herself to confinement, Sarah signifies in bodily discourse the dissent censored by southern gender systems, and, ironically, creates a space of her own.[12]

For Sarah Morgan, as for Mary Chesnut and others, the diary serves, above all, as the site of challenge, of potentiality: in (the act of) writing, Sarah invents a feminine space. Like other women (writers), she struggles against constant interruptions – by family

---

9. Cp. Wilson, p. 276: "Her slowness of recovery suggests that she has also at last broken down under the continual strain on her nerves."
10. Elaine Showalter, *The Female Malady: Women, Madness and English Culture, 1830-1980* (New York: Pantheon, 1985), p. 147.
11. Dianne Hunter, qtd. in Showalter, *Female Malady*, p. 157.
12. See Showalter, *Female Malady*, p. 134 for a discussion of hysterics' "desires for privacy and independence." The hysterical attacks of Sarah's sister Miriam and their mother in March 1864 serve a similar function.

members, social visits, cannon fire and enemy assaults. After losing her writing desk (and her home), Sarah writes with her knees for support in asylums, guest houses and aboard the schooner taking her to New Orleans. "I would die without some means of expressing my feelings," she confesses in explaining her efforts to keep her diary intact through losses of practically all other earthly possessions (436). Writing was therapy, a space of privacy undisturbed by the systems of power enclosing it. By recording in minute details the destruction of her house – from her mother's shattered armoir to heaps of broken china – Sarah is able to laugh at her losses. And restricted by feminine propriety, she can retreat into the more permissive world of her journal: "how many times it has proved a relief to me where my tongue was forced to remain quiet!... [Pens, ink and paper have] acted as lightning rod to my mental thunder, and have made me happy generally" (117).

Through writing, Sarah also attempted to escape her status as text-object, forever surrounded by masculine eyes and performing according to masculine scripts. Sarah is constantly wary (and weary) of the male gaze. "We are certainly watched," she writes about the Yankee officers passing and repassing her home (146). "I prefer solitude where I can do as I please without being observed," she records about the small town of Clinton, where everybody is "reading" her (244). In recounting her buggy accident, Sarah feels more pain from being "the centre of attraction" (335) than from her injured spine: "I only wanted to get home, away from all those eyes" (336). Though this young lady, like Gertrude Thomas, has internalized her object-role to the extent of discussing herself in the third person (158), her writing nonetheless deconstructs the observer/observed dichotomy. In her journal, Sarah becomes a recording self as well as a recorded other, a reader as well as the text. Sarah's diary amply illustrates her eye for people and, moreover, suggests the visionary powers with which this seventh child of a seventh child was thought to be endowed (Rob xiii). By presenting herself as a "seer" and observer, Sarah struggles to become the subject of her own existence.

The Confederate girl's efforts to master discourse serve a similar function, much in the style of early African American autobiographers' search for literacy. Having received only ten months of formal schooling, Sarah is painfully aware of her own linguistic shortcomings. She repeatedly refers to her diary as "trash" and "stupidity" and further demonstrates anxiety of authorship in describing her reservations about writing for public eyes: "I ... got in a violent fit of the 'trembles' at the idea of writing to a stranger" (109). Within this frame, Sarah's disdain of "ain't" and "her'n" and "his'n" (306) becomes a wish for mastery and control (also) in linguistic terms. She intensely admires Mr. Bradford and Colonel Breaux for their conversational and argumentative skills, and takes a similar pride in her own facility with words, as when she catches gentlemen's puns before they are half-spoken (367, 373-74). In search of literacy, Sarah studies "the masters" long hours every day, reading and thinking of reading even as the Yankees are approaching (426). Unconsciously looking for "a different voice," Sarah nonetheless criticizes Boswell ("a vain, conceited prig") and Johnson ("an old brute of a tyrant" [163]). Indeed, Sarah announces her desire to read "only what I absolutely love, now" (137) and writes with excitement about a discussion with Colonel Breaux on phrenology and health (289). Sarah's intellectual arousal testifies to an intense desire for selfhood. Her fantasy is largely fulfilled. At the end of the journal, the Confederate girl of Warrington Dawson's title proudly declares herself a woman (609).

As Barbara Johnson suggests, the primary autobiographical motivation is the desire to create a being in one's own image, the "desire for resemblance."[13] Yet the expulsion of otherness necessitated by the dream of resemblence is sabotaged by the "monstrosity" of autobiographical writing: the possibility of giving birth to "a filthy creation," a monster. As Johnson states, the "monstrousness of selfhood is intimately embedded within the question of female autobiography," due to the socially prescribed repression of discourses and emotions transgressing "the amiableness of domestic affection."[14] The "woman" of Sarah Morgan's journal is thus not quite the genteel Louisiana lady Sarah wishes to be. What she confronts in her writing is, ultimately, the other within. In moments of scriptural fervor,

---

13. Barbara Johnson, "My Monster/My Self," *Diacritics* 12 (1982), p. 3.
14. Johnson, pp. 4, 10.

she reveals a "monstrosity" related to her difficulty in adapting to a feminine ideal shaped by the masculine imagination.[15] In the words of Mary Jacobus, "what is repressed necessarily returns, in the language of the unconscious, as an avenging monster."[16]

The face of the other woman – the *impropre* of Sarah's discourse – again shows itself in moments of great emotional intensity. One such moment occurs after an evening spent in the company of educated southern gentlemen. I am quoting the passage at some length:

> Why was I denied the education that would enable me to be the equal of such men as Col. Breaux and the others? He says the woman's mind is the same as the man's, originally; it is only education that creates the difference. Why was I denied that education? Who is to blame? Have I exerted fully the natural desire To Know that is implanted in all hearts? Have I done myself injustice in my self taught ignorance, or has injustice been done to me? Whose is the fault.... (290)

The carefully modulated voice of the southern lady has here given way to an anxious questioning, a syntax ruptured by pain. Other passages, often signaled with "Oh, if I was a man," scream out Sarah's despair at having been made "with a man's heart, and a female form..." (183). The monster of *Sarah Morgan's Civil War Journal* is caged in a feminine (textual) body but has a feminist face.

While Sarah's questioning of boundaries was largely confined to the private space of her journal, her writing entered into a dialogue with other sexual/textual practices that allowed for similar dislocations. In and outside her diary, Sarah merged her voice with those of other women, thus establishing the sort of feminine community across masculine borders that Carroll Smith-Rosenberg first identified. Like Kemble and Chesnut, she fills her textual space with women – most notably her mother and sisters – and she consistently emphasizes the contribution of her sex to the war effort:

---

15. Johnson, p. 10.
16. Mary Jacobus, *Reading Woman (Reading): Essays in Feminist Criticism* (New York: Columbia U P, 1986), p. 9.

"Honestly, I believe the women of the South are as brave as the men who are fighting…" (182). Her feminine loyalties extend beyond enemy lines, to "the many mothers, wives, and sisters who wait as anxiously, pray as fervently in their far away lonesome homes for their dear ones, as we do here" (123).

This female bonding also surfaces in moments of fun and jollity. As Natalie Davis demonstrates in "Women on Top," an essay in *Society and Culture in Early Modern France*, the privileged time of carnival and festivity allowed for female disobedience to traditional hierarchical power structures. Though Davis limits her discussion to pre-industrial Europe, the frolic of Sarah and her sisters during the Louisiana sugar-cane harvesting echoes the "unruly" women of Davis's account.[17] Entering the dark of the sugar-house, described as a sensuous underworld, Sarah and her female companions discard all dignity and abandon themselves to disorderly merriment: "Anna flew around like a baloon, Miriam fairly danced around with fun and frolic, while I laughed…" (327). In the sugar purgery, the young women cleanse themselves of genteel restrictions as they chase their gentlemen friends from corner to corner. In the process, they establish a symbolic, if temporary, inversion of gender roles.

Interestingly enough, Sarah's opposite move – towards calm and control – functions as a similar usurpation of masculine territory. Throughout the diary, Sarah identifies with her father, both psychologically and politically. Against her mother's weakness, she posits a self-imposed coolness reminiscent of the balanced, dignified Judge Morgan. Moreover, she contrasts the quiet, gentlemanly speech of Yankee soldiers with the abusive violence of female secessionists (111). To "cry, faint, scream or go off in hysterics," she argues, will only land one in prison (514). While Sarah in this passage has in mind the Custom House jail, she implies nonetheless that to avoid feminine incarceration, one must assume a phallic position. On this background, her first meeting with Yankee officers in Baton Rouge takes on new significance. While the Confederate flag pinned on her bosom signals sexual and political difference, the pistol hidden in

---

17. Natalie Z. Davis, "Women on Top," in *Society and Culture in Early Modern France* (Stanford: Stanford U P, 1975), pp. [124]-51.

her skirt covertly denies this difference, making her in several ways one of "them." "A pistol in my pocket fills up the gap," she writes in describing what she might do if attacked. "I am capable, too" (65). Sarah presents herself, in other words, as a phallic woman. And, as Jane Gallop reminds us, "for a woman as woman to assume power is to introduce a crack in the representation of power."[18]

Sarah's fantasies of cross-dressing signal a similar desire to efface gender boundaries. In describing the "Home Guard" of Louisiana men, Sarah expresses her longing "to give them my hoops, corsets, and pretty blue organdie in exchange for their boots and breeches!" (183). While this statement serves to ridicule "cowards," it also suggests Sarah's own wish to get her hands on the paraphernalia of masculinity. In another, extended passage, she again indulges in dreams of putting on men's clothes (and roles):

> If I was a man – Oh, wouldn't I be in Richmond with the boys!... What is the use of all these worthless women, in war times? If they attack, I shall don the breeches, and join the assailants, and fight.... How do breeches and coats feel, I wonder? (166-67)

The entry then describes Sarah's (unsuccessful) attempt to try on a suit belonging to her brother Jimmy. "If only I had a pair of breeches," she writes awaiting a Yankee attack, "my happiness would be complete" (184). This (proposed) blurring of gender distinctions amidst the chaos of war implies that women need not be confined to a uni-form, to what Sandra M. Gilbert in "Costumes of the Mind" calls "a single form or self."[19] "If some few Southern women were in the ranks," Sarah speculates, "they could set the men an example they would not blush to follow. Psahw! there are *no* women here! We are *all* men!" (65).[20]

---

18. Jane Gallop, *The Daughter's Seduction: Feminism and Psychoanalysis* (Ithaca: Cornell U P, 1982), p. 120.
19. Sandra M. Gilbert, "Costumes of the Mind: Transvestism as Metaphor in Modern Literature," in *Writing and Sexual Difference*, ed. Elizabeth Abel (Brighton: Harvester, 1982), p. 196.
20. George C. Rable discusses the prevalence of these "martial fantasies" in Con-

Sarah's costume fantasy is, following Gilbert, an attempt "to name not what is fixed but what is fluid in herself."[21] The elastic ego boundaries of the "woman-as-process" born on the pages of Sarah's diary resist closure and integration, as the writing subject dissolves into other characters and emerges as kaleidoscopic selves.[22] Sarah dives into the minds and hearts of Anna and Miriam, projecting her own emotions onto her sister and companion and, in turn, finding their feelings and actions mirrored in her own. This extension of "self" is evident also in the various Sarahs writing the journal. Not only does the mature Sarah Morgan Dawson add footnotes and postscripts to the diary of her youth, but the young woman of the Civil War constantly displaces selves, strategies, solutions. As Judith K. Gardiner notes in "On Female Identity and Writing by Women," "the model of the integrated individual was predominantly male, and women writers show that this model of characterization is inappropriate to their experience."[23] Much like the "knowing" mirror squinting at Sarah "from a thousand broken angles" (240) as she returns to her destroyed home, the signifying subject reflected in *The Civil War Journal of Sarah Morgan* reaches the reader from numerous directions. And considering that Sarah wrote primarily for her own I's, the mirroring process becomes as open-ended as the diary itself.

The merging of self and other is a source of energy *and* fear in Sarah's writing. The deconstruction of difference leads, on the one hand, to a dissolution of North/South hatreds, as in Sarah's compassion for Yankee soldiers and her identification with northern mothers and sisters (182, 123). Writing from a feminine position, Sarah challenges traditional representations of meaning and

---

federate women's diaries in *Civil Wars: Women and the Crisis of Southern Nationalism* (Urbana: U of Illinois P, 1991), pp. 151f.
21. Gilbert, "Costumes," p. 215.
22. On "woman-as-process," see, for example, Jardine's *Gynesis*, Julia Kristeva's "Woman Can Never Be Defined," in Marks and de Courtivron, pp. [137]f, or Judith Butler's *Gender Trouble: Feminism and the Subversion of Identity* (New York: Routledge, 1990).
23. Judith Kegan Gardiner, "On Female Identity and Writing by Women," in Abel, p. 185.

ideology. In a recurring nightmare, for example, a soldier leads Sarah to a hill overlooking a scene of battle: "I could see the Garrison, and the American flag flying over it. I looked, and saw we were standing in blood up to our knees, while here and there ghastly white bones shone above the red surface" (128). In writing her unconscious, Sarah floods masculine symbolic systems with bodily fluid(s), thus exposing the non-meaning within. Sarah states in 1865 that she considers her writing impulse perverse, since she has nothing to say." The nothingness of Sarah's discourse of desire represents precisely the meaninglessness surrounding her.

On the other hand, the stirrings of unconscious drives caused Sarah to exorcise otherness in its most recognizable shapes and forms: "vulgar" women, the lower classes, slaves (cp. 517). In distancing herself from the other(s), Sarah hoped, of course, to eliminate alien(ating) parts of herself. Even Sarah's Yankee sympathies might originate in a desire for sameness: what the Confederate writer tries to establish across political borders is perhaps the resemblance between enemies of similar zest, class, and race. In describing a group of Yankee officers, Sarah thus writes with approval: "Fine, noble looking men they were, showing refinement and gentlemanly bearing in every motion; one cannot help but admire such foes!" (68).[24]

Sarah's (de)construction of boundaries thus establishes her diary as an electric zone, in which concepts such as woman, truth and war are endlessly vibrating. Sarah tries to keep "truth" from "lies" but ultimately has to erase the distinction. Wondering about news from Vicksburg and Port Hudson, she speculates: "if it is true, it is all for the best, and if it is not true, it is better still. Whichever it is, it is for some wise purpose; so it does not matter..." (515). She emphasizes that she does not record "events" or "reliable information" (186) and scorns people who can "only take in one idea at a time" (261). Predictably, Sarah thus expresses the deferral and

---

24. For comparison, see what George C. Rable calls a "fire-breathing and unreconstructed 'secesh female'" responding to enemy soldiers in Daniel E. Sutherland, ed., *A Very Violent Rebel: The Civil War Diary of Ellen Renshaw House* (Knoxville: U of Tennessee P, 1996). Rable uses the term in his review of the volume for the H-Civ War list, December 1996.

plurality characteristic of her medium – writing. And by reversing and traversing traditional hierarchies of order and belief, Sarah constructs herself as a deconstructionist.

In the end, however, Sarah's questioning of limit(ation)s was silenced by male gatekeepers. At the close of the journal, Sarah, Miriam and their mother are forced by physical, mental and financial necessities to seek admittance to the occupied city of New Orleans and the house of the eldest Morgan brother. In a scene resonating with symbolic significance, the crippled, mute and almost unconscious Sarah takes the Oath of Allegiance administered by Yankee soldiers. In a Kristevan reading of the situation, she enters a system of signification that in women's writing "is seen from a foreign land ... from the point of view of an asymbolic, spastic body."[25] In this (linguistic) realm, she is increasingly reduced to silence. The representative of masculine authority, generically if appropriately called Brother, forbids her to write letters and notes. Even Sarah's diary entries become short and scarce.

Nonetheless, Sarah ends her journal on an important note of ambiguity. Despite her enclosure in masculine (sign) systems, Sarah enjoys a certain independence in New Orleans: she regains her health and enjoys considerably more freedom of movement than the imprisoned Confederate officers who invite her to visit the Custom House jail. As Sarah comments, "Positions of affairs rather reversed since we last met!" (525). To an extent, at least, the women of the Confederacy emerged from the war in triumph – the heirs of a system that had for so long disinherited them.

The silence of the last pages of *The Civil War Diary of Sarah Morgan* – and beyond – originates ultimately in what Alice Jardine calls "an inability of words to give form to the world – a crisis in the function of the *technē*."[26] At the opening of her journal, Sarah writes, "There is no word in the English language that can express the state in which we are, and have been, these last days" (47). Three years later, after the death of two brothers within a week, Sarah no

---

25. Julia Kristeva, "Oscillation Between Power and Denial," in Marks and de Courtivron, p. 166.
26. Jardine, p. 100.

longer searches for words to describe her pain. Instead, the pistol fired at Lincoln concludes her (printed) diary and, indeed, sets the Confederate girl of the title free.[27] The shot marks Sarah's entry into modernity – the collapse of "master discourses"[28] and the chaos and fragmentation of Western existence. Sarah's dislocations of traditional conceptual habits – woman, meaning, region, etc. – thus place her in the intellectual company of today's (theoretical) *haut monde*. This fashionable circle would undoubtedly have pleased both Sarah the Louisiana lady and Sarah the feminist deconstructionist.

---

27. Cp. Florence Nightingale's demand for the right to pain as an antidote to the (mental) inactivity of women's lives, discussed in Showalter, *Female Malady*, p. 65.
28. Jardine, p. 100.

Frances Butler Leigh

CHAPTER SIX

"Over the Water": Frances Butler Leigh's *Ten Years on a Georgia Plantation Since the War*

"I consider outside influence by far the worst evil Southern planters have to contend against," Frances Butler Leigh concludes on the experiments with rice cultivation and labor management she describes in *Ten Years on a Georgia Plantation Since the War* (1883).[1] At the time of writing these lines, she had given up farming and in 1877 sailed for England with her husband, Rev. James Wentworth Leigh, and her mother, Fanny Kemble. Both mother and daughter constituted nonetheless "outside influences" in that, three decades apart, they had traveled from Philadelphia to the Butler plantations in coastal Georgia and recorded their encounters with totally alien customs and surroundings. Fanny Kemble's *Journal of a Residence on a Georgian Plantation in 1838-39* criticizes in letters addressed to a northern friend the institution of slavery, which the temperamental former actress found abhorrent and degrading to masters and slaves alike.[2] It records as well the disharmonies that would result in the separation and divorce of Frances's parents. Though the youngest product of their union grew up to

---

1. Frances Butler Leigh, *Ten Years on a Georgian Plantation Since the War* (1883; Savannah: Beehive, 1992), p. 156. Further references will be given parenthetically in the text.
2. Frances Anne Kemble, *Journal of a Residence on a Georgian Plantation in 1838-39* (1863; Athens: U of Georgia P, 1984). Further references will be given parenthetically in the text.

side with Pierce Butler in more ways than one, Fanny Kemble's journal constitutes the subtext for her daughter's account of island rice plantations. Most readers have nonetheless focused on differences between the two records.

Frances Butler Leigh was indeed her father's daughter. An infant during the 1838-39 sojourn in Georgia, she returned with Pierce Butler in March of 1866 to reclaim the family holdings on St. Simon's and Butler Islands and to reestablish the racial and economic hegemony that had for generations been lucrative to the Butlers.[3] Frances shared, in short, both her father's labor, such as it was, and the racial and political views underpinning his enterprise. However, like her mother, she wrote what Alfred Hornung has labelled "extraterritorial autobiography."[4] Despite her equation of "outside influence" with "the worst evil" that textually positions her among southern planters, Frances too recorded Georgian life and history from an outsider's perspective, from a marginal position essential, in Hornung's view, for describing the center. Similarities and differences, insider and outsider perspectives, thus make for the tensions and visions of the two Georgia journals – one famous, the other obscure, but both significant for the conception of southern autobiography.

A letter to her mother, written on May Day of 1881, leaves no doubt as to Frances's dislike of Fanny Kemble's *Journal of a Residence*. Kemble had additionally published the letters and autobiographical insertions collected as *Records of Later Life* in 1882 and was planning a sequel. Frances emphatically disapproved: "I have never lost in the least degree ... the bitterness I have always felt about the publication of your first Southern book – which nothing would ever induce me to have in the house." Her emotional letter ends in threats and pleadings: "now that my Father is dead, if you repeat those stories – I never can forgive it...."[5] Nonetheless, when Frances pub-

---

3. Malcolm Bell, *Major Butler's Legacy: Five Generations of a Slaveholding Family* (Athens: U of Georgia P, 1987); Constance Wright, *Fanny Kemble and the Lovely Land* (New York: Dodd, Mead, 1972), p. 175.
4. Guest lecture, University of Southern Denmark, Odense, November 1999.
5. J. C. Furnas, *Fanny Kemble: Leading Lady of the Nineteenth-Century Stage* (New York: Dial, 1982), p. 413; Bell, p. 439.

lished her own account of Georgia life, possibly to set the record straight,[6] reviewers immediately linked the books of mother and daughter. The *Darien Timber Gazette* of April 14, 1883, thus reprinted the response of one New York correspondent to the Philadelphia press, which began: "Fanny Kemble's daughter, Mrs. Frances Butler Leigh, has been going over the ground that her mother traversed and wrote about a number of years ago." In *Early Days on the Georgia Tidewater*, Buddy Sullivan reserves his admiration for Kemble: "Like her famous mother, Frances Butler kept a record of occurrences.... Her journalistic prose, while lacking the style and polish of that of her mother, nonetheless offers a intimate glimpse of life around Darien during the difficult Reconstruction years."[7]

Not just degrees of stylistic polish set off Frances Leigh's text from Fanny Kemble's. While Pierce Butler's wife had visited the Georgia coastal region in 1838-39, when her husband's overseeer, Mr. Richard King. Jr., ran a so-called model plantation, Miss Butler arrived on the property in 1866 amidst postwar chaos. Fanny Kemble wrote of privilege and sloth among white southern planters; Frances, of the next generation's defeat and despair. The political sympathies of the two clearly separated their accounts. Kemble's lazy, antebellum South compares unfavorably to the enterprising, abolitionist North, while Frances's conquered South, as in the opening quotation, might blame the North for most of its troubles. Mother and daughter did not share the impetus for traveling to Georgia in the first place. Kemble had wished to experience first-hand the institution of slavery and, romantically, to alleviate slave suffering through feminine benevolence. Frances, however, shared Pierce Butler's business concerns: "I went to the South with my father to look after our property in Georgia and see what could be done with it" (1).

Allegiance to Pierce Butler – or not – certainly makes for mother-daughter differences. Mrs. Butler had in 1838-39 found his slave-owner's paternalism degrading and desexualizing, while their

---

6. Bell, p. 442.
7. Buddy Sullivan, *Early Days on the Georgia Tidewater: The Story of McIntosh County and Sapelo* (Darien, Ga.: McIntosh County Board of Commissioners, 1990), p. 338.

daughter outright celebrated his patriarchal authority.[8] In the words of the *Darien Timber Gazette*, "Miss Butler seems to have adored her father; her whole book is about him and his exceptional character."[9] Different responses to gender relations and the nineteenth-century separation of spheres account for the contrasting responses of Mr. Butler's wife and Mr. Butler's daughter. The former promoted in dress and behavior, in letters to friends such as Harriet St. Leger and Elizabeth Sedgwick, as well as in her journal entries, notions of female equality and independence, while, at least in theory, Frances Butler deferred to masculine authority. She describes in detail the muslin curtains edged with pink calico (as well as the portrait of Robert E. Lee) with which she attempts to alleviate the Georgia home's crude "barbarism" (6). When her father and one Mr. J returns from an outing, she proudly records that "they looked round in perfect astonishment, and quite rewarded me by their praise" (8). She dwells on Pierce Butler's kind gestures toward his "people," as when he prevents the separation of the head driver, Bram, and his wife, Juba, in 1859, when this philandering grandson of old Major Butler saw fit to sell upwards of 460 slaves to pay off his creditors.[10] In Frances's representation, this event made for acts of loyalty and confidence, and prompts the old head driver to declare after Emancipation: "And now that we free, I come back to my old home and my old master and stay here till I die" (16). She comments on Pierce Butler's "fondness" for his St. Simon's people, and, following his death in August 1867, she finds comfort in the words of the former Butler slaves: "They never spoke of him without some touching and affectionate expression..." (39).

The Georgia journals of mother and daughter thus contrast most strikingly in attitudes towards slavery. Fanny Kemble abhorred the institution and regularly opposed it in her writings. In *Journal of a*

---

8. In order to distinguish between Frances Anne Kemble and her daughter and namesake, I have chosen to call the author of *Journal of a Residence* Fanny Kemble, Fanny Butler, and Mrs. Butler, while I refer to her daughter, also known as Fan and Fanny, as Frances: Frances Leigh, Frances Butler, Miss Butler, etc.
9. Sullivan, p. 339.
10. Bell, p. xix.

Residence, her tone intensifies as she discovers the full extent of the cruelties that sustain her family, as well as her own inability to ease them: "I am getting perfectly savage over all these doings," she writes to Elizabeth Sedgwick, "and really think I should consider my own throat and those of my children well cut if some night the people were to take it into their heads to clear off scores in that fashion" (216). Frances, however, shared her father's pro-slavery convictions. As Sullivan writes, "she never ceased to believe that blacks fared better as slaves than as free people."[11] She states in the final pages of her journal that "the negroes are so like children" (156) and stresses their devotion to their former owners. "The masters are far better off – relieved from the terrible load of responsibility which slavery entailed." "But for the negroes," she concludes, "I cannot help thinking things are worse" (157).

Though Frances reacted with "bitterness" to Kemble's "Southern book," the anxiety of its influence prompted her own. She writes, it seems, *Ten Years* as a sequel to Kemble's *Journal*, and simultaneously acknowledges and rejects the first volume by inscribing a decade rather than a year in her own title. Also formal choices between the covers suggest intertextual links. Like her mother, Frances mixes in her journal genres and forms, interspersing autobiographical entries with letters and postings, such as her correspondence with General George G. Meade. Like the Kemble performers in her family, she thrives on dialogues for dramatic effect and, like her mother, plays various roles in the course of her journal – dutiful daughter, "supreme dictator" (96), despondent rice planter and submissive wife, among them. As in the Kemble journal, Frances herself sets up intertextual connections based on her own readings. While Fanny Kemble invited into her text William Bartram and Harriet Martineau, Frances goes to Defoe to describe her experience: "I feel like Robinson Crusoe with three hundred men Fridays" (8). Despite the male subject position Frances here occupies, she models herself on her illustrious mother by inviting her husband to co-author the text. While Fanny Kemble has Pierce Butler co-write her journal by structuring it round his (wrong)doings, Frances literally brings in James

---

11. P. 338.

Leigh's letters to authenticate her writings. Chapters on topics such as "The Emancipated African" and "Negro Minstrelry" thus separate the final chapters Frances herself produced: "A New Master, 1871-73" and "Over the Water."

With this disappearance from her own text, Frances also joins her mother, who in *Journal of a Residence*, not to mention her later autobiographies, remains thunderously silent especially on issues of marital discord. Modern readers have speculated, for example, on Kemble's reasons for rowing away from husband and sleeping children one tumultuous night in Georgia,[12] and frequently sense this vibrant woman's efforts to submit her will to that of Mr. Butler. Also the daughter seems to hide some impatience with his person. Notorious, apparently, for procrastination (if not sloth), Pierce Butler agrees with his daughter and their company to meet at 5 a. m. to depart for St. Simon's plantation by raft. At 8 a.m. he materializes on the wharf in his dressing-gown, hands clapped to his head. Both in real life and in her story, Frances speaks her irritation with silence: "Without a word I had his bedroom furniture put on, and ordered the men to push off..." (13).

Mother and daughter shared further the silence of delayed publication. In *Record of Later Life*, Kemble explains how after the war broke out she wished to oppose the southern sympathies of her London circle: "Hearing daily and hourly the condition of slaves discussed, in a spirit of entire sympathy with their owners that nothing but the most absolute ignorance could excuse, ... I determined to publish my record of my own observations on a Southern plantation." She acknowledges as well that she withholds certain information. "I refused to place the whole in the hands of the printers," she explains, "... as the book was my personal diary, and contained matter of the most strictly private nature..." (261).[13] Frances also chose to publish with delay – mostly, perhaps, to shut

---

12. Cp. Catherine Clinton, *Fanny Kemble's Civil Wars* (NY: Simon & Schuster, 2000), p. 124.
13. Frances Anne Kemble, *Records of Later Life* (London: Richard Bentley, 1882), p. 26. Critics of autobiography have argued against the notion that diarists write for their own eyes only. See, for ex., Lawrence Rosenwald, "Some Myths about Diaries," *Raritan* 6.3 (Winter 1987), pp. 98-99.

up her mother, indeed the loudest gap in the daughter's text. "I have read the greater part of it," writes the honest reviewer in the *Darien Timber Gazette*, "and have not found on any page of it a reference to Mrs. Leigh's distinguished mother."[14]

The personalities emerging from both journals nonetheless overlap considerably. Both diarists embrace, to be sure, the nurturing role of plantation mistress who supervises the health of the people in her care. Both demonstrate a love of female independence and both thrive in financial wheelings and dealings. Fanny Kemble pays caretakers for cleaning up babies and starts paying slaves for clearing paths through the bush. Her daughter, in turn, becomes a resourceful planter and fills her own pages with rice prices and labor trouble. Though Frances dutifully talks of her "sphere," she relishes, it seems, the new social order that prompted women to expand "traditional boundaries."[15] Besides, the scripts of lady and farmwife shared various traits, at least in terms of mothering, nursing, and other domestic virtues.[16] Ladies or farmwives, both mother and daughter took after Marie-Thérèse De Camp, wife of Charles Kemble and given to hysteria. Like her Swiss-born mother, Fanny Kemble speaks emotional turbulence with bodily fits, and even Thérèse's granddaughter might lose her head, as when closing contract negotiations with the former slaves: "I had a violent attack of hysterics afterwards, from fatigue and excitement" (45). Both diarists further write with the notorious directness of Thérèse De Camp. Fanny Kemble had in the early *Journal of Frances Anne Butler* (1835) gotten herself into trouble by denouncing American hosts and habits and remained throughout her life (in)-famous for her "candid" opinions.[17] With considerable verbal bru-

---

14. Sullivan, p. 339.
15. Terrell Armstrong Crow, "'As Thy Days, So Shall Thy Strength Be': North Carolina Planter Women in War and Peace," *Carolina Comments* 28.1 (Jan. 1980), p. 30.
16. D. Harland Hagler, "The Ideal Woman in the Antebellum South: Lady or Farmwife?" *The Journal of Southern History* 46.3 (August 1980), p. 410.
17. J. W. Leigh, *Other Days* (New York: Macmillan, 1921), p. 219; cp. Henry James, "Frances Anne Kemble," *Essays in London and Elsewhere* (London: James R. Osgood *et al.*, 1893), p. 125.

tality, Frances writes off the unprofitable portion of her father's workforce: "I do not see what else is to become of the negroes who cannot work except to die" (10). Both mother and daughter describe themselves, with measures of irony, as island queens, but both surrender control to their kings, as in Frances Leigh's chapter "Abdication."

While Fanny Scarlett impulsively married her Rhett, who resembles Pierce Butler not only in name, Frances Scarlett more patiently waited for Ashley.[18] Fanny Kemble shared with Scarlett O'Hara her passion and temper; Frances Leigh, her business sense and love of the land. Both Scarletts take up the challenge of just habitable dwellings. In *Journal of a Residence* Kemble describes the complete absence of luxuries in her home. It is, she writes, "certainly rather more devoid of the conveniences and adornments of modern existence than anything I ever took up my abode in before" (63). Frances Leigh agrees. The younger Scarlett does wonders, we know, with curtains, and monitors food supplies like her fictional counterpart. Frances lives, in short, just like Scarlett on Tara: "the roof of the kitchen leaked badly, and as we had frequent showers, I often had to cook, holding up an umbrella in one hand and stirring with the other" (18-19).

Unlike Mitchell's heroine, who thinks of beaux during family prayers, both nineteenth-century Scarletts draw their strength from religion. As John A. Scott notes in his 1984 introduction to Fanny Kemble's journal, "much of abolitionism in the 1830's flowed from a Christian belief in right action and a Christian desire to turn fellow citizens from the path of sin."[19] Responding to William Ellery Channing's contribution to the debate, *Slavery* (1835), the new Mrs. Butler found it, "like everything else of his, written in the pure spirit of Christianity, with judgment, temper and moderation, yet with abundant warmth and energy."[20] Inspired by his tract, which proposed a gradual easening of slavery through persuasion of southern plantation owners, she cast herself as Mr. Butler's Chris-

---

18. For the comparison to Mitchell's Scarlett O'Hara, I am indebted to Russell Duncan, University of Copenhagen.
19. James A. Scott, "Editor's Introduction," in Kemble, *Journal*, p. xxx.
20. John A. Scott, p. xxxii; cp. Furnas, p. 178.

tian conscience. She hoped, as she put it, to place the Butler slaves "upon a more humane and Christian footing."[21] Pierce, of course, was not amused.

Three decades later, their daughter also drew on Christianity for sustenance in Georgia. Like her mother, she prayed for southern slaveholders and frequented local chapels. Unlike her mother, however, the new plantation mistress hoped the Bible might help defeated southern planters win back their strength and privileges, as she herself set out to do. Upon arriving with her father in Savannah, she writes: "I consoled myself by going off to church to hear Bishop Elliott, who preached one of the most beautiful sermons I ever heard, on the Resurrection, the one thought that can bring hope and comfort to these poor heart-broken people" (4).

These people, incidentally, formed also Fanny Kemble's circle in Georgia in 1838-39. The young girls hiding round cheeks behind black crape veils and widows' caps were not, of course, around in earlier days. The gallery of neighbors and fellow planters entering and exiting the pages of *Ten Years on a Georgia Plantation* overlap, however, with that entertaining Frances's mother with antebellum hospitality. Through her own vigorous example, Frances distances herself from the frail southern belles and ladies who had so bored her mother. Like the young Mrs. Butler, however, she appreciates the neighboring Couper family and attends with her father the funeral of Fanny's friend, Mr. James Hamilton Couper. This funeral becomes to Frances a symbolic event. The steps of the church are broken, the roof fallen, and the graveyard itself overgrown with weeds and moss. The coffin, she records, "was in a cart drawn by one miserable horse" (23). Though Frances continues her mother's drama, and the cast of Act II remains the same, the stage and the props have changed indeed. "The whole thing," Frances writes, "was sad in the extreme; and a fit illustration of this people and country" (22).

Frances's imagery of southern defeat echoes the symbolism of her mother's journal, where landscape descriptions function as political commentary. A "most beautiful species of ivy" grow in a

---

21. Furnas, p. 179.

"slimy, poisonous-looking swamp" (56, 55), this combination and others representing southern plantation life, where aristocratic gentility flourishes in the soil of slavery. Both diarists interact vigorously with the exotic terrain they inhabit, for example as fishermen. Like her mother and her grandmother, who would go fishing while her children roamed the English countryside, Frances explores Butler Island with an old man, who is "quite as enthusiastic about fishing" as she herself. "I have been out once or twice with him, but not for deep-sea fishing yet, which however I hope to do soon," she writes. She comments as well on "the most magnificent bass" he catches, as well as "blue fish weighing twenty and thirty pounds" (20-21). In the spirit of her mother, Frances also likes horseback-riding and even hunting, a sport Kemble links to regional savagery (58). Her daughter takes a more pragmatic view of hunting. She goes on a deer hunt "with some of the gentlemen," she explains, "quite as much in hopes of getting some venison as of seeing any real sport" (32).

Less poetic than her mother, Frances nonetheless relishes the freedom of the wilderness, which both writers describe with the feminine sentence Virginia Woolf would promote in *A Room of One's Own*: "the tender new spring green of the deciduous trees and shrubs, mingling with the dark green of the evergreen cypress, magnolia, and bay, all wreathed and bound together with the yellow jessamine and fringed with the soft delicate grey moss which floated from every branch and twig" (13). Though Kemble might also have written this passage on Butler Island vegetation, the words belong to the no-nonsense Frances, whom Henry James thought "inferior to her mother and sister."[22] Like Kemble and James himself, for that matter, Frances nonetheless sounds the realm of the unspoken, and listens to the silences around her. Framed by the phrase "beautiful beyond description" and the sentence beginning "Not a sound broke the stillness but the dip of our oars in the water," the passage quoted above sounds the silence of a feminine languagescape and, like Fanny Kemble, makes it speak.

The boatsmen hiding in "our" oars also break through Frances's

---

22. Furnas, p. 431.

sentences in what she labels a "wild minor chant" (13). Even Fanny Kemble had on occasion hid slave labor in constructions such as "I persisted in having my pine tree planted" (103-04), which in Frances's journal becomes, well into a sentence enumerating her own efforts, that she "had the windows mended" (7). Both join, at times, Pratt's "seeing-man" in erasing from the landscape the subaltern population. While Kemble, however, would row out alone so as to escape for a time the slaves (and their master), Frances goes further, as she explains in a sentence once again ignoring the labor of African Americans. "I hope to improve it," she writes of her Butler Island residence, "by removing the negro houses away from where they now are, close to this house, to where I can neither see, hear, nor smell them" (63).

Though Frances sided with the southern planters and her mother with the slaves, the racial views of mother and daughter occasionally merge. Both women feel that their personal influence would make a difference in the lives of the people around them. Fanny pleaded, of course, with Pierce Butler to improve the conditions of especially their female slaves, and, following Channing's scheme, thought vaguely that her personal example might improve their "conduct" and gradually prepare them for freedom.[23] Frances hoped that her personal behavior might teach her workmen industry: "They are affectionate and often trustworthy and honest, but so hopelessly lazy to be almost worthless as labourers" (11). Both diarists later revised their positions. Kemble distanced herself from what she came to see as youthful fanaticism and confessed to having "*bitterly* regretted many things" included in her book.[24] She believed, moreover, that Frances's presence on the Butler plantations "tended to prolong the dependent feelings of old relations." As she summed up the situation, "An estate cannot be made to depend upon a woman's coaxing or scolding the cultivators.... Personal influence is one thing and the laws of labor another."[25] Frances herself admitted to underestimating the workforce. Footnoting her

---

23. Furnas, pp. 178-79.
24. Bell, p. 448.
25. Margaret Armstrong, *Fanny Kemble: A Passionate Victorian* (New York: Macmillan, 1938), p. 179.

statement on laziness above, she writes in 1883: "I was mistaken. In the years 1877 and 1880 upwards of thirty thousand bushels of rice was [sic] raised on the place by these same negroes" (11).

A subtext of African American enterprise thus runs through the texts of both mother and daughter. Kemble mentions, for example, two carpenters who had found the time to make a boat and sold it to a neighboring planter for $60. On meeting the former slaves in 1867, Frances notes that "many of them had planted a considerable quantity of corn and cotton..." (15). Only reluctantly does she acknowledge the connection beteween industry and ownership. "The old people," she writes, "were far too old and infirm to work for me, but once let them get a bit of ground of their own given to them, and they become quite young and strong again" (29).

The respect that hesitantly surfaces in the diaries of mother and daughter branched into the bonding, even love, that led Fanny Kemble to side with the female slaves, whose situation, she realized, resembled her own. As Mary Chesnut had sighed a quarter of a century after Fanny's trip, "poor women, poor slaves" (15).[26] Frances Butler would hardly consent to this equation, yet she too describes emotions close to love for her African American dependents. She subscribed, no doubt, to the "domestic metaphor," the image of an orderly, hierarchical social arrangement in which every southerner contentedly had a place and stayed in it,[27] and thus saw herself as part of an extended family, white and black. She comments on her father's close ties with his former slaves and mentions herself that "they generally are singularly gentle and courteous in their manner" (49). Upon Pierce Butler's death, she finds comfort only in their company and words.

This closeness, imagined or not, might group mother and daughter with local white women, who feared, nonetheless, the company of African American men. Kemble, in contrast, rowed

---

26. C. Vann Woodward, ed., *Mary Chesnut's Civil War* (New Haven: Yale U P, 1981), p. 15; on marriage as "the dominant metaphor for slavery," see Stephanie McCurry in *Divided Houses: Gender and the Civil War*, ed. Catherine Clinton and Nina Silber (New York: Oxford UP, 1992), p. 36.
27. Anne Firor Scott, "Women's Perspective on the Patriarchy in the 1850s," *Journal of American History* 61 (June 1974), p. 52.

about with crews of slaves, to whom she trusted her life and what happiness she might possess. Her daughter lived alone among her father's ex-slaves for seasons on end, but when they reached, in her view, a "climax of lawless independence" (72), she began sleeping with a loaded pistol under her pillow. In the spirit of her cross-dressing mother, Frances invents herself as a phallic woman.[28] As Charles Joyner notes about Elizabeth Pringle in *A Woman Rice Planter*, Frances portrays herself as "'the indestructible woman,'" who copes on masculine terrain and gains financially and emotionally in the process.[29]

Like a hidden gun, views now labeled racist joined Fanny Kemble and her daughter. Despite the empathy and pity Mr. Butler's wife feels for mr. Butler's slaves, she recoils from closer contact with adult African Americans, both in terms of hygiene and physical traits. Frances Leigh, of course, constantly voiced her beliefs in Caucasian superiority and hesitated to abandon her dependents to their futures. Encouraged by Paul Du Chaillu's *Travels in Africa*, which argues that Africans will work only if supervised by whites, Frances confided to a southern friend that God had willed American slavery.[30] Charles Wynes, who edited Frances Leigh's diary for Beehive, sums up her position: "In tone, the contents of *Ten Years on a Georgia Plantation Since the War* are decidedly conservative, and Southerners, who hated her mother, Fanny Kemble, for her critical account of slavery, should have loved Frances for her account of those same blacks trying to adjust to freedom" (xvi).

Though Wynes perceptively emphasizes tone in comparing the Georgia writings of Fanny Kemble and Frances Leigh, the journals share, as we have seen, a series of stylistic and thematic concerns, from creative uses of silence to issues of gender and race. In fact, the tensions critics tend to identify exist not as much between, but

---

28. Cp. Charles Wynes's introduction to *Ten Years*: "Frances Leigh's account tells what it was like for a woman to struggle alone in a man's world" (xvii).
29. Charles Joyner, "Introduction," in Elizabeth Pringle, *A Woman Rice Planter*, ed. Charles Joyner (Columbia: U of S Carolina P, 1992), p. xlv; Mary Louise Weaks, "Three Women of Letters in the South, 1863-1913," *Mississippi Quarterly* 46.4 (Fall 1993), p. 624.
30. Wright, p. 184.

within, mother and daughter. Both women traveled to Georgia from Philadelphia, and both reacted with mixed feelings to their rice plantation experiences. Both Fanny Kemble's *Journal of a Residence* and Frances Leigh's *Ten Years* thus dramatize the conflict between insider and outsider viewpoints that haunted both writers.

As Fanny Kemble in 1838 arrived at the wharf in Darien, Georgia, she felt as if her family of travellers "had touched the outer bound of civilized creation" (47). As she confides to her friend Elizabeth, she feels "very much like one in another planet from yourself" (58). Kemble emphasizes, as travellers will, the exotic elements of her new surroundings, which she simultaneously attempts to domesticate through comparisons to English customs and landscapes. Over the course of her stay, however, she takes on the role of insider, in that her marital and financial involvement with slavery cannot remain unacknowledged. Well into her journal, she records that "for the first time, almost a sense of horrible personal responsibility and implication took hold of my mind, and I felt the weight of an unimagined guilt upon my conscience" (138). Kemble, in short, finds out that she is outsider and insider both. Henry James comments in a character sketch of Kemble on the "remarkably fine cluster of inconsistencies" in her disposition, brought out especially in discussions of North America: "The United States commended themselves to her intensely conservative taste; she relished every obligation to them but that in living in them; and never heard them eulogised without uttering her reserves or abused without speaking her admiration."[31]

Also Frances initially emphasizes the difference between Philadelphia and Butler Island, which upon arrival she sees as a world turned upside down. "The whole country," she writes, "had of course undergone a complete revolution" (1). She constructs herself and Pierce Butler as outsiders through statements such as "into this state of things we came from the North" (2), yet her journal reads as well as an insider's account of Reconstruction Georgia. She talks derogatively of Northerners who "figured it all out on paper" (63) and speaks in a southern voice: "If they would frankly say they in-

---

31. James, pp. 92, 116.

tend to keep us down, it would be fairer than making a pretence of readmitting us to equal rights" (34). Like her mother, Frances Leigh vacillates, sometimes within a paragraph, between outsider and insider's roles and actually seems to recognize the complexities of this dual vision: "we very often found ourselves taking entirely opposite views of things from day to day, which will explain apparent inconsistencies and contradictions in my statements" (3). What Alfred Hornung labels the "extraterritorial perspective" of the outsider looking in thus contributes to the parallels between the journals of a mother and daughter notoriously dissimilar. Their extraterritorial voices become, in Michael Schudson's phrase, "a performance in society's subjunctive mood."[32] Both performers – and surely Kemble has the advantage here – enact, in short, a drama of what might be, a script of the future that their roots elsewhere help them imagine.

The two lived together in London during the Civil War, years that must have called for considerable tact and silence, since Frances passionately supported the Confederacy; her mother, of course, the Union. Both chose to edit and publish their Georgia journals in England, and so inevitably added a transatlantic lens to their original outsider's vision. As Frances Leigh writes in her introduction, "I copy my impressions of things as they struck me then, although in many cases later events proved how false these impressions were, and how often mistaken I was in the opinions I formed" (3). Like her mother, Frances Leigh hoped through this apparent honesty to strengthen her credibility. She thus sets off her account from those "written either by travellers, who with every desire to get at the truth, could but see things superficially, or by persons whose feelings were too strong either on one side or the other to be perfectly just in their representations" (2-3).

Though Frances attempts to distance herself from her mother, surely a traveller, and surely an emotional one, both women's journals help us re-read mainstream American autobiography, in Hornung's view written from outside(r) perspectives from the early Puritans onwards. In the pre-national stage, colonialists inevitably constructed

---

32. Qtd. in Kathleen Diffley, *Where My Heart Is Turning Ever: Civil War Stories and Constitutional Reform, 1861-1876* (U of Georgia P, 1992), p. xviii.

their experiences in the New World through Old World paradigms, and in their conversion narratives began from an extraterritorial perspective to map their journey from outside the Church to inside. Benjamin Franklin wrote his story of self- and nationhood when stationed in Europe, and surely enacted a drama between outsiders and insiders in possibly the most American of autobiographies. Frederick Douglass speaks from an extraterritorial position of his desire for American citizenship, as do, in various ways, twentieth-century writers such as John Dos Passos, Malcolm X, and Maya Angelou. Even southern writers such as Grace King and Eudora Welty continue in their literary and autobiographical works the struggle between insider and outsider visions, communal and (inter)personal, that engages Fanny Kemble as well as her offspring.

In his biography of Kemble, J. C. Furnas confesses to having "insufficient data for hoping to understand the Butler sisters." He comments on the "unstable equilibrium" of the group consisting of Fanny, her daughters and their husbands, and ascribes the "abiding sourness between mother and younger daughter" to "daughter's heedless extravagances and invidious cleaving unto Pierce."[33] Surely this sourness comes out in Frances Leigh's outbursts against her mother's Georgia journal, which, in fact, she claimed not to have read.[34] Like the dykes and canals crisscrossing the Butler rice plantations, Fanny Kemble's *Journal of a Residence* nonetheless nourishes her daughter's book, as "that great mother stream underneath."[35] Both women reside on islands ruled by their co-authors, and both struggle with issues that continue from one generation to the next, as do the people inhabiting their pages. From a margin of genre, gender and geography, they write their stories in order to define, and influence, the center, thus propelling their texts into not just southern, or northern, but American autobiographical and utopian traditions. In this sense, both Fanny Kemble's *Journal of a Residence on a Georgian Plantation in 1838-39* and Frances Leigh's *Ten Years on a Georgia Plantation Since the War* help construct – or reconstruct – a global South.

---

33. Pp. 383-84.
34. Wright, p. 174.
35. Anne Goodwin Jones, *Tomorrow Is Another Day: The Woman Writer in the South, 1859-1936* (Baton Rouge: LSU P, 1981), p. [93]

CHAPTER SEVEN

Battle of Brains: Andrew Sheffield, a Southern Madwoman

In June, 1930, Virginia Woolf wrote in a letter to Ethel Smyth: "As an experience, madness is terrific, I can assure you, and not to be sniffed at; and in its lava I still find most of the things I write about."[1] Woolf's correlation of madness and creativity might apply as well to the roughly ninety letters written by Andrew Moore Sheffield, a mental patient in Bryce Hospital, Alabama, from 1890 until her death in 1920. Sheffield would hardly, however, embrace the term "terrific" to describe the source of her writings, nor would she, even sardonically, accept the label of "madness" for her own mental condition, despite the volcanic temper and combative personality her correspondence delineates. On the contrary, the many letters Sheffield wrote to various Alabama governors and hospital physicians, most notably to Dr. James T. Searcy, Superintendent of Bryce Hospital from 1892 to 1919, sought to establish her sanity and bring about her removal to the penitentiary, where Sheffield felt she belonged. Prior to her admission to the former Alabama Insane Hospital, she had been addicted to chloral hydrate, administered to her by Dr. William May, with whom she had carried on a violent, presumably intimate relationship. Most recently, she had attempted to burn down the house of a neighbor quarreling with the doctor.

With the prospect of the forty-one-year-old spinster's trial and imprisonment for arson, the men of her family committed their

---

1. Nigel Nicholson, ed. *A Reflection of the Other Person: The Letters of Virginia Woolf IV, 1929-31* (London: Hogarth P, 1978), p. 180.

troubled relative to Bryce Hospital, where she remained against her will for twenty-nine years, seven months, and twenty-three days. John S. Hughes's edition of her letters charts Sheffield's experience as a Victorian mental patient and her negotiations with the masculine authority figures who defined her existence.[2] Despite her considerable verbal skills, neither the political nor the medical establishment, with Dr. Searcy as the most prominent embodiment of institutional power, bent to her wishes or, perhaps, lent her an ear. Sheffield's letters persisted nonetheless in presenting her needs and desires to governors and doctors, and employed a range of persuasive strategies intended not only to make a case for her sanity but also, in the face of abuse and depersonalization, to clear for herself sufficient space to allow for a (written) identity. *The Letters of a Victorian Madwoman* accordingly enacts the battle over her brain that Sheffield fought throughout her career at Bryce. Moreover, the correspondence fills the historical silence characteristic of the Victorian mad. After all, Yannick Ripa reminds us in *Women and Madness: The Incarceration of Women in Nineteenth-Century France*, insanity may be perceived in two ways: "it can be observed from the outside or experienced from the inside." Sheffield's surviving letters not only begin what Ripa calls "the hidden story of madness"[3] but also speak of gender and powerlessness in the late-nineteenth-century South.

Andrew Sheffield seemed in various ways destined for the asylum. Despite her name she was, for one thing, female and accordingly lucky to have escaped insanity for the first forty-one years of her life. The weak physical frames of women, Victorian doctors believed, corresponded to a mental fragility that might at any point snap, thus enveloping the female sex in pure insanity.[4] Victorian theories of female madness thus grounded themselves in biology:

---

2. John S. Hughes, ed., *The Letters of a Victorian Madwoman* (Columbia: U of South Carolina P, 1993). References to Andrew Sheffield's correspondence will be given parenthetically in the text. Following Hughes, I have retained Sheffield's idiosyncratic spelling and grammar.
3. Yannick Ripa, *Women and Madness: The Incarceration of Women in Nineteenth-Century France* (Cambridge, UK: Polity P and Basil Blackwell, 1990), p. 5.
4. Ripa, p. [2].

the inconstancy of the female reproductive system "interfered" with women's nervous system and diminished their sexual and rational self-discipline.[5] Women's wombs, in short, devoured their minds. The predominance of female patients in Victorian asylums thus reflects the association of the female body with passion, irrationality, loss of control, and confinement.

As an unmarried, middle-aged and educated woman, Sheffield was particularly exposed to the label of madness. The psychiatrists of her time linked eruption of insanity specifically to "the biological crises of the female life cycle – puberty, pregnancy, childbirth, menopause." Moreover, to move into an age bracket without conforming to the expected family role – such as belle, wife, mother – constituted in itself abnormal behavior.[6] Stigmatized as "odd" and "redundant," the Victorian spinster was thus a perfect candidate for a mental hospital.[7] Intelligence and education might facilitate a single woman's confinement. In the famous case of Elizabeth Packard, doctors ascribed the insanity she contested to "excessive application of body and mind."[8] Leanings towards intellectual pursuits distracted the female sex from its preordained destiny: the accomplishment of "true womanhood."[9] Describing events leading up to her commitment, Sheffield writes: "I was 39 years of age – at that time – had for years been of age, my own woman…" (55). Once inside the asylum, she dreams of life in prison, where she might work for her own support rather than remain idle. "Had you done your duty," she tells Superintendent Searcy, "I would have been in the Penitentiary at work – earning my bread for the past five years" (70).

---

5. Carroll Smith-Rosenberg and Charles Rosenberg, "The Female Animal: Medical and Biological Views of Woman and Her Role in Nineteenth-Century America," *Journal of American History* 60.1 (June-Sept. 1973), p. 335.
6. Elaine Showalter, *The Female Malady: Women, Madness and English Culture, 1830-1980* (New York: Pantheon, 1985), pp. 55, 54.
7. Showalter, *Malady*, p. 61; Smith-Rosenberg and Rosenberg, p. 336.
8. Myra Samuels Himelhoch and Arthur H. Schaffer, "Elizabeth Packard: Nineteenth-Century Crusader for the Rights of Mental Patients," *Journal of American Studies* 13.3 (1979), p. 352; cp. Ellen Dwyer, "A Historical Perspective," in *Sex Roles and Psychopathology*, ed. Cathy S. Widom (New York: Plenum, 1984), p. 21.
9. Smith-Rosenberg and Rosenberg, p. 340.

Andrew Sheffield could muster few of the Victorian woman's ideal features: submissiveness, passivity, gentleness, morality, nurturance, and whatnot.[10] She did not conform to the physical ideal of femininity with which Victorian doctors tended to measure female sanity.[11] "When a patient comes here," Sheffield observed at Bryce, "matters not how poor – what her condition may be financialy, if her personal appearance is all right, a genteel pair of kid gloves on ... (matters not how crazy she may be) she is placed on a front first class ward..." (48). In contrast, Sheffield was not only middle-aged and poor but let what looks she may have had deteriorate completely. "I have no pride as to my personal appearance," she writes a decade into her incarceration. At sixty-one, she describes herself as having a "head almost snow white but few natural teeth and face more wrinkled than most woemen at seventy years of age" (187).

Neither did Sheffield, like Sarah Morgan and other nineteenth-century women, respond to the century's narrow[ing] boundaries of respectable feminine behavior with hysteria; instead, she exhibited opposite gender traits such as anger, aggression, and disobedience. She was duly punished by a society that saw women's "masculine" dissent as madness.[12] Not only did she cross legal boundaries of acceptability with her attempted arson; she also began a pattern of sexual transgression and thus became prey to the doctors who, as Stearns asserts in "Liberty and Lunacy: The Victorians and Wrongful Confinement," blurred the lines between insanity and (particularly sexual) immorality.[13] Madness, Victorian alienists theorized, was often rooted in moral causes. Sheffield's former addiction to chloral hydrate hardly promoted her case for sanity. That her dependency presumably was iatrogenic, i. e. caused by a physician, or that opiates in the nineteenth-century South served

---

10. Carroll Smith-Rosenberg, "The Hysterical Woman: Sex Roles and Role Conflict in 19th-Century America," *Social Research* 39.4 (Winter 1972), pp. 655-56.
11. Dwyer, "Historical Perspective," p. 27; Showalter, *Malady*, pp. 87, 89.
12. Dwyer, "Historical Perspective," p. 19; Phyllis Chesler, *Women and Madness* (Garden City, NY: Doubleday, 1972), pp. 55, 164.
13. Peter Stearns, "Liberty and Lunacy: The Victorians and Wrongful Confinement," *Journal of Social History* 11.3 (Spring 1978), p. 367.

among women, such as Mary Chesnut, as a "semirespectable substitute for alcohol"[14] did not save Sheffield from judgment. For a middle-to-upper-class woman, the familial concern was above all respectability. Though her male relatives had apparently long considered her insane, she was presumably committed to Bryce Hospital to save the family's honor and perhaps to help her father's case. Having shot and killed Dr. May as the agent of Andrew's "ruin," James Sheffield stood trial in November, 1890, and was acquitted.[15]

The daughter's confinement thus supports Allan V. Horwitz's view in *The Social Control of Mental Illness* (1982) that "the degree of exclusion of individuals who are labelled mentally ill varies inversely with their power."[16] Within the nineteenth-century family, the wills of fathers, brothers, and, for Sheffield, nephews determined the lives of their female relatives and controlled the social definition of deviance.[17] "I fully agree with you that she should not be permitted to write letters to whomsoever she wants to," Sheffield's half brother and guardian T. A. Street observes to Dr. Searcy. "I would certainly suppress her letters" (49). Though Sheffield does not blame her male relatives, she inadvertently reveals their desire to keep her behind bars: "I was well convinced many years ago that it was useless to write any of my 'use-to-be' kin on the subject of going out of the Hospital – much less to the Penitentiary," she tells Dr. Searcy in a confidential letter from around 1906 (102).

Yet Andrew Sheffield was a marginal character in more ways than one. Always a difficult and temperamental woman, she resided in the ambiguous terrain of "the borderland," in Darwinian

---

14. David T. Courtwright, "The Female Opiate Addict in Nineteenth-Century America," *Essays in Arts and Sciences* 10.2 (March 1982), p. 162; "The Hidden Epidemic: Opiate Addiction and Cocaine Use in the South, 1860-1920," *Journal of Southern History* 49 (Feb. 1983), p. 66.
15. On sexual transgressions of white females and the law, see Mary Frances Berry, "Judging Morality: Sexual Behavior and Legal Consequences in the Late Nineteenth-Century South," *The Journal of American History* 78 (December 1991), p. 855.
16. Allan V. Horwitz, *The Social Control of Mental Illness* (New York: Academic P, 1982), p. 115.
17. Ripa, pp. 32, 35.

psychiatry a no-man's land between reason and madness, inhabited by the eccentric and the deviant who, like decadent men and New Women, might at any time be recruited by patrolling psychiatrists.[18] Having read one of her long letters, Governor William C. Oates found Sheffield at least sufficiently rational for him to write Dr. Searcy for specifics. His postscript testifies to the Governor's suspicions of psychiatric conclusions: "I want her case investigated & thoroughly tested as to her mental condition" (52).

Once behind the walls and locks of Bryce Hospital, which she entered in 1890, Sheffield seemed nonetheless destined to stay. Whether or not one agrees with Horwitz's gloomy assertion that "professionals label as mentally ill virtually all individuals who are brought to their attention," the nineteenth-century labeling and commitment process might, as in Sheffield's case, prove difficult or impossible to reverse.[19] What Ellen Dwyer in *Homes for the Mad* (1987) calls the "devastatingly permanent labels" tended to keep those stigmatized as mentally ill within the hospital setting, where, critics argue, the labeling itself caused patients to act in accordance with their deviant roles.[20] Women like Sheffield thus became (in)voluntarily engaged in life-long "careers" as chronically insane. Within the overcrowded Victorian asylums, the constant moving and mixing of patients suffering from nervous disorders with full-fledged lunatics further erased the boundaries between madness and sanity.[21] To stay in the institution turned out to be considerably easier than to leave it.[22]

Furthermore, those who remained in close contact with their families were more likely to be designated "improved" or "cured" than those who, like Sheffield, retained fairly loose kinship bonds.[23] As was typical in cases of family-initiated committals, her male rela-

---

18. Showalter, *Malady*, pp. 105-06.
19. Ellen Dwyer, *Homes for the Mad: Life inside Two Nineteenth-Century Asylums* (New Brunswick, NJ: Rutgers U P, 1987), p. 114.
20. Dwyer, *Homes*, p. 54; Agnes Miles, *Women and Mental Illness: The Social Context of Female Neurosis* (Brighton: Wheatsheaf, 1988), p. 14.
21. Cp. Dwyer, *Homes*, p. 13.
22. Ripa, p. 149.
23. Dwyer, *Homes*, pp. 114-15, 127.

tives showed a minimum of concern for their confined daughter, sister and aunt once asylum doctors had taken over responsibility for her care.[24] Her distant relationship with kin deprived Sheffield of emotional ties that might have strengthened her fight to escape Bryce Hospital and the label of insanity.[25] "Sometimes," she confesses to Dr. Lanford, "I give down and wish that I had some one to speak one kind word to me – just one comforting word, and then I think that I'm not worthy *one* comforting word" (207). Besides, in a region that saw kinship as all-important and relied on family to provide (female) identity,[26] a woman cut off from her relatives became, in essence, a nobody. Without the support of a father or a brother, except for occasional minor gifts, Sheffield could add poverty to lack of identity and prepare herself to be forgotten.[27]

Most detrimental to Sheffield's release from the asylum was nonetheless her unwillingness to, in her phrase, "come under" to the hospital professionals, for example by conforming to a feminine mold. As Phyllis Chesler explains, "women are often psychiatrically incarcerated for rejecting their 'femininity' as defined by those close to them – and are released or considered 'improved' when they regain it."[28] Sheffield retained her aggressive, opinionated, occasionally violent attitude throughout her long incarceration. Perhaps she could not control her fury because, as Chesler speculates, the basically feminine world of confined mental patients enrages men less than women, who have been restricted and "maddened" by the boundaries of femininity once before.[29] Sheffield, at least, consistently expressed dissatisfaction and disagree-

---

24. Ripa, pp. 40-41.
25. Horwitz, p. 103.
26. Elizabeth Fox-Genovese, "Family and Female Identity in the Antebellum South: Sarah Gayle and Her Family," in *In Joy and Sorrow: Women, Family and Marriage in the Victorian South, 1830-1900*, ed. Carol Bleser (New York: Oxford U P, 1991), p. 19.
27. Ripa, p. 92.
28. Chesler, p. 94; cp. Peter McCandless, "'A House of Cure': The Antebellum South Carolina Lunatic Asylum," *Bulletin of the History of Medicine* 64 (Summer 1990), p. 241; Stearns, p. 368.
29. Chesler, p. 55.

ment with her surroundings and occasionally acted out her emotions through her body, a violent behavior that, to doctors and staff, confirmed her insanity and sent her to the institution's back wards. She did, on rare occasions, engage in feminine stroking of masculine egos, as in this opening letter to Governor J. F. Johnston: "First, allow me to congratulate you upon your renomination, if an honest, faithful and capable discharge of duty will insure your reelection, you will be Alabamas next Gov." (82). Her compliments serve, she communicates self-consciously to Searcy in an accompanying note, a strictly persuasive function: "perhaps he [the Governor] will answer this, as I've flattered him a little" (84). Unable or unwilling, however, to respond consistently to incarceration with the submission and passivity that might have won her much-desired removal from Bryce Hospital, if only to the state penitentiary, Sheffield was left, as Dwyer writes, with "self-conscious sabotage" as her only recourse to power over those who supervised her life and determined its course.[30] For Sheffield, this sabotage became, above all, the letters with which she bombarded Superintendent Searcy, Alabama governors, and others.

Like other inmates' delusions of grandeur and (sexual) power, Sheffield's writing enacted the mental patient's "doomed search for potency."[31] Through demonstrations of syntactic coherence and symbolic control, she hoped to persuade the authors of her confinement of her sanity. The asylum itself, of course, framed her life and her combat with authorities, but the scene of action was the sign. Her supervisors provided only reluctantly the sheets of paper she needed. Asylum doctors at Bryce and elsewhere habitually limited, censored, or confiscated inmates' mail.[32] The rationale was the necessity to protect ladies from "possibly shameful self-revelation"[33] as well as from the danger of kindling patients' obsessions and constant attention to their illness. These arguments might cover asylum administrative and medical staff's fear of the legislative in-

---

30. Dwyer, "Historical Perspective," p. 41.
31. Chesler, p. 31.
32. Dwyer, *Homes*, p. 126.
33. Showalter, *Malady*, p. 79.

vestigations and inspections that critics of psychiatric practices initiated from the 1850s and 1860s.[34] Victorian alienists, Showalter notes, "tended to *silence* the female patient." Moral managers of the nineteenth-century insane rested therapeutic reputations on their ability to control (or eliminate) patients' language.[35]

Dr. James T. Searcy, Superintendent at Bryce almost for the duration of Sheffield's incarceration and her primary correspondent, thus constituted a reluctant, at best indifferent audience. Despite the many years they both spent at Bryce, their relationship was characterized by distance and antagonism. Hospital staff filled up the space between superintendent and inmate, thus impeding immediate contact; medical visits to asylum halls served not least a disciplinary purpose.[36] A difference of interest further separated the two: the medical expert wished to implement his therapy, while the patient wished to escape it. Most crucially, however, the different access to influence permanently unbalanced their relation. As John S. Hughes concludes in his introduction, "the Superintendent possessed both power and freedom. Sheffield held but little of either."[37]

Though various metaphors suggesting a differential authority thus might describe the Searcy-Sheffield association, critics of Victorian psychiatry, like Elizabeth Packard, prefer to represent doctor and (female) patient as inquisitor and witch or as father and daughter. Certainly Searcy's diagnosis and forceful therapy might throw a medieval light upon their correspondence. Closer to home, the paternalistic institutional hierarchy emerging from *Letters* casts Searcy as the stern patriarch (with a "stark view of sex roles")[38] intent on infantilizing and remolding his unruly daughter. She, in turn, seeks to overthrow or infect the patriarch's system of order. Their correspondence reveals as well the mutual dependence hid-

---

34. Himelhoch and Schaffer, p. 345.
35. Showalter, *Malady*, p. 154.
36. Ripa, pp. 147, 139.
37. Hughes, "Introduction," p. 45.
38. John S. Hughes, "The Madness of Separate Spheres: Insanity and Masculinity in Victorian America," in *Meanings for Manhood: Constructions of Masculinity in Victorian America*, ed. Mark Carnes and Clyde Griffen (Chicago: U of Chicago P, 1990), pp. 54, 62.

ing in both sets of metaphors. Not only do their long-standing affiliation with Bryce and their bouts of shared vocabulary suggest inescapable parallels; each becomes, in a sense, a mirror for the other's identity. *The Letters* thus illustrates the dialogic principle that Stuart Hall (following Bakhtin, Volosinov and others) discusses in "Metaphors of Transformation." Dialogism, he writes, "celebrates altererity.... As the world needs my altererity to give it meaning, I need the authority of others to define, or author, my self."[39] The doctors, in Sheffield's view, "swear the patients are crazy to keep them there," while simultaneously mirroring their charges by "appearing to be *somewhat demented themselves*" (48).

Sheffield did not unambiguously conceptualize her antagonistic, yet complementary, relation to the medical staff in terms of gender. Superficially, at least, she lived up to her unusual first name by distancing herself from virtuous femininity and by seeming distinctly male-identified. Her awareness of appropriate feminine behavior surfaces, as we have seen, when for persuasive purposes she stages herself according to the standard role. Having mailed a vituperant attack on Governor Joseph F. Johnston in 1897, in which she paints him as a friend of rapists and murderers, she subsequently apologizes most humbly, casting herself as a dutiful daughter, so to speak, in the very act of transgression: "Were my Father living," she writes to the Governor, "and knew that I had written such an insulting note to a nice good old gentleman he would be very much mortified over it. Hope you will pardon me..." (74). Andrew Sheffield recognized as well the price of her refusal to act the feminine part more consistently. "I could bid prison walls farewell tomorrow if I would only agree with Dr. Searcy," she writes to Gov. Johnston the following year (85). Well into the next century, in 1911, she no longer bothers to evoke traditional femininity, except negatively: "I am not a good woman, lay no claims to being good..." (204). In the end, then, she defines herself in contrast to southern womanhood, only her emphatic repetition revealing the cost of her self-positioning.

---

39. Stuart Hall, "Metaphors of Transformation," in Allon White, *Carnival, Hysteria, Writing: Collected Essays and Autobiography* (Oxford: Clarendon P, 1993), p. 18.

Battle of Brains: Andrew Sheffield, a Southern Madwoman

Andrew Sheffield identified with the men of her family. Though they had declared her insane and committed her to Bryce, she never blamed them and unconsciously chose to ignore what southern historians have called "the theme of male failure."[40] Any doubts or disappointments she might have felt about her male relatives, she counters efficiently with extensive expressions of pride in her father. Col. James F. Sheffield had lost his fortune in the war and had declined in status from planter, war hero and office-holder to a clerkship in the State Superintendent of Education office.[41] To Andrew Sheffield, however, he epitomized American success and masculine virtue: "Was conscientious, just, and honest .... Was remarkably handsome, said to have been the handsomest man in Laws Brigade. Like Carnegie was a *book worm*. Like yourselves [Drs. Partlow and Lanford] was '*poor raised*' and '*self made*'" (155). She invests less emotion in writing of her nephew O. D. Street, the U. S. District Attorney for northern Alabama, yet unfailingly mentions him with respect and awe. Anticipating a rare visit, Sheffield writes to Drs. Searcy, Partlow and Lanford around 1910/11:

> It is him wanting to see me, not me wanting to see him.... I will let him come, at the same time I feel that I am doing him a great injustice to allow him to come here and call for me as his aunt – the 'worst disgraced woman in the State of Ala [.'] (200-01)

Sheffield's hesitations in terms of facing her nephew might hide a resentment she did not allow herself to feel about the man who escorted her to life-long incarceration. But without other emotional or familial ties, she held on to male kin despite all, and possibly transferred her anger and hurt onto the patriarchal figures at Bryce – the doctors at whom she fired innumerable accusations and complaints.

Both groups of men presumably took part in what Ripa calls "the conspiracy of silence,"[42] the tacit agreement between familial

---

40. See Bleser, p. 256.
41. Hughes, "Introduction," p. 14.
42. Ripa, p. 35.

and psychiatric representatives of power to end disturbingly deviant behavior through so-called voluntary committals. Certainly Sheffield's correspondence reveals the male bonding between members of her family, doctors and politicians who kept her in insanity wards. A letter from Governor Johnston written to Sheffield on July 19, 1887, thus begins by praising her father as "a gallant Confederate soldier and a good man and citizen." After professing complete ignorance of her case, the Governor proceeds to emphasize the respect and prestige enjoyed by the Bryce Superintendent: "*You will understand of course that what Dr Searcy would say about your case would have great weight, because he is a man of such high character that one would be very reluctant in believing that he would report other than the matter as he sees it*" (63, 64). Sheffield's underlining and marginal comments here show not only her awareness of this masculine gatekeeping but also the anger and frustration it inspired. "You men had as well stay away from me," she writes to Dr. Lanford around 1907, "for I will not speak to any of you, will not multiply words with you" (116). "You men," she concludes some pages later, "have done your do" (118).

Despite the wrath Sheffield lavished upon the "prejudiced physicians, calling themselves insanity experts" (85), whom she addressed as "you men," she did not gang up with female members of the hospital community. She found suffocating the web of female gossip that, she argues, caused her removal to back wards (117) and resented more than her scheming fellow patients the young hospital nurses. Often recruited from rural families while still in their teens, these transient staff members represented everything Sheffield had lost[43]: youth, beauty, ignorance, freedom. She disliked being in the hands of a "pettycoat government," a phrase she repeats throughout her correspondence, and felt superior to "the more common class nurses, unable to write legable, or read a paragraph in a newspaper correctly" (125). She pinpoints the tendency of lower-rank (female) hospital staff to carry out even implied wishes and dictates of male superiors[44] and expects no alliance with Bryce

---

43. Hughes, "Introduction," p. 38.
44. Chesler, p. 63.

"pettycoat government": "The Dr's and nurses play on into each others hands – one does not counteract or check the other – both are reaping mutual benefits, and the *patients* in their graves" (163).

Yet Sheffield's resentment of Supervising Nurse Mary Buck propels her to speak out for all women patients and thus express feelings of solidarity with "the afflicted and unfortunate of this State" (134). In a letter to Governor Comer of March 1908, Sheffield writes on behalf of the Bryce "female department": "We, the patients, beg of you to protect us, and remove the woman supervisor who is responsible for most of the wrong things that go on here" (133). Despite the attack on "you men" and her sense of a female patient community, however, Sheffield saw herself as an isolated case, correspondence with masculine authorities her only hope for space, justice and truth.

Because many of her letters ended up in hospital files, received little or no attention, or did not survive to be printed in Hughes's collection, Sheffield's voice reaches it audience only through filters and mufflers. What rings out clearly, however, is her resistance to having others speak *for* her. In the very first letter of the ninety preserved, she addresses Governor Thomas G. Jones in order to prevent Dr. Bondurant's evaluation of her (in)sanity from representing the truth about her mental state (47-48). Sixteen years later, her resistance to having her voice usurped by doctors has merely hardened: "Dr Partlow told me in No 14 that I 'was not insane', but '*we*' want to do what 'we' think is for the best. There is no '*we*' in my case, that is, the law part, so he should have said Supt instead of '*we*'" (165).

Sheffield's unruly voice preserves her individual identity, despite doctors' efforts to bring about a manageable, feminine silence. "'[P]atients and nurses must not talk,' 'must not speak of what they see' – must be *mute*," she quotes Dr. Lanford as saying (171). Dr. Searcy admits in 1896 to Governor William C. Oates that he keeps Sheffield "on the demented ward," where, he explains, "she could not frighten others with her horrible tales" (60). Though the Superintendent thus objects to Sheffield as narrator/writer, she persists in generating language. "My tongue has never been silenced, and never will be," she writes in 1909. "When I know that it is right to use it I will do it regardless the punishment" (171).

Victorian madwomen, Showalter notes, did not take to silence: "Their talkativeness, violation of conventions of feminine speech, and insistence on self-expression was the kind of behavior that had led to their being labeled 'mad' to begin with."[45] The effect is, in Sheffield's case, an outpouring of words spilling onto her pages as if to swamp her readers. Her wordiness might, of course, originate in lack of writing experience – "the trouble with myself, is, that I have to say so much to express a *little*," she writes in an early letter (53). Obviously, she also "multiplies" words simply for the sake of doing so, as if to fill the blankness of her life with language and to remind the outside world, and herself, of her existence. Sheffield's verbal diarrhea served a therapeutic function. As in the tribal societies discussed by Horwitz, the ritualized confession of sins constituted a standard cure for insanity and social disruption.[46] Through linguistic inclusiveness, Sheffield managed, despite odds, to contain her identity for almost thirty years.

Repetition, a founding movement in *Letters*, worked in similar fashion. Repetition operates in Sheffield's texts stylistically, or through a compulsive return to favorite words and phrases: "I was sent here a sane woman"; "petticoat government"; "a prostitute and a criminal"; "I never saw a drunk woman until I came here," etc. Thematically, Sheffield returns again and again to her own case story, to her desire to leave Bryce Hospital for the state penitentiary, to nurses' and patients' intrigues, and to the abuse and neglect she suffers from doctors. As Hughes notes in introducing the last segment of the ninety letters, this Victorian madwoman repeats in essence only one story. Sheffield's compulsive repetition of the same narrative tells, of course, its own story of trauma and (self-)therapy. But repetition suggests as well that even language closed in upon Sheffield. As her mental and verbal horizon shrunk during the decades she spent on asylum back wards, her linguistic imprisonment mirrored only too accurately her physical one.

At the same time, Sheffield's many repetitions – her retelling of her case story to a sequence of governors, her repeated pleas to be

---

45. Showalter, *Malady*, p. 81.
46. Horwitz, p. 151.

transferred to the state penitentiary, and her explanations concerning squabbles and fights with nurses – constitute attempts to persuade doctors, governors and Bryce trustees of her sanity. Since incomprehensibility in Horwitz's analysis is a "central attribute" in lay definitions of madness,[47] Sheffield tried consistently to establish a rationale for the events leading to her committal to Bryce Hospital as well as for her moods and actions once there. As neither her attitude nor her situation changed for close to thirty years, however, Sheffield's repetitive facts and explanations tend to defeat her purpose. Covering the same argumentative ground *ad nauseam*, she evinces not comprehensibility but compulsion.

Other argumentative strategies nonetheless strengthened Sheffield's case and must have caused her correspondents at least to wonder about her (in)sanity. She seeks, for example, to minimize the relational and cultural distance between herself on the one hand and psychiatrists and politicians on the other. The tendency is for labels of mental illness to move from those with rank and power to those without[48]; thus, persons socially and culturally at the level with medical/political authorities are least likely to be declared insane. Accordingly, Sheffield repeatedly highlighted the assumptions and background she shared with her doctors. She bridged the gap between patient and physician with phrases like "you know that" (on one occasion repeated four times in four lines [68]) and "were I in your place" (95), which suggest a common pool of insight and ability despite a concrete relational distance. Sheffield further evokes a familial parallel to ensure Dr. Searcy's compassion: "you know that it has gone hard with me – as much so as would with one of your daughters if forced to spend seven years on the back wards of this Hospital..." (68). This appeal apparently unsuccessful, Sheffield tries again: "it was reasonable to suppose that as you had children of your own, you would be merciful on other peoples" (70).

Most persistently, Sheffield focuses on the high-status class and race that in her mind collapsed the distinction between herself

---

47. Horwitz, pp. 19, 27.
48. Horwitz, p. 78.

and the Bryce medical staff. "You must remember," she writes to Searcy in 1907, "that my use to be kin, rank as you and yours do" (111). Her family's prominence, she believes, entitles her to treatment as good as that received by private, paying patients (142). On one occasion, she sketches her whole family history so as to prove to Drs. Partlow and Lanford that she is "not far behind your private, and educated weomen, so far as *prominent*, and *wealthy* relatives are concerned" (155, cp. 210). Besides, she reminds her most stubborn opponents, the whiteness she shares with them ought to wipe out remaining differences: "You are not a friend to white weomen," she writes in the angry note to Governor Johnston she later regretted (73); in another to Dr. Lanford she complains that Dr. Rau failed to treat her "with the courtesy that was due a good negro" (129). Sheffield's insistence on rank and race attempted to narrow the distance between those controlling the labeling process and those controlled, as well as to ensure a tolerable treatment during her asylum stay. Class and money determined, after all, an inmate's "psychiatric career" and also left open the possibility of wrongful confinement, in Stearns's analysis primarily "a middle- and upper-class concern."[49]

To veil the issue of gender, which, despite her first name, would increase the relational and cultural distance to the men she wished to approach, Sheffield enlisted for her cause male experts and authority figures. In her first letter to Governor Johnston written in 1897, Sheffield immediately mentions Ex-Governors Jones and Oates and proceeds to identify herself through male kinship: "I am a daughter of Col. J. L. Sheffield who died at Montgomery 1892." To authenticate that she is indeed wrongfully confined, she calls upon "the Supt and his physicians" (61). Nine years after this first letter to Johnston, she still supports her case for sanity with male experts, this time addressing the Hospital Treasurer (98).

Persuasive devices such as detail, enumeration, and a rhetoric of deprivation further impress upon her audience the inclemency of Sheffield's situation. She lists, for example, all relatives she can

---

49. Elaine Showalter, "Victorian Women and Insanity," *Victorian Studies* 23.2 (Winter 1980), p. 161; Stearns, p. 369.

think of to establish her family's respectability and provides, when possible, details of employment, education, and even drinking habits. Her description of asylum back wards exemplifies as well her technique of minute cataloguing:

> behind the scenes are the neglected, sick, and dying patients, tho bruised and bleeding from nurses hands, calling to the Dr to receive his refusal of protection or aid, tho distressed, mistreated, ill used in any form, with no hope, no chance of reaching a genuine, honest, human heart.... (163)

The emphasis on what is not there, with which this passage closes, recurs in Sheffield's prose. In one vignette of hospital back wards, her rhetoric evokes especially the sensory deprivation she endures:

> nothing to hear but the unearthly shrieks of the maniacs, nothing to see but the poor incurably insane beings, nothing for the mind or body to feast upon, deprived of books or papers, in fact deprived of every thing which might lighten confinement and pass the dreary hours. (62)

Yet Sheffield hoped, with her emphasis on deprivation, not for liberty, but merely for removal to the penitentiary. As she writes to Governor W. C. Oates in 1895, again expressing her intentions negatively, "I did not appeal to you thinking that I could, or wanting to gain my liberty, freedom through you, for I am not entitled to my freedom – neither do I want it" (56).

While these lines to Gov. Oates might employ negation to veil Sheffield's desires as feminine (non)assertions, her words reveal as well the contours of traditional morality and phraseology. Echoing Victorian rectitude, Sheffield distinguished between "lewd" and "virtuous" women (154) and accuses the Supervisor of Nurses, Mary Buck, of having "two sisters of disreputable character" (115). Without hesitation, Sheffield places herself in the lewd and disreputable category, repeatedly referring to herself as "disgraced" and a "prostitute and criminal." "I am a deep dyed criminal," she opens a letter to Governor William D. Jelks (105); in another to Dr. Searcy, she employs the slight variation of "'houseburner' and prostitute"

(183). By using a moral vocabulary indistinguishable from that of her doctors, Sheffield might, of course, seek to ingratiate herself to those in charge. Her phraseology reflects as well what Ripa calls inmates' "guilt," i. e. their internalization of society's judgment and subsequent desire for punishment (66). Sheffield, for one, has total confidence in the judicial system: "My only wish and desire, is that justice be meted out to me," she writes in her letter to Jelks. "I crave justice, I yearn for it, I pray for it, for that alone will *attone* for the crime" (106). However, Sheffield's self-labeling as a "criminal" and a "prostitute" could simply be the terms with which she describes her confinement to the hospital back wards[50] or her way of mocking the self-righteous language of her keepers.

Sarcasm certainly helped Sheffield scorn those in power. Not only did she matter-of-factly place "Dr" within quotation marks in many letters to hospital physicians; she also questioned the systems of belief they so vigorously endorsed. "If I have been so unfortunate to violate the laws of Moral Society and deserve Capital punishment," she writes to Governor Thomas G. Jones in 1893, "please commute my case to the Penitentiary instead of the Insane Hospital" (48). Anticipating a visit from Governor Johnston five years later, Sheffield addresses Searcy with intensified sarcasm: "You need not fear to trust him alone I will not ask him for *Tobacco* or *money*, neither will I ask him to have *intercourse* with me, so you need not have him *guarded*" (80, cp. 76).

The vaccillation between straightforward usage of a Victorian moral vocabulary and a sarcastic jeering of the behavioral codes it upholds suggests, of course, Sheffield's own moral pendulations. Her indecision, or her endeavor to occupy several positions at once, nonetheless serves her well in the contest of language that makes up her correspondence. Throughout her letters, she rewrites, so to speak, the terms both she and the medical staff employ by imposing new meaning on traditional words, thus enlisting them on her side in the ideological battle she hoped to win. When assistant physician Thomas F. Taylor calls her "the most prominent woman in the State" (114), i. e. the most "disgraced," Sheffield uses his language to argue for renewed attention to her case: "As I am so very promi-

---

50. Hughes, "Introduction," p. 23.

nent I think it but right and just that I should cost the State enough to pay a commission of lunacy to interview me" (129); moreover, she begins to emphasize her family's prominence (153-55). She even signs herself "Prominent woman," an act that simultaneously accepts, denounces and redefines for her own purposes the attack on individual identity that labeling and confinement brought about.

The mixed responses to Victorian ethics characteristic of Sheffield's writings account as well for their blend of discourses. Sometimes Sheffield addresses her correspondents with utmost politeness and apologizes for any discursive slippage that might occur. In her 1893 appeal to Governor Jones, she begins with all due respect: "I beg to be excused for the liberty I take in annoying you with my many complaints." As she zooms in on the Supervising Nurse, a woman she never learned to like or accept, Sheffield remains genteel. "If she takes a dislike to a patient (excuse my slang expression) the patient had better be in *Purgatory*" (47-48).

Sheffield's somewhat prudish attention to diction disappears in other sections of her correspondence. In her family overview, she mentions maternal relatives as *descendants of the old time blue blood arristocracy*" and immediately afterwards writes: "Only three drunkards in the family..." (158). She tells Governor Johnston that Dr. Searcy has "money, station, and is a social and religious ornament," then proceeds to call her doctor "the most artful and cunning piece of flesh that I ever had to encounter with" (83). Sheffield's mixed language reveals that the education she boasted might have gone further. It discloses as well her hesitation between Victorian femininity and earthier rhetorical and behavioral modes, as well as between a wish to persuade and anger at having to do so. Most certainly, Sheffield's fluctuating diction originates in fatigue and impatience with official uses of language and power. "Be positive and plain," she asks of Governor Jelks in 1906. "I have been undermined and baffled with until I want nothing but candor" (106). In fact, Sheffield might opt for colloquial candor to invade from "below" the respectable "high," thus confusing and contesting the hierarchical construction and administration of Victorian insanity.[51]

---

51. See White.

Confined to back wards for years on end, Sheffield yearned, of course, for variation and amusement, yet her desire to go to a circus may similarly relate to a Bakhtinian carnivalesque. Having written, perhaps needlessly, to Drs. Partlow and Lanford for permission to join the circus-going party, Sheffield received it too late to get herself ready. In a letter of Dec. 7, 1909, she fumes over such "mean treatment" and points out that she "would not have been the only disgraced woman on the grounds, all kinds go to circuses" (173). She rejoices particularly in the escape from her status as "most disgraced woman in Alabama" that the circus could offer. But Sheffield remained, on this day as on others, within the boundaries of her moral and mental labels. Aided by a street parade, animals, and a minstrel show, other patients, doctors and nurses abandoned established distinctions and became a group (173). The whole party enjoyed, in Hall's formulation, "the temporary licensed suspension and reversal of order"[52] – exactly what Sheffield in her own life and writings (had) hoped to accomplish.

From behind Bryce Hospital locks, she reached instead for equality, or power, by issuing ultimata and threats to representatives of "the high." "Read my letter and return it," she tells Dr. Searcy (52). In another letter, she threatens with violence and arson, should a grand jury ever decide to acquit her and thus send her to Bryce rather than punish her with jail (71). By using authoritative language, Sheffield hoped to persuade the Superintendent to attest to her sanity, so that she might accomplish her goal of going to the state penitentiary rather than stay on at Bryce. Yet she wanted to leave on her own terms. As she impresses on Dr. Searcy in 1910, "I am ready, willing, and waiting to go at any time that you 'dance to *my* music, ['] not me to yours" (195). Sheffield's commanding tone originated, as we have seen, in her impatience with the feminine submission that won other patients their freedom: "I cannot say *please,* never have said it in all my life – I'll *never, never,* say *please,* please please" (233). She usurps the language of power out of a strong belief in democratic and genderic rights: "I've as much right to my opinion as you have to yours," she lets Dr.

---

52. Hall, p. 6.

Lanford know in 1911, "and as much right to spend it – as little as you think" (209).

Through orders and threats, Sheffield hoped to clear a space for herself in the overcrowded Bryce community. She implores a succession of governors and doctors to exchange her hospital room for a prison cell, or to have her confinement to back wards exchanged for the quiet monotony of convalescent halls (49). Though private space was needed for patients' recovery, and though the ward classification was initially intended to facilitate successful cures, transfers to and from back wards were also at Bryce and elsewhere employed as punishments and detonators in patient-staff relations.[53]

With acquiescence not among her virtues, Sheffield failed to secure the quiet room she yearned for and transferred her struggle for space from a physical to a mental level. "I can see nothing ahead of me but the noise and confusion of violent wards," she writes to Dr. Lanford in 1919, "so all that I have to ask of you Dr's Searcy and Partlow is to stay away from me" (186). Intent on staying sane among the incurably insane, Sheffield carved out a negative space, where non-existence meant freedom from interference. "I do not appreciate your making any inquiry as to my self," she lets Dr. Lanford know. Instead, she writes, "I would appreciate your not giving me a moments thought." Outside her doctors' horizon, she would be simply "a '*nothing* and *nobody*,'" and thus free at last (119). Similarly, Sheffield withdrew from communication with staff and fellow patients. She confides to Dr. Searcy that she "never speak[s] to any patient except in answer – and then in as few words as possible" (141). "I have not spoken to Dr. Searcy this year," she sums up in 1909, "and I'm none the worse off. I have concluded that under the circumstances it would be right that you all quit speaking to me, and me to you" (164).

Only in the silence she herself constructed could Sheffield avoid conflict with agents of power and her own ensuing powerlessness: "With you all, there is only *one side* to any thing and that is *your* side, you always in the right, and the defenseless patient in the *wrong*" (164). Moreover, by cutting off communication, Sheffield hoped

---

53. Showalter, *Malady*, p. 37; Dwyer, *Homes*, pp. 13-14, 24, 124.

to preserve her sanity, against heavy odds (166), and to fight in writing for the space most cruicial of all: her brain.

Because of the centrality of her brain to her crusade for justice, Sheffield surrendered her body to Bryce Hospital. During a bout of illness in 1907, she finds her eyesight weakening, and notes to Dr. Searcy: "I'm under the impression that when blind I would be put on a violent ward, but it is only the *body* that can be hurt here" (108). She does not mind that her body blends in with others on hospital wards; she becomes indifferent to hospital discipline and treatment as relating to her physical existence. She writes to Dr. Partlow, "if you want to give any more punishment give it" (161); her tone remains apathetic: "I don't care what you all do with me, I feel indifferent, am willing to go to the annex, even to No 18" (168). Sheffield's surrendering of her body to authorities might be her way of calling attention to it, or might help her escape from the restraints imposed upon the female anatomy in the Victorian South. Most likely, she gave up on her body in order to hold on to her brain. After dreaming of her death, Sheffield communicates to Dr. Lanford, "My body would be at your disposal," but she excludes from this arrangement the part of her remains most essential to her cause: "I intend to make lawful arrangements as to my head, that is, my brain" (190).

The battle for brain space spanned the close to three decades of Sheffield's Bryce career. "My brain was, & is yet in a healthy condition," she states in 1895. It remains the pivotal point in her correspondence with doctors and politicians, as she explains to Governor Johnston a few years later: "I want Dr's Searcy, Wright[,] Bondurant and Somerville to seal my fate, they are the men to pass sentence upon me, so far concerns the condition of my *brain*." She insists on mental health: "I was sent here a sane woman – for I was – and my mind is the same now as was when sent here – perfectly sound, my brain in a healthy condition..." (66). Her brain takes on a tangible, physical quality, with almost a life of its own. Indeed, Sheffield prepares to continue her battle beyond death by means of gray matter alone: "I intend to request it of the next Legislature that they appoint Dr. Leach to remove and examine my brain at my death, and make a public statement as to its condition, it of course would be found to be in a healthy condition..." (190).

Battle of Brains: Andrew Sheffield, a Southern Madwoman

For now, however, Sheffield was stuck in her body and at Bryce. Shunning domestic metaphors, Sheffield represents the asylum as a prison and her stay there as hell on earth. She emphasizes the lack of fresh air and sunshine, and comments on the gloom of her "cell" (63). Her "contrariness," she realizes, has "pinned [her] to the prison" (76), to her a world of torment. The patients who endure as well the Supervising Nurse's resentment may as well "be in *Purgatory*" (48). To Sheffield, Mary Buck is a devil in disguise: "the woman supervisor of the Institution is a Fiend, devil, monster in human form ... a *fiend* incarnate" (133-34). While patients thus lived not in a home but in Hell, Sheffield found the Hospital "an earthly Heaven for employees..." (111).

Other metaphor clusters illustrate the asylum's unequal distribution of power. She compares physicians and nurses to kings and queens (48) and sarcastically addresses Searcy as your "Lordship" (177). At the end of his term as Superintendent, she begins a request for spending her own money, "As you are soon to abdicate your throne..." (233).

Separated from medical royalty, Sheffield writes elsewhere, "come the poor old state paupers (as we are called) who bear the burdens of the day." Envisioning the asylum as a battlefield, Sheffield sees this group of patients as "similar to that of a poor old private in war, who does all the work and fighting, receives no pay and get nothing to eat, and subject to the whims of those who have been placed over them" (48). Dr. Lanford, she complains, dehumanizes the impoverished insane in his care, but ought at least to give every one "the chance of a 'good yard dog'" (149).

Sheffield's favorite metaphor for degradation and marginality remained, however, race. She asks to be treated with the courtesy due "a good negro" (129) and states, as a measure of her desperation, that she "had rather marry a nice, clean, genteel looking mulatto negro rather than remain here" (90-91). Her most spicy attack on Governor Johnston accuses him of "doing all in [his] power to shield, protect, and defend the negro rapeist" (73). Sheffield's construction of race represents the supremacist notions of her region, and more than hints at her anger and despair. Like her fellow inmate Mrs. Roper, who constantly raves about "negro men assaulting southern white weomen and little girls," and specifically states that a "negro ought to rape Fowls [a patient] cut her open from throat to regina" (143), Sheffield hoped by violating taboos of race and gender to pierce the indifference of those meting out (in)justice.

Sheffield chose extremes so as to maximize her correspondents' attention. At one end, she casts herself as a powerless victim, at the mercy of medical supervisors. "I'm old, homely, ignorant, poverty-stricken, friendless, homeless, and disgraced" (95), she writes to Dr. Searcy. At the other extreme, however, Sheffield chooses to be a devil, emphasizing the stubbornness, anger, and temperament that will, she hopes, overthrow her enemies. "I am not boasting only wanting you to know your supervisors did not 'outdo' me so much after all, with their lies," she informs the Superintendent. "Neither of them are the devil that I am for they have not the sense to be" (80-81). Sheffield takes pride in her personality, reminding Dr. Searcy that she will "never come under," "never '*bow* in humble submission'" (168). As she matter-of-factly states, "I am the meanest woman here" (137). Whether representing herself as victim or as victor, Sheffield reveals in her construction of identity the binary thinking informing the linguistic and thematic choices of *Letters*. Her addiction to opposites – doctor/patient, virtuous/lewd, asylum/penitentiary, to mention just a few – originated not just in her culture, her personality, or her supposed mental illness but also in a desire to resist institutional and personal erasure. By writing herself in boldface, she hoped not to appear as "demoralized" and "dehumanized" as she sometimes claimed to be (71).

While the dehumanization Sheffield experienced often came from the noise and "filth and insanity" that surrounded her, her loss of individuality or humanity resulted as well from institutional maneuvers. Her doctors, after all, sought to deconstruct the patient selves that they, or members of family/community, had judged to be insane. Sheffield constantly found herself objectified by staff and visitors, as she explains in a passage worth quoting in full:

> The physicians have lain aside my real name – am addressed as "the prominent woman." I have been, against my will, forced on public exhibition in the Hospital, forced to be gazed at by the curious, (those coming and going,) as the most "prominent woman in the State." Exhibited and gazed at as though

> I were a curio in a museum, and if fashionably dressed, one would suppose that I had been placed here, not only to be gazed at, but to blaze as a paragon for some fashionable Metropolitan. (99)

Sheffield makes clear with the passive voices, metaphors and repetitions of her writings that hospital authorities had constructed her inmate's life so as to deconstruct her self. Nameless, and powerless, she must surrender her humanity, or, as her subtly gendered prose implies, accept her femininity. She resists, however, objectification and dehumanization, as when reminding Dr. Lanford that "crime, and disgrace, doesn't transform women into brutes" (174). But her vision in 1910 of a fragmented body tells a story of its own:

> I dreamed again of dying.... I have no hope of being buried should I die here. I was told soon after I came here that a great many of the bodies – not claimed by relatives, were shipped to "Mobile and Birmingham Medical Colleges to save the students the expense of buying subjects." That is why I have such a horror of dying here through the winter months – while those schools are in session. If my body was dissected in either of those colleges the fragments would be thrown into a waste pool and washed into the gulf. (189)

As Allon White explains in his discussion of "one of the most common of dreams, fantasies," this image of corporal disintegration "occurs at those times when the unified and transcendent ego is threatened with dissolution."[54] After two decades of asylum confinement, Sheffield struggled to keep her self together, if only to secure a burial plot. Ten years later, she would have escaped into the Hospital graveyard – physically, if nothing else, in one piece.

"The sooner I die out, the better" (160), Sheffield writes towards the end of her long incarceration, her statement spanning an array of meanings: hopelessness, endorsement of social and medical evaluations, indifference, freedom. Dr. Searcy took a rather different, if somewhat muddled approach to his patient's situation. In his

---

54. White, p. 77.

most succinct diagnosis of Sheffield, he mentions delusions, physical and verbal violence, and constant misinterpretations. He concludes, if behind a cover of passive voice, that "she is always cited in the Hospital as a most typical case of '*moral insanity*'" (59). However, as Hughes points out, Sheffield's files make no mention of this diagnostic label, which by the end of the century seemed outdated at best. The diagnosis indicated, nonetheless, Searcy's determination to withstand the pressure from Sheffield, and potential allies, to win her removal from the Bryce asylum. The many persuasive devices she tried out in her thirty-year correspondence thus won her only the chance to escape her daily life through writing. Her fantasies of space and freedom induced her to ask Dr. Searcy if he would bring her back, should she attempt to leave (93), yet the stony silence that met this inquiry, as well as many others, eventually led to Sheffield's withdrawal from language, as well as from hope.

If, as Horwitz would have it, the exclusion of the insane stems from a break-down of cohesive community structures, the South in which Sheffield existed was on the brink of collapse.[55] She belonged to a powerless, vulnerable group of individuals who did not consistently share the values of "official controllers" and thus suffered the exclusion of the culturally distant. As a (disobedient) woman, in short, Sheffield constituted a threat, her "insanity" a signifier of inherent otherness. The asylum investigation she lived through in 1907 did not improve her situation. In Dwyer's analysis, such probes into conditions of the mentally ill increasingly came to resemble morality plays, with stock characters such as angry (ex-) inmates and exhausted attendants enacting a predictable script. Far from leading to improved situations and moral victory, asylum investigations merely ended in confusion and, presumably, increased depression and despair among patients.[56] The phrase imaginatively inscribed above the entry hall of Utica thus applies to Bryce as well: "Who enters here must leave all hope behind."[57] Conscious of this waste, Sheffield sums up her life in confinement:

---

55. Horwitz, p. 102.
56. Dwyer, *Homes*, p. 187.
57. Dwyer, *Homes*, p. 9.

Battle of Brains: Andrew Sheffield, a Southern Madwoman

> No one who has never been a sane uncared for person in an Insane Asylum, can imagine what it is to be immured within its walls for years, subject to the power of prejudiced physicians, calling themselves insanity experts, and without hope of ever getting out. It is a life of repression and depression, it is the acme of weariness; the life is narrowing, the thoughts run in one channel so long. It is worse than death, it is a living death. It is an indescribable situation. (85)

Though this Victorian madwoman thus found herself beyond hope, beyond life, and beyond language, she deserves to win, no matter how belatedly, what she so long fought to have: the last word.

Grace King

CHAPTER EIGHT

Festival of the Dead: The Stories of Grace King

"Old New Orleans" (1926), a sketch of her native city that Grace King published towards the end of her career, takes its readers on a guided tour of the old French Quarter and the "new" or American quarter, returning up Chartres Street to St. Louis Cathedral. At the end of the text, we have entered the old St. Louis Cemetery, "the spot most interesting to artists," and are left by our guide in front of some fragments of stone carrying a name, "Cydalise Coeur de Roi," but nothing more. Throughout the walk in the French Quarter, the imagination of the little crowd of tourists that King's reader joins has been stimulated with an ever-ready stock of stories and histories about the founding fathers of this picturesque and charming city. The unkempt grave, however, remains silent. "Ah, what romances might be attached to such a name, what photographs made of its bearer! Who was she? What was she! We shall never be able to find out; the oldest memories of the old quarter do not hold her. Even the Cathedral archives carry no record of her. 'Cydalise Coeur de Roi!' A name, that is all!"[1] Yet the urgent, almost insistent voice of the narrator in this closing paragraph tells its own tale. In the quiet, enclosed space of the graveyard, so interesting to artists, is buried the story of the patriarchal southern culture's muted other. Her story, the blank page following the narrator's words reminds us, must be invented. While Grace King's histories of Louisiana have a decidedly masculine focus (e.g. *Jean Baptiste Le Moyne, Sieur de Bienville* (1893); *De Soto and His Men in the Land of Florida* (1898)),[2] other works of hers unearth the margin-

---

1. Grace King, "Old New Orleans," *The Bookman* 63 (March 1926), pp. 77, 78.
2. Grace King, *Jean Baptiste Le Moyne, Sieur de Bienville* (New York: Dodd, 1893), *De Soto and His Men in the Land of Florida* (New York: Macmillan, 1898).

al, often shattered existence of women, and women artists, in the South.

As an advocate of womankind, writing from and of marginality, Grace King was, perhaps inadvertently, a feminist. Since her family had also lost estate and fortune in the turmoil of the Civil War, King did not belong to the economically and socially privileged group of southern suffragettes who, as Ann Firor Scott explains, could "afford to be radical."[3] She left to others the rallies and the barricades and became, in reward, the Grande Dame of Louisiana letters, celebrated by the New Orleans genteel establishment. Yet King's writings speak as eloquently, if more discreetly, of sexual and social discriminations against (southern) women and subtly posit alternatives to existing gender arrangements. As a result of an unresolved conflict between a conservative and a militant self, Grace King preferred her pen to the picket line and, like the Confederate diarists preceding her, advocated change in a way befitting a southern lady.

This strategy was in many ways expensive: contemporary critics confined her to the feminine role she, at least partially, sought to escape. In "A New Orleans Lady of Letters" (1936), John S. Kendall describes Grace King as intellectual, but hastens to emphasize that she was "an exemplary daughter, a devoted sister." In fact, he later adds, "she also had a talent for household work. She was really a very competent dressmaker."[4] Henry P. Dart comments in "Miss King's Historical Works" (1923) on her talents as a secretary[5]; Fred Lewis Pattee finds in *American Literature Since 1870* (1915) King at her best "while depicting these whimsical, impracticable, tropic femininities," although, he adds, "she makes them not so bewitching as does Cable."[6] Most telling is perhaps the long silence that after King's death in 1932 (and the appropriate obituaries) surrounded her

---

3. Ann Firor Scott, "The 'New Woman' in the New South," *South Atlantic Quarterly* 61 (Autumn 1962), p. 475.
4. John S. Kendall, "A New Orleans Lady of Letters," *Louisiana Historical Quarterly* 19.2 (April 1936), pp. 438, 452.
5. Henry P. Dart, "Miss King's Historical Works," *Louisiana Historical Quarterly* 6.3 (July 1923), pp. 347-53.
6. Fred Lewis Pattee, *American Literature Since 1870* (1915; New York: Cooper Square, 1968), p. 363.

writings. Like the quiet stone in the St. Louis Cemetery, her life and work have called for an author.

Robert Bush responded first with *Grace King of New Orleans: A Selection of Her Works* (1973); later, with *Grace King: A Southern Destiny* (1983), both of which have helped fill the vacuum in which the King canon was put to rest. Yet as the titles of some of his articles on King would suggest – "Grace King and Mark Twain" (1972), "Charles Gayarré and Grace King" (1974) – Bush has focused on King's relationship to the male intellectual establishment. Despite its attention to Julia Ward Howe as a catalyst for King's intellectual awakening, even his "Grace King: The Emergence of a Southern Intellectual Woman" (1977) concentrates on the father figures, biological and literary, who engendered King's career.[7] David Kirby's monograph, *Grace King* (1980), traces, less convincingly, King's similarities to Henry James.[8]

While neither Bush nor Kirby are blind to the importance of women's issues in King's life and work, feminist critics such as Helen Taylor and Anne Goodwin Jones have placed this topic at the center of their scholarship. Taylor makes a case for "the liberalizing and liberating effect which the lives, works and friendships of other women writers were to have on her own,"[9] though she here excuses herself from a detailed analysis of King's works. Jones, however, identifies in readings of central King texts such as *Monsieur Motte* (1888), "The Little Convent Girl" (1893), and "Bonne Maman" (1886) a distinct, if undeveloped, feminist thrust in King's fiction.[10]

With her conservative stance on region, race, and class, and her flirtations with genteel femininity, Grace King would appear an

---

7. Robert Bush, ed., *Grace King of New Orleans: A Selection of Her Works* (Baton Rouge: LSU P, 1973); Robert Bush, *Grace King: A Southern Destiny* (Baton Rouge: LSU P, 1983); "Grace King and Mark Twain," *American Literature* 44 (March 1972), pp. 31-51; "Charles Gayarré and Grace King," *Southern Literary Journal* (Fall 1974), pp. 100-31; "Grace King: The Emergence of a Southern Intellectual Woman," *Southern Review* 13 (Spring 1977), pp. 272-88.
8. David Kirby, *Grace King* (Boston: Twayne, 1980).
9. Helen Taylor, "The Case of Grace King," *Southern Review* 18 (Fall 1982), p. 687.
10. See Anne Goodwin Jones, *Tomorrow Is Another Day: The Woman Writer in the South, 1859-1936* (Baton Rouge: LSU P, 1981), pp. 93-134.

unlikely candidate for feminist attention and popularity. Indeed, King's deference to men, her dainty helplessness and her impatience with radical suffragists signal above all the perfect southern lady. Letters to her sisters written during King's visit to Hartford in 1887 when, as a house guest of Charles Dudley Warner and his family, she met prominent members of Nook Farm society, abound with descriptions of Mrs. Clemens's dresses and other feminine details, including table decorations and silver candelabra.[11] In 1903 King wrote with pride to the president of Tulane University that "if it were not for the South – the term gentleman and lady would fall out of our vocabulary, which would contain only man and woman."[12] Two years later, at the tender age of fifty-four, King was devastated by the loss of her brother Branch, whose death left three southern ladies, herself and two unmarried sisters, without gentlemanly protection in the house they all shared: "What were we to do without him! What could we do! He was the head of the family – the elder brother being married and settled away from us. Everything was dark and confused before us. We became not only frightened but demoralized."[13]

King responded to contemporary feminists with little enthusiasm. She granted that Julia Ward Howe, who was in New Orleans to head the Women's Division at the Cotton Centennial Exposition in 1884, "gave us a peep at Boston & the position the women occupied there...."[14] Yet the southern lady denounced the table manners of Howe and her daughter, Maud: "They literally 'grabbed' for food – & ate & drank like cormorants."[15] A suffragist "disturbance" in England in 1913 elicits no comments in King's memoirs except the recollection that the King sisters' wraps and umbrellas were confiscated at the door of the York Cathedral. In a biographical sketch of "Theo. Bentzon – Madame Th. Blanc" (1896), a literary friend from King's stay in Paris in 1891-92, she suggests that

---

11. Bush, "Grace King and Mark Twain," p. 36.
12. Bush, *Grace King of New Orleans*, p. 388.
13. Grace King, *Memories of a Southern Woman of Letters* (New York: Macmillan, 1932), p. 237.
14. Bush, *Grace King of New Orleans*, p. 380.
15. Bush, "Emergence," p. 275.

"the particular and brilliant distinction of Theo. Bentzon's *salon* is its high-bred avoidance of 'blue-stockingism,' and all that suggests it, however remotely...."[16]

At the same time, King obviously chafed at the limitations of the southern gender system. She eagerly joined the Pan Gnostics, a literary club formed on the initiative of Julia Ward Howe, and, despite her misgivings about this visiting northerner, praised Howe's performance in New Orleans in 1884. With ironic distance to traditional sex roles, King noted that Howe organized the Woman's Department at the Exposition "with what used to be called, 'masculine competence.'"[17] When the president of Tulane University expressed the city's gratitude to Howe at the close of the Exposition, King winced at his condescension:

> Preston Johnston's answer was a ludicrous effort on his part to come down to the occasion. He tried to be very grateful for the volumes of *women's* books, – complimented books and women['s] work in general, vague, terms – & then by a happy thought finished up by an eulogium of Mrs Howe and her accomplished daughter.[18]

During her visit to Hartford three years later, King proved herself receptive to feminism. She met Isabella Beecher Hooker, "a tall, handsome woman, who talked to me about 'Woman's Rights' and converted me to her point of view."[19] King's quotation marks and the little narrative energy devoted to her encounter with Hooker in *Memories of a Southern Woman of Letters* (1932) hint at later skepticism. Despite her appearance in 1913 before the Era Club in New Orleans, which advocated progressive legislation, King did not openly support radical feminists, as she impressed on her nephew, Carleton King:

> They are an important & influential set of women & I needed them for, rather than against me, that is all. They were delight-

---

16. Bush, *Grace King of New Orleans*, p. 351.
17. King, *Memories*, p. 54.
18. Bush, *Grace King of New Orleans*, p. 380.
19. King, *Memories*, p. 77.

ed to hear that in my opinion the Eng[lish] women deserved the vote & would get it. Their lawlessness consists of breaking a few windows & trying to horsewhip Asquith, who deserved it. But to tell you the truth, I have lost confidence in the business and political efficiency of our men.... I don't think giving the vote to women will correct the depravity & extravagance of the men, but it will certainly not help them in their extravagance & depravity.... But as I have always said, I am not a clamourer for the suffrage & not a militant.[20]

The "but"s of the passage speak of ambiguity, even confusion. Yet King seems, despite her pessimism concerning the political importance of women's suffrage and her own unwillingness to mount the barricades, to sympathize with the Cause.

King's own strategies for professional and personal independence spoke less cautiously about her desire for female emancipation. In furthering her own career, King showed little ladylike reticence but shrewdly made contacts with literary luminaries.[21] Her ambitions paid off in several ways. Upon the receipt of her first paycheck (for "Monsieur Motte" [1886], her first published story), King tasted the sweetness of financial independence: "I went out to get some white toweling ... and as I walked on the street I felt very proud I can tell you, the first really well satisfied moment of my life."[22] Encouraged by her first success, the budding writer sought the company of her neighbor in Hartford, Mark Twain, not least because of his disregard of gender distinctions: "He is quick to catch your idea – and nice to it, after he catches it. He does not impose his opinions, at least on me he did not – and he listens – at least to me – with attention." Later in this "Second Impression" of Mark Twain, King continues: "He treats ladies generally as if they were nice clever boys – like himself. If they need his advice or protection – he treats them as if they were nice, good sort of sisters – without any sentiment, or exaggeration of his services."[23] Upon

---

20. Qtd. in Bush, *Southern Destiny*, pp. 259-60.
21. See Taylor; Bush, "Emergence."
22. Qtd. in Bush, "Emergence," p. 285.
23. Qtd. in Bush, "Grace King and Mark Twain," pp. 39, 40.

returning from Europe after a visit to the Clemenses in Florence five years and three books later, King had become downright assertive, as is apparent from a letter to Warner: "I saw myself losing time & money, awaiting the convenience of a lot of men – which made me furious. I sent Nan around to Dodd, Mead, with an insistent request that any one of the firm should come to see me before afternoon."[24]

Grace King remained single, at least partly from choice. Her journal and correspondence during the 1880s and 1890s occasionally reveal a strong resentment of male dominance. The unmarried woman would suffer "the degradation of being dependent," but a wife, bound by "a hollow sham called matrimony," would have to submit to the "martyrdom" of the marriage bed, "painful, yes – degrading, humiliating."[25] In considering "Subjects for a Southern Novel" in her journal, King later raged against southern "gentlemen," much in the manner of Mary Chesnut:

> The public chivalrous talk and bearing of the men; their utter contempt of the claims of women in private. Their reckless extravagance in regard to themselves; their parsimony towards women – their egotism – their dissipations – their terrible, wild depravity.... Is slavery accountable for the degraded position of women in the South? for degraded they are, beyond belief, beyond imagination – .[26]

Though lack of suitable partners strengthened King's decision not to marry, she devoted herself to intellectual pursuits in order to escape the physical, economic, and mental subservience of her sex.

Spent in the company of her mother and two unmarried sisters, King's life thus signals a resistance to male control, but her fiction questions most strongly established southern gender roles. Instead of flaunting her feminist sympathies, King joined "a feminine and feminist underground."[27] Like numerous other nineteenth-century

---

24. Qtd. in Bush, *Southern Destiny*, pp. 136-137.
25. Qtd. in Bush, *Southern Destiny*, pp. 39, 40.
26. Qtd. in Bush, *Southern Destiny*, p. 33.
27. Helen Taylor, p. 687.

women writers, she hid her "improper" anger and militancy behind a becoming imaginative veil.

The titles of King's writings immediately stress her strong interest in gender. With titles such as *Bienville* and *De Soto and His Men in the Land of Florida*, King trespasses on the traditionally male territory of history (writing), but her fiction titles are even more frequently gender-marked: "One Woman's Story"; *La Dame de Sainte Hermine*; *Monsieur Motte*; "The Flitting of 'Sister'"; "The Self-Made Man"; "A Splendid Offer: A Comedy for Women"; *Memories of a Southern Woman of Letters*; "Bonne Maman"; "The Little Convent Girl"; "La Grande Demoiselle"; "Mimi's Marriage"; "Anne Marie and Jeanne Marie"; "The Old Lady's Restoration"; "Grandmother's Grandmother," etc.

In accordance with the female emphasis apparent in these titles, King claims in her fiction an intimate knowledge of womankind. She usurps the position of interpreter and advocate of her sex[28] through repeated, usually narratorial generalizations about women, as in the following excerpts from "Le Chevalier Alain de Triton" (1891), a historical romance, and *Monsieur Motte* (1888), her first novel: "women from birth are anticipators, always, by a species of atavism, fixing their eyes on the oasis before them, instead of the desert around them"[29]; "a woman's affections are always her deceivers and betrayers"[30]; "Men are the serious occupation, women are the playthings, of fate."[31] In *Balcony Stories* (1893), King authoritatively describes one female protagonist's week-long lovesickness but surrenders expertise as to the condition of her beloved: "A man could better describe his side of that week...."[32] Nonetheless, King considers women the superior interpreters, in part because "God keeps so little of the truth from us women."[33] As if to prove her point, she demonstrates with a reading of Mrs. Talbot's face in *The Pleasant Ways of St. Médard* (1916) her adeptness with (female)

---

28. Bush, "Emergence," p. 278.
29. Grace King, "Le Chevalier Alain de Triton," *Chautauquan* 13 (July 1891), p. 435.
30. King, "Chevalier," p. 448.
31. Grace King, *Monsieur Motte* (New York: Armstrong, 1988), p. 159.
32. Grace King, *Balcony Stories* (New York: Century, 1893), p. 84.
33. King, *Balcony Stories*, p. 116.

signifiers: "Her blue eyes showed thoughts behind them other than the ones that lighted his dark eyes with heroic fire...."[34]

The well-tuned interpretative skills of King's female characters are, at least in part, the result of the social and spacial restrictions imposed on southern women. "Is there any thing in the world that a woman's life cannot contain?" asks the narrator of "The Chevalier Alain de Triton" in a passage of considerable emotional intensity, only to exclaim: "cloister a woman's life, you but increase the horizon of her soul."[35] Despite this fringe benefit, the feminine enclosures of King's fiction, as in Sarah Morgan's diary, induce suffocation. Male characters are free to roam the city of New Orleans, the American continent, and most of the world, but King's female protagonists are symbolically immured in stultifying prisons of sex. "A Domestic Interior" (1895), for example, recounts a story of childbirth, set in a room described as "a narrow cage," from which a "narrow hall" leads to "the little closet of a kitchen." Only the return of the father brings to the overcrowded household stories of "the outside world": "politics, business, opera, gossip, chit-chat, bon-mots, mimicry, burlesque."[36] In "Mimi's Marriage" (1893), the little bridal chamber is "really not larger than sufficed for the bed there, the armoire here, the bureau opposite, and the washstand behind the door, the corners all touching."[37] Secluded on a remote plantation much in the style of the King sisters' sojourn on L'Embarras during four Civil War years, the three sisters of "Bayou L'Ombre" (1887) remain "passively quiet," their appearances advertising "an unwholesome lack of vitality, an insidious anamorphosis from an unexplained dearth or constraint."[38] King's criticism of cloistered female lives surfaces perhaps most clearly in "Bonne Maman." "What tomb could be lonelier or uglier than this little cabin,"[39] speculates the title figure and thus explicitly equates a sequestered female destiny with death.

---

34. Grace King, *The Pleasant Ways of St. Médard* (New York: Holt, 1916), p. 16.
35. King, "Chevalier," p. 444.
36. Grace King, "A Domestic Interior," *Harper's* 90 (Feb. 1895), pp, 407, 408, 409, 411.
37. King, *Balcony Stories*, p. 39.
38. Bush, *Grace King*, p. 105.
39. Grace King, "Bonne Maman," *Harper's* 73 (June-Nov. 1886), p. 300.

Among Grace King's most significant representations of enclosure is the convent, whose thick wall metaphorically divides an inner, domestic world of contemplation from an outer world of action. Jones observes that King's discussion in her memoirs of a typical female education indicates no questioning of its emphasis on manners and morals.[40] King's fictional rendering of convent life, however, includes vitriolic attacks on female socialization in the South. As the breeding ground of traditional feminine virtues – silence, obedience, innocence, passivity – the convent prepares young girls for lives of inaction, for living death. "It enrages me every time I think of it," exclaims Claire of "Bonne Maman" in recalling years spent among the Ursuline sisters. "It was killing! Study! When I was thinking all the time about something else, straining my ears to listen, just to see if I could hear the cannon shooting 'way out there in the distance.'"[41] Her author obviously agrees. In "At Chenière Caminada" (1894), the narrator observes that "Like death, Dominique and his wife entered their brood and took one out, and buried her from themselves in a convent in New Orleans."[42] At the end of her story, the young lady designed by the Sisters is literally dead, floating passively in the Gulf as a bride of God.

Since the convent prepared young women for wife- and motherhood, King's fictional resistance to the narrowness of female lives included reservations about the institution of marriage. "The Self-Made Man: An Impression" (1890) communicates perhaps most explicitly the ill-treatment of wives by husbands in King's imaginative work. The self-made man, a fleshy, ignorant hypochondriac, spills his ego in endless self-congratulations over King's pages, completely silencing and, ultimately, effacing, his young wife and the female narrator. The latter eventually escapes the smug professor, but his grief-stricken wife is imprisoned in a room – and a life – of misery. King's description of this beautiful woman and her boy-child suggests female victimization and sexploitation:

---

40. Jones, *Tomorrow*, pp. 131-32; King, *Memories*, p. 24.
41. King, "Bonne Maman," p. 295.
42. Grace King, "At Chenière Caminada," *Harper's* 88 (May 1894), p. 872.

with a six month's progress of nose and mouth toward the original self-made type, and breakfasting as if he too had chronic dyspepsia, his heavy little hands grasping and pulling the breasts to which his large mouth clung determinately. And *she* had to be the mother of *this*, and the wife of *that*! Oh destiny![43]

In "A Drama of Three" (1892), the aging Madame Honorine endures the poverty and the tirades of married life with the General and silently concludes that in matrimony, "One can give everything, and yet be sure of nothing."[44] To King, marriage typically interfered with "the soul-culture of women"[45] and condemned wives and mothers to life-long sexual and social slavery.

The trafficking in women that Eve Sedgwick, with Gayle Rubin, considers the essence of patriarchal society surfaces thematically in King's last novel, *La Dame de Sainte Hermine* (1924). As a young girl, the motherless title figure is placed in a convent, and, upon the death of her father in her sixteenth year, becomes the ward of his brother, "a savage rustic of brutal manners and of frightful tyranny."[46] La Dame de Sainte Hermine, christened Marie Alorge, is married off to a red-faced sailor, shut up in her guardian's castle, and pursued by an ardent young admirer, only to be shipped off as a *fille de cachet* to the New World, where she is received by a group of French officers. Throughout her decidedly melodramatic adventures, Marie Alorge is a passive commodity exchanged by men amidst the rustling of contracts, letters, and delivery notes.

Almost a century before Luce Irigaray's "When the Goods Get Together," King metaphorically exposed the patriarchal notion of women as merchandise. The debutantes in "The Evening Party" (1894) are carefully packaged for the marriage market. "It seems to me that for women it is the most profitable use for time and money in the world – dressing," confesses one mama to another,

---

43. Grace King, "The Self-Made Man: An Impression," *Harper's Bazaar* 13 (5 April 1890), p. 258.
44. King, *Balcony Stories*, p. 19.
45. King, "Chevalier," p. 430.
46. Grace King, *La Dame de Saint Hermine* (New York: Macmillan, 1898), p. 22.

her economic word choice suggesting a clear understanding of the function of her sex in a patriarchal economy.[47] The woman unable or unwilling to sell herself in marriage thus fails, as King satirically demonstrates in her description of the aging Aurore of *Monsieur Motte*: "Now, economical Nature seemed stealthily recalling one by one charms which had proved a useless, unprofitable investment; flattening her chest, straightening her curves, prosaicising her eyes, diluting her voice...."[48] To secure the highest return on her capital, a woman should marry young. In the words of Aurore's more worldly friend, "a disappointment cracks us all, – us women, – as if we were fine vases. *Ma foi*! we ought all to be sold as bargains, – damaged goods."[49]

Like Gertrude Thomas, King uses art metaphors to describe her female characters and further to display the decorative, but dehumanized, status of her sex in the gender economy of her time. After being exhibited in the ballroom of "The Evening Party," the sobbing Louisette takes off her newly acquired feminine paraphernalia and, "like an edifice falling down amidst all its carpentry and masonry, she fell on her bed."[50] The Demoiselles San Antonio of *The Pleasant Ways of St. Médard* are reduced to artifacts by their enterprising companion, who rearranges their hair, their postures, their very bodies, for maximum effect. In her biographical article on Madame La Comtesse Tascher de la Pagerie (1893), King notes that "inestimable piece of workmanship that she is, she might justly by an art-loving committee be placed on a cushion all to herself in a glass case of some museum."[51]

Like a jewel in a museum case, a woman in the world of Grace King finds herself closed off from a life of independent action, trapped in a female body exploited by men. The chateau of *La Dame de Sainte Hermine* becomes, for example, like other female enclosures, an image of the sexual body in which Marie Alorge at sixteen must dwell. The castle is attacked by men, one of whom finds refuge in

---

47. Bush, *Grace King of New Orleans*, p. 168.
48. King, *Monsieur Motte*, p. 126.
49. King, *Monsieur Motte*, p. 108.
50. Bush, *Grace King of New Orleans*, p. 171.
51. Bush, *Grace King of New Orleans*, p. 344.

an overgrown arbor, a thinly veiled image of the female genital area. Complete with drawn swords and bloodied sheets, the castle imprisonment of La Dame de Sainte Hermine symbolically describes the incarceration of women in bodies besieged and invaded by masculine desire. At three, the son of the competent protagonist of "The Clodhopper" (1907) still suckles his mother's breast and viciously beats her face. Eventually reduced to a thin, wrinkled wreck, the Clodhopper concludes about her grown son that "He's been suckling me all his life!"[52] King repeatedly casts female life in bodily images, as in a narratorial aside in "Earthlings," a novel published in *Lippincott's Monthly Magazine* in 1888: "Experience lies between womb and tomb, and each woman has to bear her own experience, as she bears her own children, through individual joy and suffering."[53] Engendered by men, a woman's fate is rooted in biology and apparently as inescapable as the body she inhabits.

King avoids this biological trap, however, by proposing social alternatives to only superficially natural gender constructs. First on her list is economic independence. Her female characters, however destitute, are generally an enterprising lot, sewing, baking, teaching and nursing their way to financial self-support, and, in the process, changing from ladies by birth to ladies of worth.[54] Moreover, the majority of King's women characters inhabit female communities that subtly question the patriarchal ideal of "home." The old ladies' home of "A Quarrel with God (1897)," the five-sister household of "The Flitting of 'Sister'" (1903), and the recurring Ursuline convent are all hotbeds of female, if not feminist, culture. They constitute alternatives to the isolation and exploitation of women in traditional families with images of female bonding and self-sufficiency. Often made up of white and black women together, King's female communes implicitly advocate gender solidarity across established lines of race and class.

King constantly pairs white and black women, thus establishing a mirror relation between the two groups of characters: Bonne

---

52. Grace King, "The Clodhopper," *McClure* 28 (March 1907), p. 491.
53. Grace King, "Earthlings," *Lippincott's Monthly Magazine* 42 (Nov. 1888), p. 663.
54. Marie Fletcher, "Grace Elizabeth King: Her Delineation of the Southern Heroine," *Louisiana Studies* 5 (Spring 1966), p. 51.

Maman/Aza ("Bonne Maman"); Madame Odalise/Didon ("Chevalier"); Tante Liane/Agrippine ("An Interlude" (1894)), etc. Even the languid story-tellers of "The Balcony," King's preface to *Balcony Stories,* are mirrored in the gossipping nannies on the gallery of "The Drama of an Evening."[55] The black women serve as daring others to timid white selves, as projections of King's desire for (and fear of) the emancipation of her sex. While she describes the passion between the convent girl and her cousin in "At Chenière Caminada" in muted images of storm, waves, tides, and drowning, King openly acknowledges the sensuality of the high-spirited laundry women of "Bayou L'Ombre." Though King's distinction between white restraint and black indulgence reflects southern racist stereotypes, it also maps for her African American women characters a terrain of sexual independence. Similarly, King reserves for women entrepreneurs of color the greatest economic success. In "Bonne Maman," for example, the white grandmother has become the financial responsibility of her niece, who secretly takes in sewing and embroidery from the surrounding African American community. But Bonne Maman's ex-slave, Aza, has risen to become a prosperous madam of the local brothel. Unrestrained by the moral and racial code of the southern lady, King's African American women characters apply their various talents to the positions available to them and thus gain a sexual and social freedom only imagined by their European American counterparts.

Simultaneously nurturing and threatening, powerless and powerful, the women of color in King's fiction are "phallic mothers," i.e. speaking and acting from a position of omnipotence and omniscience usually associated with masculinity. Like the phallic mother, the muscular woman slave embodies what Jane Gallop calls a fraudulent power, a paradoxical mixture of femaleness and phallus, of bondage and influence. By occupying an impossible location of power, the phallic mother questions the very notion of power and so implicitly expels the Phallus.[56] The phallic mammies of King's

---

55. King, *Monsieur Motte,* p. 212.
56. Jane Gallop, *The Daughter's Seduction: Feminism and Psychoanalysis* (Ithaca: Cornell U P, 1982), p. 117.

imaginative work thus outrageously unveil the ideological equivalence of phallus/father/man/power/white, exposing the traditional sexual, racial and social hierarchies of southern society.

King further questions customary conceptions of gender by promoting an androgynous character type, represented as either a (wo)man of action or a feminized man. In *La Dame de Sainte Hermine*, the helpless Marie Alorge is set off by the resolute Dame Catherine, a six-feet-tall Canadian trapper with the clothes, the look, and the strength of a man. The "Clodhopper," an African American parallel, is "as tall as any man present," shows her bony legs in trousers "like the men's,"[57] and earns a man's wages for a man's work. In her biographical article on Madame la Baronne Blaze de Bury (1893), King relates a description of this writer-turned-activist as "A man, a woman, and a lion."[58] Conversely, the "good" men of King's textual and moral landscape are decidedly feminine.[59] Bienville, the hero of King's first historical work, appears in *La Dame de Sainte Hermine* as "a man of presence but insignificant in his person; small, slight, and careless of his appearance."[60] The adored husband of "Mimi's Marriage" is "blond, and not good-looking, and small!"[61]; the faithful fiancé of the title figure in "Annette: A Story of the Street" (1930) is "very delicate, slight of figure, narrow of chest, pale."[62] King's androgynous hero(in)es may signal their author's retreat from sexual imperatives, but they simultaneously traverse the gender divisions and restrictions of her time and region.

As a turn-of-the-century woman experimenting with gender, King nevertheless provides more questions than answers to the rearrangement of sexual and social roles. Her characters' quest for new selves appears in King's choice of imagery, which reveals the fluidity of female identity in the late nineteenth century. The mask, for example, suggests not only the woman disguised for the

---

57. King, "The Clodhopper," p. 488.
58. Bush, *Grace King of New Orleans*, p. 341.
59. Jones, *Tomorrow*, p. 117.
60. King, *Hermine*, p. 4.
61. King, *Balcony Stories*, p. 53.
62. Grace King, "Annette: A Story of the Street," *New Orleanian* 1 3 (20 Sept. 1930), p. 36.

social theater but also the author's search for her true face. In "Annette" King thus explores the terror of finding that this original self has been lost during a life of suffering. Annette's invincible enemy, Time, is significantly represented as masculine: "Little by little have the years taken from Annette her youth ... her beauty ... as they took her love ... they have indeed taken her very self, as they took him ... leaving her only the mask and costume that Time throws to those he despoils."[63] As the gaps of King's own sentence hide an unspeakable fate, Annette's mask covers only the nothingness of a self suppressed.

The metaphor of voyage, however, indicates a continued search for new horizons. Young Misette of "Earthlings" constantly dreams of travel: "It was the fantastic idea that ran through all her musings, voyaging. She had been so stationary all her life."[64] Suggesting a passage from one level of understanding to another,[65] the voyages of King's female characters may – if only superficially – result in disaster, as in "The Little Convent Girl" (1893), or they may prove worth the risk, as in *La Dame de Sainte Hermine*, whose French protagonist eventually finds self and satisfaction in the New World. The passage to freedom frequently runs through a distinctly sexual seascape. "At Chenière Caminada," for example, leaves its heroine in the arms of her lover, while "they were floating above the trees – and the rushing waters still carrying them up higher and higher..." (874). To find themselves, King's fictional women obviously have to explore their sexuality, to take a dive into "that great motherstream underneath."[66]

The liminal mist that occasionally enwraps King's southern settings and her contemplative heroines further hints at transition and reflection. With an image cluster of silver fog, moons, and mirrors, King presents a group of women looking for themselves. At times, this impulse is purely narcissistic, as in the self-admiration of the debutantes of *Monsieur Motte*. The narrator, however,

---

63. King, "Annette," p. 37.
64. King, "Earthlings," p. 638.
65. Jones, *Tomorrow*, p. 100.
66. Bush, *Grace King of New Orleans*, p. 154; Jones, *Tomorrow*, p. 126.

secretly points to the dangers hiding in the mirror, to the destiny awaiting the dancing daughters of disillusioned mothers: "[the débutantes] looked at themselves in the mirrors, or at their partners, not at the crow's-feet and wrinkles which had travelled from the hearts to the faces of the débutantes of twenty-five years ago ...."[67] By stressing the hidden similarities between the daughters and the mothers, King seeks to awaken her readers from the trance that has glazed the eyes of the waltzing Creole maidens. "A Delicate Affair" (1893), on the other hand, demonstrates its protagonist's escape from the fixity of the mirror. Madame Atalanta has furnished the four walls of her drawing-room with mirrors, so that "the apartment, in spots, extended indefinitely," giving an effect "full of gaiety and life."[68] Her elderly beau, Mr. Horace, vainly attempts to awaken past emotions in Madame, who is absorbed in a card game very much of the present. Discouraged, Mr. Horace lets his eyes wander to a painting of Madame in early youth, and further, to the painting's reflection in a mirror, "so much softer and prettier, so much more ethereal, than the original painting."[69] The aged original of the painting has meanwhile left to give her servant a lusty scolding, thus evading her companion's desire to fix her in time and place. With her multiple representations, multiple mirrors, and multiple tempers, Madame avoids codification and remains unassimilated by that emissary of the symbolic, Mr. Horace.

King's preoccupation with names, and with naming, indicates her desire to invent her own language and to write her own life. Towards the end of "A Delicate Affair," Madame Atalanta has admittedly acted out the plot written by Mr. Horace – she has visited and forgiven her dying childhood friend and rival, Myosotis – and so is, after all, encoded in a masculine sign system. Yet the two women use each other's secret pet names, Amour and Divine, and thus manage to establish a feminine linguistic underground. The narrator hides still another ace up her sleeve: "If Mr. Horace had not slipped away, he might have noticed the curious absence of

---

67. King, *Monsieur Motte*, p. 229.
68. King, *Balcony Stories*, p. 197.
69. King, *Balcony Stories*, p. 202.

monsieur's name, and of his own name, in the murmuring that followed. It would have given him some more ideas on the subject of woman."[70] In the barely audible female discourse, the masculine signifiers – and their signifieds – are conspicuously absent. At the end of King's story, all three of the old friends rest in the St. Louis cemetery, but the final trumpet imagined by their author might very well sound for a female victory, *malgré lui*.

"Madrilène; Or, The Festival of the Dead" (1890), again set in a New Orleans cemetery, presents more fully Grace King's conception of gender and creativity. On the surface, however, this story focuses on race. Madrilène, short for Marie Madeleine, has spent fifteen joyless years as the drudge of Madame Laïs's house of ill repute, crowded with the wealthy quadroon's numerous relatives and customers. Whenever her duties leave her a moment, Madrilène rushes from this "colored" household to the nearby cemetery, where her pleasure is to stay "with the good dead, with the white dead."[71] To enjoy this privilege, Madrilène has become the unofficial assistant to the besotten sexton, Monsieur Sacerdote, himself a member of the coveted race. The story, which takes place on October 31, just before All Saints' Day, climaxes rather unpleasantly with Madrilène's accidental discovery that she, too, is white and thus entitled to a private resurrection from darkness and misery.

On another level, however, "The Festival of the Dead" becomes an allegory of woman on the edge. Suspended on the color line, Madrilène is also divided between the female enclosures of the brothel and the graveyard, further separated into white and "colored" territories. Outside of this woman-space, inhabited by the fatherless, the husbandless, even the nameless, lies the masculine territories of the streets, where "any moment something might happen to a woman all alone" (882). King frequently positions Madrilène at the gates of the graveyard and the bordello, literally neither inside nor outside and symbolically inhabiting a shadowy

---

70. King, *Balcony Stories*, p. 219.
71. Grace King, "Madrilène; Or, The Festival of the Dead," *Harper's* 81 (June-Nov. 1890), p. 874. Subsequent references to this story will appear parenthetically in the text.

borderland. The gatekeepers, Monsieur Sacerdote and Madame Laïs, are significantly androgynous: the one, a benevolent feminized man; the other, a belligerent (wo)man of action. Both the cemetery and the brothel thus represent a revolutionary world of *différance*, in which fixed definitions of gender give way to fluid boundaries subject to interpretation. Both gatekeepers are conveniently expert readers – Monsieur Sacerdote of inscriptions and books; Madame Laïs, of customers' faces and clothes.

"The Festival of the Dead" is thus above all a story about woman-as-artist, suspended between two sorts of creativity: a life of the body, represented by Madame Laïs and her rainbow-colored progeny; or a life of the spirit, the graveyard. King unhesitatingly promotes the latter. While she associates the physical existence in the brothel with violence, with servitude, and with people of color, she links the cemetery with life elevated into art, a communal space of tradition, serenity, and eternity. It is, significantly, a refuge for female artists, whether specialists in voodoo, flower arrangement, or, like Madrilène, in the creation of wreaths. The graveyard functions as a place for poetry, tales, and gossip. It is also the setting for Madrilène's lessons, offered by the sexton, in reading and writing, with the gravestones as convenient exercises. Most importantly, the cemetery allows Madrilène an identity. Until her final discovery of her whiteness, only Monsieur Sacerdote "ever called her by her name [Marie Madeleine], instead of by the vulgar contraction of it" (872). But the graveyard is the domain of the select few: "It was a closed cemetery lifetimes ago; burial in it had become an inheritance, or a privilege of society partnership...." (869).

The notion of a male gatekeeper to this world of creativity and spirituality deserves further attention. Madrilène visits Monsieur Sacerdote at his convenience only; many a night she is left standing by the heavily bolted gate, reduced to silence: "she did not attempt to make herself heard. That would have been a noisy process. She leaned, as usual, against the fence and waited" (879). The woman artist, in other words, inhabits a linguistic landscape designed, owned, and protected by "men." In Lacanian terminology, she is alienated from the masculine symbolic order, marginalized not only socially but also linguistically. King sums up Madrilène's alienation:

> Her own words, from the common store of language about her, could not have expressed her thoughts; or perhaps the words as well as the thoughts were foreign to her; perhaps the thoughts were transplanted with the words from the books read aloud to Monsieur Sacerdote in surreptitious hours.... (876)

As the representative woman writer, Madrilène is, furthermore, constantly followed by the male gaze, by an unidentified stranger watching her every move. King describes him as "a grave, sedate, middle-aged scholar, with eyes that gathered as much in a glance as Madame Laïs's" (881). This reader of female activity manages to help rescue the swooning Madrilène from her violent housemates and thus plays a largely positive role in the young woman's search for a (white) identity. Yet, as a symbolic representative of the male literary establishment, the greying scholar is at the same time an irritating appropriator of female freedom and creativity. Whether wrapped in the arms – and the gaze – of a father-mentor, or in linguistic marginality, the woman writer is enclosed in masculine sign systems. Though this creative space is her only refuge, she is surrounded by discomfort, by walls, and, ultimately, by death.

Yet King's story takes place just before All Saints Day and thus holds out hope for resurrection. On this festival of the dead, the cemetery is filled with flowers, with artifacts, with "housecleaners" and women vendors. Gossiping voices fill the silence, and female artists emerge victorious. Zizi, the conjure woman, for example, wins a sweet revenge over the powerful Laïs with effective voodoo packets, and Madrilène herself invents her first text. Her story – "Negroes are murdering a white girl in here!" – jars on the ears of later readers, but it is nonetheless "an unheard-of, an unknown, an uncodified cry" with which the woman artist speaks (or screams) herself. Her voice is enough "to awaken the dead in the cemetery," and it restores – if only temporarily – the muted female other to her (white) self, and to her audience: "White faces and white gowns, white paper wreaths of her own manufacture, dressed for the morrow's festival. They had come at her cry..." (882, 883).

As Madrilène articulates her first narrative, "she knew not herself what her lips were screaming," but her alarm originates in "something within her driven to voice by extremity of pain and humiliation." Her pain and degradation are authored by the Phallus, the cutting knife that threatens her very existence and in whose presence Madrilène feels "the naked fleshy mass crowding her, the blows, the darkness, the epithets, the hot, puffing breath, the odor" (882). Yet it is precisely Madrilène's struggle against the phallic weapon seeking to invade her that engenders her creativity and inspires her scream. This cry from "something within her" bridges the gap between the graveyard and the brothel and thus unites the spiritual and the bodily fictional landscape into a new text.

The birth pangs of the woman writer are all but deadly. Supported by the scholar-stranger, Madrilène labors to bring forth herself: "I – I – I am – I am not – I only – called..." (883). Mutely, she continues: "If she could only push the words between her lips! They burst on her tongue like bubbles. She felt them in her hands; if only she could shove them where all would see them!" (883). Instead, her head falls on the stranger's shoulder, her eyes closed, her body bleeding. When the police demand her identity, she leaves to others to name her "Marie Madeleine – nothing" (885). Towards the end of the story, Madrilène's selfhood is almost erased. In her unconsciousness, "she sank down, down, through sightlessness, dumbness, deafness, to nullity" (886).

The darkness of the unconscious, however, is pregnant with creativity. Like the nothingness that follows Marie Madeleine's true name, her nullification signifies a feminine refusal to accept the Name of the Father. It is time for woman to explode the symbolic, argues Hélène Cixous in "The Laugh of the Medusa" (1976), "taking in her own mouth, biting that tongue with her very own teeth to invent for herself a language to get inside of."[72] At the close of "The Festival of the Dead," old Zizi is pleasurably "sucking" her words "like sugar between her toothless gums"; though deprived of sharp instruments, she is the victorious author of the text's final paragraph of semiotic chatter. Simultaneously mother and newborn, Madrilène has given birth to herself with a barely audible

---

72. Hélène Cixous, "The Laugh of the Medusa," in *New French Feminisms*, ed. Isabelle de Courtivron and Elaine Marks (New York: Schocken, 1981), p. 257.

sigh. This writing of the body, in King's words, "joined past to future" and (in triumphant *différance?*) "filled ... the world" (886).

In contrast, Grace King's own story ended in silence. The deaths of her mother and two brothers shortly after the turn of the century dried up much of King's creative energy, which she lavished instead on a memorial journal, and foreign travel. Also her feminist aspirations eventually came to an end. Recording in a notebook her last conversation with George C. Preot, a literary mentor, King wrote as early as in 1901: "I told him, that I was happier, since I had got rid of all my hopes – and had my future behind me – that I strive no more – ."[73] Upon her own death in 1932, King seemed destined to share the fate of the unknown Cydalise Coeur de Roi and quietly fade from Louisiana (literary) histories.

Nonetheless, King's posthumously published *Memories of a Southern Woman of Letters* communicates from the grave the author's pride in her accomplishments and her unwillingness to be silenced. After the obligatory "FINIS" that ends her autobiography, King adds, repetitiously, "Enough!" only to include an italicized poem, whose presence implicitly speaks of a desire to escape the anonymity of the blank page. This desire has only recently been gratified. After decades of obscurity, King is appearing at conferences and in journals in a belated, but significant, resurrection. Like the celebrating ghosts in "Madrilène; Or, The Festival of the Dead," the muted southern others are dancing in the graveyards.

---

73. Bush, *Grace King of New Orleans*, p. 386.

Mamie Garvin Fields

CHAPTER NINE

Pirates' Treasures: Mamie Garvin Fields's Carolina Memoir

One chapter of Mamie Garvin Fields's autobiography *Lemon Swamp and Other Places* (1983), which her granddaughter Karen E. Fields assisted her in putting together, recounts how in the 1890s Fields's teacher, Miss Anna Izzard, would take the older students from her school on walking tours to visit landmarks of Charleston. The children favored particularly the dungeon where pirates used to be incarcerated; occasionally, they were so lucky as to find brass coins and arrowheads in the yard. "Pirates' treasures," they called their findings, and wondered whether a whole box full – or even the pirates themselves – might still be in the dungeon. As Charlestonians of color they were kept wondering. "Of course," Fields reports, "we couldn't go in." Nonetheless, Miss Izzard's (or Lala's) students learned about pirates transporting contraband in and out of tidal creeks, of the one-eyed captain sporting a red bandana and of the squint-eyed sailor leaving Wadmalaw Creek with his sails on fire. "Lala knew how to tell a story," Fields notes, thus emphasizing the power of narrative.[1] Fields's own life story is a case in point. A little girl at the beginning of the Jim Crow era and a retired teacher at its end, she describes a rich and fulfilling existence as a teacher, wife, mother, and community activist, with the 1920s and 1930s as her most formative and prominent decades. Despite the ground-breaking events that make up Fields's story,

---

1. Mamie Garvin Fields, with Karen Fields, *Lemon Swamp and Other Places: A Carolina Memoir* (New York: Free P, 1983), p. 53. Further references to *Lemon Swamp* will be given parenthetically in the text.

her telling of this story is equally significant, if, as poststructuralists would argue, such a separation is desirable or even possible. Though African American autobiography fulfills an American desire to face up to the nation's history, the "auto" of color constitutes itself – "difference" and all – with(in) the spoken and written text.[2] Fields's and Karen Fields's formal choices – authorial/editorial, narrative, genderic, linguistic – thus shape not just the life choices from which they take shape but reimagine American autobiography as well as American history. A pirate in her own right, Fields navigates, sails ablaze, from the "Forbidden Places" of her chapter heading straight towards an American mainstream of her own design.

Lemon Swamp originates in a red folder marked "Letters to My Three Granddaughters" full of loose-leaf pages, on which Fields had written of her Charleston, South Carolina, childhood at the close of the nineteenth century. Around her, in Karen Fields's words, she saw "surries clopping down narrow streets, hard-working craftsmen in wood and brick, decorous ladies wearing elegant laces" (xi). Fields had in the early 1970s sailed into a family Christmas celebration in Washington, D.C., her red folder that year's Christmas present to Karen and Barbara, both graduate students at the time, and their cousin Marcia, still in elementary school.

Fields's motivation derived from several, if related sources. She shared the symptoms that in Michel Beaujour's theory of the self-portrait defines this literary form. The "inaugurating experience" of the autobiographer, he argues, "is one of emptiness and absence."[3] While this sense of loss and depersonalization might relate specifically to the advanced age in which many an autobiography is undertaken, Beaujour's terms hold specific meaning for an old African American woman who has lived most of her life in the Jim Crow South. Though Fields has inscribed her absence in the title of her published life story, she declares herself simply through the autobiographical gesture, which communicates to the world that this

---

2. William L. Andrews, ed., *African American Autobiography: A Collection of Critical Essays* (Englewood Cliffs, N.J.: Prentice-Hall, 1993), p. 2.
3. Francoise Lionnet, *Autobiographical Voices: Race, Gender, Self-Portraiture* (Ithaca: Cornell U P, 1989), p. 225.

life (and the person who has lived it) counts.[4] The preoccupation with survival characteristic of early African American autobiography has thus in the life stories of freeborn nineteenth-century women of color become a desire to articulate and identify the self.[5]

Inherent in this enterprise is a "revisionist mission"[6] seeking to exchange racial reality for racial stereotypes, the degraded images of inferiority against which African Americans have written their tradition.[7] The authorial absence in the title, which, apart from situating itself spatially, designates the text as *a* Carolina memoir, thus aims at representativeness; it offers to its audience one southern, African American, female life among others. In doing so, Fields proposes her story as an argument for racial competence and success, implicitly silencing those who have, for various reasons, preferred less benevolent narratives of her race and her region.

In 1975, Karen Fields began recording conversations with her grandmother, alternately in Charleston, where Fields still resided, and in Washington, D.C. Karen Fields's questions inspired the older Fields to write and tape further information, and the two Fieldses' late-night telephone conversations grew increasingly elaborate (and expensive). In the summer of 1978, the year Fields turned ninety, the pair worked away on *Lemon Swamp* in a Cambridge apartment, each at her separate desk. Karen Fields would transcribe the already-taped interviews and conduct new ones, while Fields would read and edit the transcripts, adding new memories that would occur to her as she read her partly recorded life story. *Lemon Swamp* thus came into existence as a product of conversations between grandmother and granddaughter, a process that blurred not just the generational boundaries separating the two Fieldses but also, in tune with African American literary traditions, the boundaries

---

4. William L. Andrews, *To Tell a Free Story: The First Century of Afro-American Autobiography, 1760-1865* (Chicago: U of Illinois P, 1986), pp. 7, 16.
5. Joanne M. Braxton, *Black Women Writing Autobiography: A Tradition within a Tradition* (Philadelphia: Temple U P, 1989), p. 10.
6. Deborah McDowell, "'The Changing Same': Generational Connections and Black Women Novelists," *New Literary History* 18.2 (Winter 1987), p. 284.
7. Henry Louis Gates, Jr., *Figures in Black: Words, Signs, and the "Racial" Self* (New York: Oxford U P, 1987), p. 25.

between speaking, writing, and reading. *Lemon Swamp* thus occupies an in-between space that bypasses traditional western notions of text and authorship, what Francoise Lionnet calls *métissage*, "the fertile ground of our heterogeneous and heteronomous identities as postcolonial subjects."[8]

Fields's narrative identity is further elasticized by the polyphonic family and community voices that blend into her prose. She discusses, for example, her great-great-uncle John, an African-born slave who attended Oxford University in England as a valet to members of the (white) Middleton family, long before she introduces her own childhood. Her ancestors thus figure prominently in her self-conception, as do the families in the Short Court neighborhood where she grew up and still resided when writing *Lemon Swamp*. Due to her strong familial and communal values, Fields writes herself as a "collective subject."[9] Throughout *Lemon Swamp* she articulates her story in "the common (female) tongue ... [, the] shared Afro-American woman authorial voice" identified as a recurring figure in novels by women of African descent.[10]

Because of its composition process, *Lemon Swamp* belongs to *métissage* territory also through the critical marginalization of so-called "ghost-written" autobiography. Stemming, no doubt, from the unequal distribution of power between the black slave narrator and the white amanuensis, who, as William L. Andrews writes in *To Tell a Free Story: The First Century of Afro-American Autobiography, 1760-1865*, "possessed the ultimate control over the fate of the manuscript and considerable influence over the immediate future of the narrator,"[11] critics have tended to disregard collaborated autobiographies as inauthentic. L. B. Jugurtha, for example, emphasizes in her appraisal of the narratives of Frederick Douglass and James W. C. Pennington "that they are not told-to or ghost-written biographies. The men wrote well...."[12] In a 1992 postscript to his

---

8. Lionnet, pp. 6, 8, 22.
9. Gina Wisker, ed. *Black Women's Writing* (New York: St. Martin's, 1993), p. 9.
10. Michael Awkward, *Inspiriting Influences: Tradition, Revision, and Afro-American Women's Novels* (New York: Columbia U P, 1989), p. 13.
11. Andrews, *Free Story*, p. 21.
12. Lillie Butler Jugurtha, "Point of View in the Afro-American Slave Narratives:

1978 essay on "Patterns in Recent Black Autobiography," Alfred E. Stone notes the absence of collaborative autobiography in the criticism of Joanne M. Braxton and Elizabeth Fox-Genovese. Stone himself, however, ascribes a critical reappraisal of this "experimental mode" of life narration to the popularity of Malcolm X/Alex Haley and Nate Shaw/Theodore Rosengarten." Indeed, he valorizes the "as told to" mode, because, he notes, "individual and collective existence ... is, for some, admirably re-created by cooperation between more than one memory and imagination."[13]

In texts by women of color, the "mixtures of speech" make up, as Karla Holloway argues, a defining trait.[14] In other words, as African American counterpoints to Hélène Cixous and Catherine Clément, who, in Cixous's line, "distrust the identification of a subject with a single discourse,"[15] the Fieldses, like the more theoretically inclined Frenchwomen, are "differently engaged" in the same discursive enterprises. As Stone writes in 1992, collaborative autobiography is "admirably adaptable to women's experience and to womanist ideology."[16] The "Acknowledgments" section of *Lemon Swamp* pushes towards the ideal(ized) mutuality that Stone implies. Though Fields gets the first paragraph to thank those who have helped along her project, and Karen Fields, the second, the two Fieldses come together in the last line of the acknowledgments, which emphasizes authorial and familial bonding: "We both thank our family and all our kin" (ix). Interestingly, the son and father who biologically and geographically links the two women is practically absent from their story. Fields mentions at the end of *Lemon Swamp* that she managed to send her son Robert off to study architecture in Washington, D.C., where Karen Fields grew up, and thus implies the

---

A Study of Narratives by Douglass and Pennington," in *The Art of Slave Narrative: Original Essays in Criticism and Theory*, ed. John Sekora and Darwin T. Turner (N.p.: Western Illinois U P, 1982), p. 119.

13. Albert E. Stone, "Postscript: Looking Back in 1992," in Andrews, *African American Autobiography*, pp. 190-91.
14. Karla F. C. Holloway, *Moorings and Metaphors: Figures of Culture and Gender in Black Women's Literature* (New Brunswick, N.J.: Rutgers U P, 1992), p. 84.
15. Hélène Cixous and Catherine Clement, *The Newly Born Woman* (Minneapolis: U of Minnesota P, 1986), p. 136.
16. Stone, "Postscript," p. 191.

missing father. Yet the female Fieldses leave empty the patriarchal space simultaneously uniting and separating their existences. They circumvent as well, when possible, another father who in Fields's segregated South defined the contours of her life: the white southern patriarch. By erasing the fathers and their claims, the women writing usurp the center and thus establish themselves as authorities. In doing so, they abandon the typical roles of American grandparents and grandchildren who, Karen Fields writes, "tend to humor and patronize one another, to sit smiling around family tables, beyond agreement and disagreement" (xii). They (over)turn, in fact, the tables: the grandmother becomes younger as she relives in memory the time when she was Karen Fields's age, while the granddaughter moves beyond her years. In taking over the autobiographical project, she speaks in her grandmother's voice and gives birth, so to speak, to the older woman by helping (re)create her life story.

A Bakhtinian "hidden polemic" nonetheless hides beneath the textual surface, which, as in the swamp that has given the Fields autobiography its title, may hide more dangerous waters.[17] Certain utterances in *Lemon Swamp* clash with others outside the boundaries of the author's discourse, understood, in Bakhtin's phrase, "only in its import."[18] In recounting her trip to Boston the year before her marriage, Fields states: "I wish I could tell you whether or not the Clyde Line ships were segregated coming out of the South" (141). She thus addresses Karen Fields's interest in "what could not be done" as opposed to her own focus on "what was done." In Karen Fields's explanation, her grandmother "was not trying to convey 'how black people fared in Charleston over the first half of this century,' but 'how we led our lives, how we led *good* lives'" (xx). The authorial and editorial differences emerging from the granddaughter's theory and the grandmother's practice thus bounce and leap within the narrative space(s) of *Lemon Swamp*.

The relation between Karen Fields's "Introduction" and "Epilogue" and the autobiographical text thus framed dramatizes the

---

17. For Bakhtin's definition of "hidden polemic" and its relation to African American double-voiced discourse, see Gates, *Figures*, p. 24.
18. Gates, *Figures*, p. 247.

differences and ambiguities that form *Lemon Swamp* as *métissage*. As in the white-authored testimonials authenticating the slave narratives, the frame makes up at least a visual beginning and end, thus ascribing to the autobiography itself the status of in-between. A textual hierarchy thus establishes itself, with the middle defined, as Raymond Hedin explains, by its relation to beginning and end, whose "means" the autobiographical narrative serves.[19] Written by a northern-educated, modern professional, Karen Fields's frame accordingly legitimizes the story of her obscure southern grandmother and claims for Fields's life story truth and value both. As Gayl Jones, following John Wideman, observes in *Liberating Voices*, the frame grants black speech the status of literature and maps out its possibilities.[20] The frame-text relation of *Lemon Swamp* thus parallels that of the early slave narratives, in which authenticating documents, as Robert Stepto points out, converse with, yet dominate, the slave's life story.[21]

At the same time, however, the authentification of the *Lemon Swamp* introduction might constitute a signifying act. Unlike white amanuenses' influence upon slaves, the intraracial alliance of the two Fieldses appears democratic and egalitarian, the granddaughter's advanced education balanced by her grandmother's advanced years. The frame enters, in fact, into a call-response relation with the narrative, posing questions later answered in the textual "middle" or commenting upon concerns of Fields's developed within the narrative proper.

Signifying or egalitarian impulses aside, Karen Fields's frame nonetheless attempts to contain the autobiographical narrative, and, most likely, the narrator, in order to wrap up its incompleteness or, as she puts it in her last line, "to *hurry up* and get through" (247). In an opposite move at the end of the framing Epilogue, grandmother and granddaughter sit down at the kitchen table,

---

19. Raymond Hedin, "Strategies of Form in the American Slave Narrative," in Sekora and Turner, pp. 25-34.
20. Gayl Jones, *Liberating Voices: Oral Traditions in African American Literature* (Cambridge, Mass.: Harvard U P, 1991), pp. 68, 131.
21. Robert Stepto, *From Behind the Veil: A Study of Afro-American Narrative* (Urbana: U of Illinois P, 1979), pp. 3-31.

sheaves of paper and cups of okra soup at hand, writing, so to speak, beyond the ending. As Keith Byerman notes about modern African American fiction, "the key characters ... are still engaged at the end in becoming a self."[22] The kitchen vignette dramatizes as well the incompleteness of autobiography as a genre, since the narrating I continues to live after the narrated I has fallen silent. At the same time, however, the tension between continuing and "get[ting] through" mirrors the indecision of the Fieldses as to how and when to stop. Uncomfortable about ending the autobiography in 1948, when, as the narrative has it, "much was coming that we couldn't imagine then" (241), Karen Fields continues her grandmother's story in(to) the Epilogue, only to cut it off at the kitchen table. Fields, on the other hand, steps out of the frame enclosing her, continuing to speak with/in the Epilogue and, as we have seen, still writing at its end. In a sense, then, the frame-main text relationship pushes *Lemon Swamp* towards Lionnet's in-between or *métissage* because of competing impulses within and between the collaborators.

Competing impulses characterize as well the relationship between the author(-function) and the audience. Just as the slave narrator had to strike a balance between the linguistic expectations of northern readers and the linguistic customs of southern blacks,[23] the Fieldses – as *métis* women and as co-authors – must negotiate between different audiences.[24] Their ideal readers would be those who, in Hurston's phrase taken up by Deborah McDowell, "enter by the 'intimate gate.'"[25] Karen Fields, of course, makes up Fields's first and most narrowly conceived audience. As a close relative, the granddaughter has the right to complain about the older woman's narrative pace and thoroughness, a right she asserts in her "Introduction." "'Now, Karen,' [Grandmother Fields] would say, 'I want you to know your cousin so-and-so, who is the daughter of such-

---

22. Keith Byerman, *Fingering the Jagged Grain: Tradition and Form in Recent Black Fiction* (Athens: U of Georgia P, 1985), p. 277.
23. Keith Byerman, "We Wear the Mask: Deceit as Theme and Style in Slave Narratives," in Sekora and Turner, p. 70.
24. Lionnet, p. 95.
25. McDowell, "Changing Same," p. 297.

and-such, our this-and-that because, you see...'" (xxvii). In the narrative proper, Fields acknowledges this immediate audience as well as Karen Fields's familiar reactions: "Really, I will make you tired if I tell you all the things that used to happen, the things that used to wear some of us down when they were happening" (195). Karen Fields's cousins so-and-so, the sons and daughters of such-and-such, literally enter by the intimate gate to become Fields's audience as well. As Karen Fields explains in her introduction, "at first we thought of the project as a booklet we would circulate at a Middleton family reunion..." (xii). Still aglow with the success of another family gathering that took place in 1982, the year she would be ninety-four, Fields makes clear that she envisions for her autobiography a private, familial and receptive audience. "Listen here," she tells her granddaughter, "we have to *hurry up* and get through with *Lemon Swamp*. All those children are clamoring to read it" (247).

An implied audience accompanies, however, the transition of *Lemon Swamp* from booklet to book. Like the nineteenth-century clubwomen who, with their emphasis on cleanliness, religion, and duty, hoped to inspire a sympathetic white response, Fields aims at an audience outside her circle of "kissin' friends," to use another Hurston phrase. She approaches this (presumably white) readership with caution, much in the style of the black congregation her mother remembers marching towards its newly-established chapel: "Let those refuse to sing/Who never knew their God./But children of the Heavenly King,/Arise and praise the Lord!" (33). Though Fields does not actively sing out hymns to get across a discreet message to less benevolent members of her audience, the fragments of song and poetry, like the musical notations of Du Bois's writings, express the exclusion of African Americans from self-expression, the problem of articulating directly what Du Bois calls the "strange meaning of being black here at the dawn of the Twentieth Century."[26] Indirectly, Fields further addresses whites by demonstrating her social worthiness and by problematizing the

---

26. Gordon D. Taylor, "Voices from the Veil: Black American Autobiography," *Georgia Review* 35 (Summer 1981), p. 343.

racial hierarchy that bounds her. Despite this criticism, her larger, white audience might listen as intently as her ideal black one. As Toni Morrison argues in *Playing in the Dark*, white Americans look towards Americans of African descent to explain themselves. This "fetishizing of color," which projects onto the racial other the fears, desires and chaos of majority society, results, in short, in the "helpless and hapless" fascination that propels white readers to black texts.[27]

Whether positioned in assent or dissent, the audience accordingly participates in shaping *Lemon Swamp*. And, like the African story-teller who holds on to the role of narrator through persistent critical commentary, Fields invites her readership to engage in an ongoing interpretation of the people and events that constitute her life (story).[28] She enters, in short, into a dialogue not just with Karen Fields but with the larger readership, black and white, of the published *Lemon Swamp*. The "you" towards whom she targets her stories as well as the morales drawn from them thus includes both those inclined to agree with her and those who need to come around to her perspective on social/racial organization. In any case, as Lionnet points out, "interaction with a real or virtual hearer is an integral part of the storytelling situation."[29]

In her introduction to *Lemon Swamp*, Karen Fields signals, to be sure, a racial (aesthetic) identity by representing her grandmother as a story-teller. Both Fields and her husband express their convictions "in the stories they told over and over," as Karen Fields writes, "without pausing to ask whether the young people want[ed] to hear – and hear again" (xv). Fields, in turn, remains conscious of her contribution to the oral history of African Americans and strives to fulfill her narrative obligations as efficiently as those who came before: "I wish I could tell this part of my story the way the people

---

27. Toni Morrison, *Playing in the Dark: Whiteness and the Literary Imagination* (Cambridge: Harvard U P, 1992), pp. 6, 7, 17, 80-81.
28. John F. Callahan, *In the African-American Grain: The Pursuit of Voice in Twentieth-Century Black Fiction* (Chicago: U of Illinois P, 1988), p. 15.
29. Lionnet, p. 162; cp. Susan Willis, *Specifying: Black Women Writing the American Experience* (Madison: U of Wisconsin P, 1986), p. 15.

who were there used to tell it..." (36). With the "telling of the tale," then, the primary motif of *Lemon Swamp*, Fields's autobiography becomes, as Andrews writes about the form in general, "a complex of linguistic acts in a discursive field."[30]

In making this field her own, Fields relies on a series of oral strategies that help her establish the audience *rapport* she envisions. Apart from interposed remarks to her reader such as "you see," "let me tell you this..." (20), she literally invites the audience to enter her local and textual landscape: "Go a little farther down the yard and you would come to the grape arbor...," she suggests in describing the home next to her own in Short Court (5); she also takes her audience on a tour of her Charleston neighborhood: "But let's keep walking down Bogard and turn at the next corner, onto Ashley Avenue. There we would find..." (19). She keeps her readers on their toes with exclamations such as "Goodness!" (among the spiciest), as well as with rhetorical parallelisms and contrasts. "Cousin Delia had to live without her people, and then she had to die without them," she writes about a former slave who had been sold away from all her Louisiana relatives (17). Again to emphasize a point she wants her audience not to miss, she notes about her own school at James Island that it "was near and far – near, because only 3 miles down the road; far, because no busses carried you down the road..." (205). With the parallelisms and antitheses of her stories, Fields not only retains the attention of her readers but points to the contradictions and ironies hiding behind the smooth surface of Carolina society. As Valerie Smith writes about Frederick Douglass's use of antithesis, it conveys his awareness of the schism between his oppressors' welfare and his own.[31]

The oratorical tradition of African American narrative appears as well in Fields's use of anecdotes as the major structural device of *Lemon Swamp*. Whether we are witnessing a young boy getting frightened by a corpse untouched by present-day morticians' means of beautifying the dead, or the attractive Goldie Borden directing

---

30. Andrews, *Free Story*, p. 23.
31. Valerie Smith, *Self-Discovery and Authority in Afro-American Narrative* (Cambridge, Mass.: Harvard U P, 1987), p. 24.

a children's choir singing the "Hallelujah Chorus" at the Morris Street Baptist Church, Fields leads her readers from one tale to another. She highlights certain stories in this string through repetition, and allows herself, in speakerly fashion, abrupt transitions as well as lengthy digressions. Phrases like "to come back" and "let me return to ..." thus dot her prose, allowing her audience to follow the circular movement through her life/text that, Gayl Jones explains, characterize "orally defined structures."[32]

Fields addresses those listening to/reading her tale in several voices. Since she devoted much of her professional life to teaching and, moreover, wants to convey to her audience the realities of African American life during Jim Crow, her loudest voice is didactic. She opens each narrative unit with a morale, which the incident she recounts then illustrates. She closes by repeating the moral lesson she wishes to convey to her readers – be it the importance of dressing properly before leaving one's house or tidiness in sewing. "'Study to show yourselves approved unto God: workmen, who need not be ashamed,'" she quotes her art program teachers at Claflin University as saying. And, adds Fields, who, after all, majored in pedagogy, "that is a saying that you can apply to many things you do in life" (89).

So as to demonstrate that her education and her middle-class status have not diminished her racial loyalties, Fields speaks as well in the voice of the folk. To be sure, the gospel and blues that pop up in her language constitute, as Houston A. Baker, Jr. argues with Derrida, the "always already" of African American culture. In Baker's words, the blues "are the multiplex, enabling *script* in which Afro-American discourse is inscribed."[33] Participating in what Akward labels a process of "denigration" – the incorporation of African American features into western systems of cultural expression[34] – Fields notes upon becoming head teacher on James Island that she and the other newly hired educators "got our chance to see how we could carry our burden in the heat of day" (205). To teach the children in her charge how to read, she needed books, no easy

---

32. Gayl Jones, p. 21.
33. Baker, p. 4.
34. Akward, p. 9.

matter in rural South Carolina in 1926: "Joshua fi't the battle of Jericho; and we fi't the battle of the books" (208). She relies, besides, on the concreteness of blues language and on its "worrying the line,"[35] a repetition with variation that allows Fields to return, from different angles, to central concerns of hers: interracial color discrimination, family, community, etc. Discussing these topics, and others, she further brings different characters, conversations, situations and time frames together, "jamming" and in this process widening their significance and possibilities.[36] With her blues voice, Fields interacts with the African American folk tradition, and its strategies for subversion and endurance.[37] Indeed, Fields incorporates the voices of the James Island population into her own prose, the result, perhaps, of an urge to "adorn" her pages with dialect, as Hurston would have it.[38] Fields's quotation marks nonetheless reveal the cultural/linguistic distance separating her from full usage of the African American vernacular, not to mention Gullah.

To allow for dimensions of her existence requiring aesthetic frills, Fields employs a feminine, lyrical voice that occasionally recites poetry both of her own and others' making. She reserves this discourse for describing beautiful dresses or women's artwork, such as the wall decorations in the Dunwalton building at Claflin, or the stacks of differently-textured and -colored material enlivening the side of the dressmaking classroom there (88). Recalling the year of her marriage in 1914, Fields speaks with equal enthusiasm – and lyricism – of her wedding gown and the azaleas and wisteria vines of the Charleston spring (157).

Yet another familiar feminine mode of expression coexists with Fields's various autobiographical voices: silence. Intensely aware of the requirements of true womanhood, an ideal subscribed to by African American women in the turn-of-the-century South,[39] she often keeps herself quiet rather than articulating an opinion. "From

---

35. Gayl Jones, pp. 94-95.
36. Gayl Jones, p. 49.
37. Byerman, *Fingering*, p. 8.
38. Holloway, *Moorings*, p. 173.
39. See Linda Perkins, "The Impact of the 'Cult of True Womanhood' on the Education of Black Women," *Journal of Social Issues* 39.3 (1983), pp. 17-28.

a child I was taught not to 'talk when you ought to be listening,'" she informs her readers. "In Charleston, a woman had a terrible reputation if people got to the place where they would say, 'Her mouth hangs on a hinge'" (165). In accordance with the Victorian feminine ideal, she remains silent on sexual issues, with narrative gaps between, for example, her wedding ceremony and the new bride and groom's departure for Charlotte the following morning. Fields erases the African American body also to reconstruct the notions of its insatiable, promiscuous sexuality held among various groups of white southerners. She maintains, moreover, a certain reticence concerning the psychological and physical violence against her race characteristic of the Jim Crow South. Rather than overtly criticizing the segregation practices hemming African Americans in, she employs a series of rhetorical questions to point to racial injustice. In discussing the Hametic, a hotel for people of color that they couldn't afford and that, due to segregation, whites could and would not use, she asks, "What do you think of that – a hotel for Negroes that Negroes couldn't go to?" And worship at the segregated St. James Methodist Church certainly raised a few questions: "How the white pastor could celebrate an authentic Methodist Communion with some of the members confined to the gallery, I don't know. And how did they baptize, I wonder, since the font is always in the front of the church, downstairs?" (32).

However, while Fields thus allows segregationist ironies a certain narrative space through her questions, she pushes physical violence to the margin of her text. She mentions briefly how in the post-WWI South, Ku Klux or redneck gangs would pull an African American soldier off the train: "Oftentimes," she says briefly, "the young man was beaten, or worse" (161). During the war, when blacks and whites fought abroad, Klan members did not "make the racial war over here," she recalls, "but I guess they were thinking all kinds of things." Her deliberate vagueness aims to deemphasize the racial violence around and toward her, presumably as a literal and psychological survival measure. Instead, she speaks of the domestic life subject to her control: "While they were thinking whatever they were thinking, Bob and I were trying to set up house in Charlotte and start our family" (162).

Fields's multiple (non)voices lend to her autobiography the performative aspect that may characterize the genre as a whole. Yet her role playing suggests not just the indeterminacy of the postmodern/feminine subject but a political motive as well. By denying "a fixed identity" subject to categorization and systemic control, role playing denies such permanence and manipulation in part, as Byerman explains, "by suggesting that the fixed identity, like the system that produces it, is only one among several possibilities."[40] To speak in different voices, in short, aligns the narrator(s) with social change.

The performance of *Lemon Swamp* participates, moreover, in the signifying textual relations characteristic of the African American literary canon. As Michael Akward argues in *Inspiriting Influences*, African American women writers tend to refigure and revise earlier texts in the tradition. This practice explains the recurring affinities between individual works that constitute, in Gates's phrase, "precisely chartable formal literary relationships, relationships of signifying."[41] Parodic or not, *Lemon Swamp* rewrites the early slave narratives that positioned the slave as a fellow human being and a truth-teller, what Andrews calls "a reliable transcriber of the experience and character of black folk."[42] Fields's integrationist impulse, and her concern with truth and justice, establish the intertextual relationship to the slave narrative and its moral assumptions, amplified in her (discursive) role as pedagogue and moral guide. Her autobiography thus shares with the slave narrative the emphasis on verbal expression. The slave narrators hoped, as Andrews and others have shown, to win religious and secular authority through the word.[43] In Fields's text, literacy and education similarly serve as tools of self-authorization. Certain passages of *Lemon Swamp* suggest, however, that Fields follows the post-bellum ex-slave narrators in shifting her (linguistic) focus from generating facts to generating "frills," what Butterfield calls "giving pleasure"[44] and poststructuralists, *jouis-*

---

40. Byerman, *Fingering*, p. 5.
41. Akward, p. 4; Holloway, *Moorings*, p. 7.
42. Andrews, *Free Story*, p. 1.
43. William L. Andrews, *Sisters of the Spirit: Three Black Women's Autobiographies in the Nineteenth Century* (Bloomington: Indiana U P, 1986), p. 1; *Free Story*, p. 13.
44. Stephen Butterfield, *Black Autobiography in America* (Amherst: U of Mass. P, 1974), p. 136.

sance. Her intertextual ties to slave and ex-slave narratives come out, moreover, in her fight to do away with the bonds impeding the free physical and mental movement of African Americans. Like the postbellum autobiographers, she dwells proudly on the contribution of her people in/to the South. Fields recounts her life within an "inspiriting" context of stories and voices preceding and surrounding her own.[45] As we have seen, the title of her autobiography inscribes the individual storyteller within a larger framework. The retrospective assessment of one life becomes an assessment of a racial, cultural and social landscape.

If *Lemon Swamp* inserts itself into the tradition of African American autobiography, it partakes as well in a distinctively feminine writing project. The plural languages of *Lemon Swamp* make of it a blend of voices and values, a writing from the edge blurring distinctions between past and present, self and other, history and memory, to mention just a few. With feminine ellipses and silences, Fields's autobiography moreover creates, as Wolfgang Iser theorizes, a tension between showing and concealing, between "what is said" and "what is meant."[46] The discursive space in between becomes a field of potentiality, a play-space in which established assumptions – of race, of gender – become destabilized. The textual gaps of *Lemon Swamp* encourage, in fact, a revised reading process – what Andrews in speaking of early slave narratives labels "creative hearing."[47] Fields's omissions evolve around abuse and violence, and especially around female physicality and bourgeois notions of impropriety. Her silences have a specifically feminine accent.

Unlike Frederick Douglass, who aims to tell "the father's story" within an androcentric form[48] and possibly, as some critics argue, is entrapped by the rhetorical/ideological structures he wishes to

---

45. See Akward.
46. Wolfgang Iser, *The Act of Reading: A Theory of Aesthetic Response* (Baltimore: Johns Hopkins U P, 1978), p. 45.
47. William L. Andrews, "The First Fifty Years of the Slave Narrative, 1760-1810," in Sekora and Turner, p. 8.
48. Deborah McDowell, "In the First Place: Making Frederick Douglass and the Afro-American Narrative Tradition," in Andrews, *African American Autobiography*, pp. 44-45.

overturn,[49] Fields chooses not to silence "the mother's story." Her autobiography stresses formally and thematically close ties to female relatives and friends, supporting Susan Willis's assertion in *Specifying* that "the black woman's relation to history is first of all a relation to mother and grandmother."[50] In contrast to Douglass's linear success story, a male plot, it is argued, charting one individual's solitary journey through adversity,[51] Fields tells of communal efforts within an anecdotal, digressive narrative mode. Indeed, the circular movement of *Lemon Swamp* not only returns her to the South after two brief sojourns in the North but also allows her to return to situations and issues already covered – what Holloway calls "recursion."[52] Of the two structural patterns Stone identifies in his seminal essay on African American autobiography, Douglass conforms to the life-as-journey tradition; Fields, to life-as-stability. In Stone's formulation, this design depicts "the self staying in one spot and confronting the challenges and vicissitudes of minority existence in racist America by remaining in Alabama or Mississippi, say, and forging an identity there."[53] Stone does not consider gender in his early discussion of African American narration, yet Fields's choice of the circular stay-at-home structuring principle constitutes as well a choice of a feminine mode of life – and of narration.

Fields articulates, moreover, her dissatisfaction with southern segregation in what Claudia Tate calls a "maternal discourse." Tate explains in her discussion of African American women's sentimental novels of the Reconstruction period that "the domestic plots rely on a tradition of politicized motherhood that views mothers and the cultural rhetoric of maternity as instruments of social reform."[54] Fields literally uses a maternal discourse of rebellion in buying her first-born a special, ivory-colored wickerwork baby car-

---

49. Valerie Smith, pp. 26-27.
50. Willis, pp. 5f.
51. Valerie Smith, p. 33.
52. Holloway, *Moorings*, p. 78.
53. Albert E. Stone, "After *Black Boy* and *Dusk of Dawn*: Patterns in Recent Black Autobiography," rpt. in Andrews, *African American Autobiography*, p. 177.
54. Claudia Tate, *Domestic Allegories of Political Desire* (Cambridge: Oxford U P, 1993), p. 14.

riage with reversible top, decorated on the inside with a crocheted ivory blanket laced with blue ribbons and bows. "Few in the city," Fields recalls, "had anything like my carriage" (9). Through her baby's fancy equipment, Fields thus asserts his – and her – equality with the white families crowding the benches at Colonial Lake, where the African American infant's mother and grandmother have to keep walking to be tolerated (9). Fields also takes on the role of "outraged mother," as defined by Joanne M. Braxton,[55] in fighting for her extended family of schoolchildren, whose education, she believes, is essential to social and racial democracy. Ultimately, the formal elements that *Lemon Swamp* shares with African American autobiography and with feminine (or womanist) narratology combine into the overall aim of Fields's life story: persuasion. By relating her life as an African American woman's text, Fields claims a space for black women within white male (literary) history; she hopes, indeed, to persuade new generations, black and white, of African American dignity, and power. In a context of southern racial practices, *Lemon Swamp* accordingly advocates social change.

To use Valerie Smith's terminology, a "concealed plot" involving resistance and activism thus hides underneath the "manifest plot" of integrationist uplift that seemingly dominates Fields's memoir.[56] And, as in many an African American autobiography, the word is the key to this resistance. As Andrews writes in *To Tell a Free Story*, "It is possible to redefine one's place in the scheme of things by redefining the language used to locate one in that scheme."[57] Fields subverts, for example, the rhetoric of bourgeois complacency in recounting her activities of the 1920s. "Bob and I finally settled in Charleston," she writes, "but we didn't settle *down*. We got ready to fight, with other black people" (186). As V. N. Volosinov theorizes, the sign becomes the locus of the class (or race) struggle, since "differently oriented social interests" within a community intersect in the language they share.[58] The African American writer, then, usurps

---

55. Braxton, p. 21.
56. Valerie Smith, p. 131.
57. Andrews, *Free Story*, p. 7.
58. Holloway, *Moorings*, p. 79.

the language of power and uses it subversively in the context of the disempowered.[59] Fields, for one, mocks the school superintendent's impolite mode of address in narrating their meeting in his private garage. On one occasion during WWII, they discuss arrangements to warn black country schools in case of an attack. "Well, no, Fields mustn't worry about that: so-and-so was going to ride all around and give everybody the alarm." "Of course," Mamie Fields adds, "Fields did worry" (240). Like African American autobiographies from Equiano onwards, parody and irony may serve as weapons of (linguistic) resistance.[60] With tricksterly duplicity, Fields thus discusses the segregation practices upheld by white Charlestonians in the language they themselves employ. "Another unwritten law, or 'custom,'" Fields recalls, "used to give the battery over to blacks one day each year, the Fourth of July" (55). The quotation marks, not to mention the holiday itself, tells its own story of black (in)dependence.

Besides signifying upon white customs, Fields exercises her linguistic skills in getting from white authorities what she needs for her classrooms. She does not, perhaps, get quite as "sassy" as some African American women whose verbal wit serves as defense and/or liberation in the absence of physical or social power.[61] The linguistic one-upmanship characteristic of Fields's verbal encounters with school trustees evokes, nonetheless, a similar feminine trickster behavior. She frequently litters her phrases with the word "government," for example, to scare southern county officials weary of federal interference (160). She also learns to use the term "social work" (226) to her advantage. Fields has to "dramatize," as she puts it, to get even a dictionary for her school (225), yet she manages to borrow the superintendent's truck for an Emancipation Day parade by describing her plans for the float. Language, in sum, serves as the site and the means of self-determination.

Fields manipulates looks as well as words in resisting the representations of racial inferiority imposed upon her in the Jim Crow

---

59. Butterfield, p. 240.
60. Byerman, "Mask," p. 76.
61. Braxton, p. 30.

South. Though segregated from white southerners, she is the target of the white gaze, as she explains in recounting her attempt to buy a crochet needle in Ehrhardt. The store owner resents her request and marks her territory with the gaze: "Ruth began to look again, the way they would do you, taking their time, and knowing they got the right to stare. She squinted like a far-sighted person standing too close to see something clear. That told you to stand back" (72). Fields's stance demonstrates that the white gaze freezes blacks into passive otherness. Not to return the gaze is essential to their survival.

Nonetheless, Fields resists the dominant gaze, directly or indirectly. Her mother sets the example by confronting the white policeman who has bent down to admire the baby she is promenading at Charleston Lake in the fanciest baby carriage around. Seeing that this supposedly rich and pampered baby is African American, the policeman stops smiling and accuses Mrs. Garvin of theft. She responds by usurping the gaze: "And she stood there, looking him right in the face, just daring him to touch anything, *daring him*, and mad enough to spit.... She just kept looking at him, right in his red face, until he got through talking" (9).

Similarly, Fields and her friend Charlotte manipulate established patterns of looking in the streetcar episode when they challenge "race" as a discriminatory category and practice:

> now, get on, keep laughing and talking, put in your money and walk right past the conductor, nonchalant, don't know what he is looking at, don't even notice that he is looking.... We kept on, not noticing the white passengers who got on and noticed us. They just looked at us and then at the conductor. The conductor looked at us. We kept on looking at each other and talking. The work of the eyes God gave us is something! (65)

In the complicated web of (non)gazes unbalancing racial hierarchies, Fields and her friend push to extremes the white aggressive and the black evasive pattern of looking. In doing so, they subtly avert the white gaze, which, as in the quoted text, begins to flicker, until the white conductor, so to speak, becomes invisible. The color line that W. E. B. Du Bois identified as the problem of the twentieth century begins to flicker as well. As Joseph P. Reidy notes about recent southern historiography, the color line can no longer be easily identified, nor, for that matter, erased. Instead, Americans must face "a more porous boundary between races."[62]

The mediation between confrontation and conciliation characteristic of Fields's rhetorical strategies and black women's autobiographies as such[63] results in part from the "double consciousness" Du Bois associated with the African American experience. The American part of this "twoness" emerges in Fields's middle-class beliefs. Though she may not have written a manual on how to succeed, like *Up from Slavery*, she constructs her life with Bob in terms of upward mobility brought about through family, education, thrift, and hard work. Like other (African) American autobiographers, she relies, moreover, on a patriotic rhetoric to communicate her victories, however small. Rather than having her schoolchildren sing and dance at the school closing ceremony like the white teacher she replaces on John's Island in 1909, she impresses upon them their national culture and duties: "if they were Americans, they ought to be able to sing 'America, the Beautiful' and say the Pledge of Allegiance" (127). That African American children in an isolated South Carolina island community achieve cultural literacy ensures, Fields hopes, their civil rights, despite the oppression of their home region: "My school was in the United States, after all, and not the Confederacy" (127). As Fields's negation suggests, her American patriotism creates a distance to southern racism. In her childhood and youth, black Charlestonians thus celebrated the Fourth of July on the Battery with much ado, while white Charlestonians chose to ignore this "Yankee holiday" (55). The texts chosen for this festive occasion imply, however, the double vision and heritage of African Americans: "The Battle of the Republic," "The Emancipation Proclamation" and assorted Lincoln pieces, as well as parts of Douglass's antislavery speeches and James Weldon Johnson's "Lift Ev'ry Voice and Sing" (56). A

---

62. Joseph P. Reidy quotes Judy Scales-Trent's phrase, in his "Calliope and Clio: The Style and Substance of Recent Historical Writing on the South," *The Southern Review* 32.2 (April 1996), p. 389.
63. Braxton, p. 204.

specifically African American perspective obviously inserts itself into Fields's patriotic rhetoric, making *Lemon Swamp* a "duplex autobiography," in Olney's phrase, not just in the sense of a "confluence of culture and consciousness,"[64] but also in its ambiguous relation to American institutions and (linguistic) codes.

While *Lemon Swamp*, like African American self-narration in general, revises the tradition of American autobiography, it redefines as well the autobiographical subject of color. Unlike the male soldier fighting his way through adversity and chaos, whom Butterfield identifies with male-authored African American autobiography, Fields is the blues singer,[65] or possibly the housewife and community worker. The rhetoric of domesticity that permeates her autobiography might, in fact, as Tate would argue, constitute an emancipatory discourse, a "gendered discourse of citizenship"[66] expressing in domestic tropology a feminine political desire. Her communal rhetoric and activities deconstruct in similar fashion dichotomies between public/private spheres and traded/domestic labor. In her emphasis on community work, Fields proposes a third sphere that partakes of both binaries but cannot be fully absorbed in either.[67] In revising (African) American autobiography, Fields accordingly constructs a different vision of social and historical action. To return to Willis's notion that African American women define their relation to history as a relation to mother and grandmother, Fields's conception of American history remains intensely personal and communal, with moments such as World War II and even the Civil Rights Movement at the edge of her vision. What stands out for her in the 1960s, her granddaughter tells us in the Epilogue, is the establishment of a public day care center for working mothers in Charleston (244).

Fields thus passes on to future generations the experiences and treasures she, in turn, has received from women in the past. She approaches her life text much in the way her "Grandma" would present to those coming of age her trousseau from the West Indies:

---

64. Braxton, pp. 104, 208.
65. Wisker, p. 128.
66. Tate, p. 51.
67. See Beth Moore Milroy and Susan Wismer, "Communities, Work, and Public/Private Sphere Models," *Gender, Place and Culture* 1.1 (1994), pp. 71-90.

Pirates' Treasures: Mamie Garvin Fields's Carolina Memoir

> Oh, it was a treat whenever she would open that trunk! She didn't open it very often. When she did, she made a big affair out of it. First to go get the key, then to open the trunk, carefully, then to remove the dried flower petals, which she had sewed into little silk bags, now to unfold the covers she had around the different things, fold them again just so and put them aside. (21)

In unfolding her life story, Fields dramatizes the details of domestic life in a manner similar to the flamboyant lady from St. Kitts who became the second wife of Fields's Grandpa Bellinger. Not only does Fields present her memories to a small group of granddaughters and family friends; she co-authors with Karen Fields the autobiography that, like the day care center she gets going in the 1960s, will reach a wider group of people, white and black. Similar to her grandmother, however, Fields combines in her text African American and feminine modes of expression, creating from domestic items a bond to nineteenth-century authors. In fact, as Annette Niemtzow writes, "to make autobiography bend to the requirements of the black family – particularly to find space for the often important role of the grandmother – has been the achievement of the modern black autobiographer, especially the female autobiographer."[68]

However, like the pirates' dungeons that Fields imagined in the 1890s, when Jim Crow prevented her visit to this historical landmark, *Lemon Swamp* hides riches of a potentially dangerous nature amidst its lavender and lace. Though a soft-spoken lady narrator of a woman's (and womanist) life, Fields resists linguistically and otherwise the authors of southern segregation and prejudice. She does not, in fact, "get so much as a doily" out of her grandmother's trunk, yet she inherits the older woman's courage, community activism, and rhetorical expertise. The trunk she passes on to Karen Fields and the younger readers mixes hemstitched petticoats, embroidered tablecloths and elaborate wedding dresses with less tangible treasures wrested from forbidden places – explosives, indeed, worth a pirate's efforts.

---

68. Annette Niemtzow, "The Problematic of Self in Autobiography: The Example of the Slave Narrative," in Sekora and Turner, p. 104.

Alice Walker

CHAPTER TEN

Woman(ist) as Artist: Alice Walker's *The Temple of My Familiar*

Two old women, both experienced artists, frame the four-hundred-plus pages of Alice Walker's *The Temple of My Familiar* (1989), a broad canvas of African and African American life from the beginnings to contemporary San Francisco yuppiedom. The opening page introduces the South American Zedé, Sr., a seamstress or "sewing magician," who creates from peacock, parrot and cockatoo feathers the traditional capes worn by priests, dancers, and musicians at local village festivals. At the close of Walker's novel, Miss Lissie, a most bewitching womanist artist, has left for posterity a self-portrait, in which Lissie-as-Lion looks daringly at the viewer, her abundant tail almost obscuring the elegant, red, high-heeled slipper on her back paw.[1] With(in) this frame, Walker paints African American feminine creativity as a marginal, magic space inhabited by goddesses, whose knowledge and power explode traditional symbolic and social codes. In the process, Walker presents a womanist interpretation of "the blackness of blackness," Henry Louis Gates, Jr.'s term for the non-essence of black difference.[2]

---

1. For Walker's full definition of "womanist," see her *In Search of Our Mothers' Gardens: Womanist Prose* (New York: Harcourt Brace Jovanovitch, 1984), pp. xi-xii. Her definition includes "A black feminist or feminist of color," "Usually referring to outrageous, audacious, courageous or *willful* behavior," "Committed to survival and wholeness of entire people, male *and* female," and "Loves music. Loves dance. Loves the moon. *Loves* the Spirit."
2. Henry Louis Gates, Jr., "The Blackness of Blackness: A Critique of the Sign and the Signifying Monkey," in *Black Literature and Literary Theory*, ed. Henry Louis Gates, Jr. (New York: Methuen, 1984), pp. [285]-321.

In creating her feathered capes, Zedé the Elder removes herself from her family hut to a location outside, a gesture through which Walker establishes the connection between feminine art and marginality. Only a few steps from the main hut, Zedé is inside yet outside the village community. Also the South American setting, off-center in relation to the main plot of the novel, establishes the foreignness of feminine creativity. Zedé's daughter Zedé, who inherits her mother's creative gift and thus, as with her name, establishes the "always" of feminine artistic tradition, further connects this tradition with displacement. Escaped from imprisonment to the United States, Zedé the Younger speaks English with a heavy Spanish accent and, in Cixousian terminology, as "woman, escapee" has marginality and dislocation inscribed in her voice.[3] An old photo of the newly arrived Zedé holding her baby daughter Carlotta shows Zedé's "drawn face ... partly in shadow," later revealing to Carlotta's husband "the stress of oppression, dispossession, flight," as well as the hidden face of the woman artist.[4] The notion of feminine creativity as "the repressed of culture"[5] recurs in Walker's description of Zedé's immigrant life. In the daytime Zedé works within masculine sign systems by making jeans and country-and-western shirts in a San Francisco sweatshop, but at night, she "furtively," at home, continues to make exotic feathered headdresses and capes (6).

The decentered existence of Walker's artist associates her with magic, even madness. The original "sewing magician," Zedé the Elder, works, as her daughter explains, "as if by magic." Without looking at her work, she operates in a dreamlike state, her fingers knowing "just what to do" (47). Miss Lissie, the most flamboyant and haughty of Walker's artist figures, proudly labels herself a "witch doctor" and a "sorceress" (97) and thus again positions female creativity in the realm of magic and miracles (104-05). Even Fanny, the granddaughter of *The Color Purple*'s Celie and an ex-academic turned masseuse in contemporary San Francisco, places a crystal

---

3. Hélène Cixous, "The Laugh of the Medusa," in *New French Feminisms*, ed. Elaine Marks and Isabelle de Courtivron (New York: Schocken, 1981), p. 249.
4. Alice Walker, *The Temple of My Familiar* (New York: Pocket, 1989), p. 18. Subsequent page references will appear parenthetically in the text.
5. Cixous, "The Laugh of the Medusa," p. 248.

at her client's head and feet and speaks, it seems to Carlotta, "the very babble of witches" (293). This feminine "chaosmos" functions as a joyous subversion of masculine logic and order.[6] The feathered artwork of the two Zedés, for example, surfaces at festivals and parades as disrespectful, bold signs of carnivalesque topsy-turvy, a discourse that breaks through grammatical-semantic and social-moral codes.[7] Carlotta observes about her mother's cockatoo and peacock-feathered ornaments worn at a Halloween parade in San Francisco that they seem "almost too resplendent for the gray, foggy city" (6); the naked, beer-drinking and crystal-carrying gay man who wears one of the enormous headdresses constitutes himself a sign of feminized, marginal and pleasuring illogic.

In fact, the feathered capes, shawls, headbands and whatnot that Carlotta's mother produces during the sixties, when San Franciscan rock stars are "into" feathers, functions within an economy of abundance and waste. With her spectacular, superfluous, ornamental artwork, Zedé creates (her) desire within an economy that, in Cixous's phrase, "can no longer be put in economic terms.... At the end of a more or less conscious computation, she finds not her sum but her differences."[8] The woman artist is, in other words, a Bataillan gift-giver, who depropriates endlessly, more, and through the mere wastefulness of her gifts transforms conventional systems of exchange and profit. Yet Zedé does in fact make a profit on her capes, but her ventures into a masculine "gift-that-takes" economy rests on a foundation of subversive theft. Carlotta steals the feathers her mother transforms into art and thus becomes a *voleuse*, a bird-robber-woman who "take[s] pleasure in jumbling the order of space, in disorienting it, in changing around the furniture, dislocating things and values, breaking them all up, emptying structures, and turning propriety upside down."[9]

The rearranged furniture and broken walls of this festive subversion include western conceptions of self and signal the fluid

---

6. Cixous, "The Laugh of the Medusa," p. 258.
7. See Julia Kristeva, *The Kristeva Reader*, ed. Toril Moi (New York: Columbia U P, 1986), p. 36; *Tales of Love* (New York: Columbia U P, 1987), p. 381.
8. Cixous, "The Laugh of the Medusa," p. 264.
9. Cixous, "The Laugh of the Medusa," p. 258.

personality boundaries of Walker's woman(ist) artists. Fanny regularly falls in love with spirits, who inhabit her or vice versa for months on end; on a journey to Africa, she discovers an African sister who mirrors her not only in looks but also in sharing her middle name Nzingha. This merging with others, living and dead, is intensified in the case of Miss Lissie, who refers to "myselves" in describing the many women, men, and even animals she has been in lifetimes spanning thousands of years.[10] In photos taken of Lissie over her present lifetime, she appears forever different: tall, short, light, dark, healthy, crippled, haughty, beaten, etc. As Lissie explains to Fanny's husband Suwelo during his stay in Baltimore after the death of his Uncle Rafe, the photographer/lover for whom Lissie modeled, "had never, in all his work as a photographer, photographed anyone like me, who could never present the same self more than once, and I had never in my life before found anyone who could recognize how many different women I was." Even to her parents, Lissie didn't seem to have, in their words, "no certain definite form" (91).

With her gesture towards fluidity and multiplicity, Walker deconstructs the impulse towards unity and wholeness of textual voice, because, to represent the dividing and incompatible forces of her existence, the woman(ist) artist of color must assume her own division. In Barbara Johnson's phrase, "the sign of an authentic voice is thus not self-identity but self-difference."[11] Through this lack of correspondence to a single referent, Walker moreover writes her female artist into the African American trickster tradition. As Jay Edwards explains in "Structural Analysis of the Afro-American Trickster Tale," the trickster figure "assumes his unique and powerful role by virtue of his crossing and violating boundaries."[12] In all the

---

10. Roland Walter discusses African American women writers' utopian intent in (re)constructing a mythic past in "The Dialectics Between the Act of Writing and the Act of Reading in Alice Walker's *The Temple of My Familiar*, Gloria Naylor's *Mama Day* and Toni Morrison's *Jazz*," *The Southern Quarterly* 35.5 (Spring 1997), pp. 55-66.
11. Barbara Johnson, "Metaphor, Metonymy and Voice in *Their Eyes Were Watching God*," in Gates, *Black Literature*, p. 212.
12. Jay Edwards, "Structural Analysis of the Afro-American Trickster Tale," in Gates, *Black Literature*, p. 91.

lifetimes Lissie recalls, she was "someone who started trouble" (54). Accordingly, through fluidity of form and irreverent behavior, Walker's trickster-artist violates symbolic and cultural codes and thus embodies what Ralph Ellison designates the liberating "joke" of the trickster.[13]

The two self-portraits that Lissie and her impotent husband-companion Hal give to Suwelo upon his departure from Baltimore express in one sense a joke on Suwelo's closed circuits of interpretation. The backgrounds of the paintings show the trees, corn, and flowers of his old friends' house, but the centers consist, instead of portraits, of mere outlines of a man's and a woman's torso, surrounded by the deep blue space of infinity. Turning over the paintings, Suwelo reads on Miss Lissie's self-portrait, "Painted by Hal Jenkins" and on Hal's, "Painted by Lissie Lyles" (193). Apart from the notions of art as a chaosmic, festive gift as discussed above, the paintings suggest the fluid ego boundaries of Walker's feminine or feminized artists, and, moreover, associates them with absence and negativity, with what is not there. As Julia Kristeva theorizes in "Oscillation between Power and Denial," woman-as-artist rejects by assuming a negative function "everything finite, definite, structured, loaded with meaning" and thus sides with revolutionary explosions of social codes.[14] Indeed, through their tricksterly signifyin(g) on the self-portrait form, Lissie and Hal break up Suwelo's conception of self and instead introduce him to invention, to change. Lissie and Hal, for one (or two?) must, in other words, be imagined. When Suwelo initially moves into his uncle's house, for example, the photos of Lissie that had decorated the hallway are missing, alerting him only with the contours of the frames in the wallpaper to their existence (40).

This invisibility is, on still another level, a Walkerly signifyin(g) on the canonical African American absence, a tradition that describes blackness as a negative essence, a transcendent signified.[15] However, rather than creating another transcendent signified of

---

13. Ralph Ellison, *Shadow and Act* (New York: Signet, 1966), pp. 61-73.
14. Julia Kristeva, "Oscillation between Power and Denial," in Marks and de Courtivron, p. 166.
15. Gates, "Blackness," p. 315.

blackness as presence, Walker posits an interpretative openendedness, the notion of aesthetic indeterminacy and play.[16] The "blackness of blackness" must, then, be constantly produced and invented, and the nonessence of black feminine creativity accordingly includes dynamic motion.

This energy is characteristic of Arveyda's mother, who before three years of physical inactivity channeled her creativity into the founding of the Church of Perpetual Involvement. This woman, as Arveyda remembers her, "did not recognize limits," to the extent that no year of birth is placed on her gravestone. Besides such connections with infinity, she invents herself as Katherine Degos instead of accepting her given name. A troublemaker and trickster in Lissie's mold, "she was a woman of such high energy she always seemed to him to be whirling, and the first time Arveyda heard the expression 'whirling dervish' he thought of it as a description of his mother" (12). Lissie herself/selves seem/s to Hal to be "so black ... like, *concentrated*" (44) and feels her brain to be "charged ... like a battery" (52). Through the non-representable energy of these characters, Walker creates the visual and verbal text of African American femininity as dynamic process and play. As Ellison writes in *Invisible Man*, "black is" and "black ain't."[17] At the same time Walker communicates with her charged images the power of African American women artists.

This power is intimately associated with their expert readings. Talking with Suwelo in Uncle Rafe's kitchen, for example, Lissie answers his unspoken question about the number of locks in her wild, glorious lion's mane, itself a sign of untamed bodily energy and creativity: "Exactly one hundred and thirteen" (53). Lissie's mirror image Hal becomes practically blind whenever, prompted by his father, he stops painting. "Like seeing someone forced to blind himself" (60), says Miss Lissie, thus denouncing the Law of the Father, that enemy of feminine revisions. "How am I to be a great painter if I never *see* anything," writes one of Walker's budding artists in her journal a few generations earlier. Despite her tradi-

---

16. Gates, "Blackness," p. 305.
17. Gates, "Blackness," p. 315.

Woman(ist) as Artist: Alice Walker's *The Temple of My Familiar*

tional female socialization, the young woman(ist) disguises herself as a man and enters the brothels of Victorian London in order "to look, to study, to contemplate" (220). This breaking of feminine boundaries becomes as well a revision of art, in that she, so to speak, invents the female gaze: woman looking at woman (looking). "I am fascinated," she writes in her diary, "by the women's eyes, their bold, aggressive stares, their businesslike appraisal" (220).

Significantly, the invention of the feminine artistic I is connected to the female body and to desire: "I must say it is this sucking that the women most seem to enjoy and their enjoyment of it in turn stirs me..." (221). The mirror relationship established here suggests, moreover, that in inventing a female gaze, woman as artist invents as well herself as (desiring) subject. Lissie, for example, looks "on people's lives as if they was plays," Hal explains. "She was always moving people around" (43). This ability to usurp power through the creation of alternative scripts resurfaces in another of Lissie's lifetimes, when she and her friend Fadpa set up shop as fortune-tellers. Not only does their crystal ball again establish Lissie's expert vision, but true to her tricksterly creativity, she mocks the world of masculinity: "For every man, they saw war, a future of fighting.... But Lulu [Lissie] and Fadpa would say, instead, that they saw a hundred pretty women locked in a room to which the man in front of them, alone, had the key..." (105).

The ability of Walker's artists to decipher their surroundings originates, perhaps, in their intuitive access to knowledge. An African scholar with "lifeless eyes" (61) becomes a "well-educated, smooth-talking zombie" in representing masculine, academic "truth," while Lissie's folk knowledge based on personal experience receives the author's endorsement, if only through the massive narrative energy devoted to her stories. Similarly, Suwelo finds his knowledge of (African) American history in work bastions such as the university and the research library, while Fanny comes upon the things she needs to know haphazardly, by coincidence. In knocking over a vase, perhaps, she will find that "the information, or whatever it was, she'd been looking for, vaguely, would appear on the wettest page of one of the books" (277), as Suwelo recounts with exasperated envy. This libidinal encircling of knowledge, of seeing, surfaces also in non-fictional descriptions of African American feminine creativity. Toni Cade Bambara states to Zala Chandler in *Wild Women in the Whirlwind* (1990) that when working on *The Salt Eaters,* she never had to leave her house: "Once you understand what your work is and you do not try to avert your eyes from it, but attempt to invest energy in getting that work done, the universe will send you what you need. You simply have to know how to be still and receive it."[18]

The endorsement of intuitive patterns of knowing possibly relates to the African aesthetics of Walker's art(ists). As defined by Sunday O. Anozie in "Negritude, Structuralism, Deconstruction," an African theory of art must reckon with "a *lived* system of signs and symbols, a sort of experiential semiology shared by all." Crossing boundaries of genre and form, African signs and symbols 'speak' "in traditional African decorative arts, sculptures, graffiti, and so on."[19] Rather than focusing on *l'écriture* and *parole,* or the artist-as-writer, Walker has consequently in *The Temple* zoomed in on painters and musicians, most of whom rely on the African continent for self-identity/ies and inspiration and express themselves through African aesthetic principles.

The colors of Walker's artists, for example, form the clear, bright, natural spectrum of African/Native American art, as with the intense, deep sky blue in the outlines of Hal/Lissie's self portraits, or the energy-instilling "complex royal blue" of Celie, a woman "very much influenced by color" (143). Occasionally, Walker draws on peacock imagery to communicate the power and dignity of her artists' color schemes. Among the first of the many Walker artists who go to Africa, Eleandra Burnham Peacock becomes a painter after her encounter with M'Sukta, an African woman imprisoned for ten years in the Museum of Natural History in London. Several generations later, Carlotta, whose roots are South American, establishes herself as a bell chimist in a San Francisco cottage, whose

---

18. Zala Chandler, "Voices Beyond the Veil: An Interview with Toni Cade Bambara and Sonia Sanchez," in *Wild Women in the Whirlwind: Afra-American Culture and the Contemporaray Literary Renaissance,* ed. Joanne M. Braxton and Andrée Nicola McLaughlin (New Brunswick: Rutgers U P, 1990), p. 350.
19. Sunday O. Anozie, "Negritude, Structuralism, Deconstruction," in Gates, *Black Literature,* p. 122.

rooms – blue, green, olive, gold – communicate "a peacockish feeling" (387).

As indicated with this relationship across time and space – what Chinosole in discussing Audre Lorde labels a "matrilinear diaspora" – the art of *The Temple of My Familiar* is in the African tradition communal and functional.[20] At the M'Sukta Art School, for example, an institution set up by Eleandra Peacock's blue-haired grandniece, students paint on walls and, moreover, express themselves aesthetically with locally woven bedspreads and brightly painted wardrobes (343). Even Lissie and Hal's gumbo, cooked with sensitivity, love, and creativity, becomes a sign of artistic and social communality, as do the many wall decorations of Walker's prehistoric cave dwellers. Above all, the African art of Walker's millenium-spanning novel is ancestral, rooted in connections to ancient pasts and selves. One of Miss Lissie's last paintings depicts "the tree of life, with everything, including 'the little white fellow' [one of Miss Lissie's many forms] in its branches" (416). With this ancestral emphasis, Walker again joins forces with women writers such as Mamie Garvin Fields and Maya Angelou, or Toni Cade Bambara and Sonia Sanchez, who in the Chandler interview "speak of the need for African people to rely upon the spirit and the bones and the knowledge of those who came before us, ancestors."[21] Or, as Hélène Cixous chooses to express this reliance on tradition, "Woman always occurs simultaneously in several places.... In woman, personal history blends together with the history of all women, as well as national and world history. As a militant, she is an integral part of all liberations."[22]

The African jungle, where several of Walker's artists discover themselves, functions as a maternal space of liberation and creativity. Lissie's dream memory of a childhood in a "forest that, for all we know, covers the whole earth...," with "no concept of finiteness, in any sense" (83) represents this space as unconscious, pre-linguis-

---

20. Chinosole, "Audre Lorde and Matrilinear Diaspora: Moving History beyond Nightmare into Structures for the Future," in Braxton and McLaughlin, pp. [379]-94.
21. Chandler, "Voices Beyond the Veil," p. 342.
22. Cixous, "The Laugh of the Medusa," pp. 252-53.

tic, without separation and difference – in other words, as a Kristevan imaginary, untouched by the Law of the Father.[23] In the contemporary American scenario, the space of maternal creativity has, to no surprise for readers familiar with Walker's work, become a garden. Hal and Lissie paint in the luscious garden surrounding their small house, amidst giant dahlias, corn, blue morning glories, and infinity: Suwelo experiences the day he spends there as "eternity itself" and soon drifts off to sleep – the unconscious, maternal landscape of feminine creativity (191-92). Similarly, Fanny's "mother-in-law cottage," the location for her masseuse activities, sits sensuously among "hibiscus and jasmine," vaguely remembered by Carlotta as "bright colors and a lovely scent" (292). Like Fanny's massage parlor, which it resembles, Carlotta's own bell chimist studio is the guest house in a garden of flowers and colors, an alternative space with waterfalls, bells, and chimes reminiscent of Kristevan imaginary babble. As a feminine space of freedom and creativity, the garden thus signals woman(ist) artists who have – finally – reinvented their identities. Carlotta has left behind the stiff bras and high heels that made her resemble a female impersonator, and, hair cut and thighs slimmed, has broken down walls into androgyny. "You don't look like a woman anymore," Suwelo exclaims, only to be confronted with elasticized notions of femininity: "Obviously," Carlotta laughs, "this is how a woman looks" (399).

As in the exchange above, where Carlotta's body is the site of change and invention, the wild gardens and the cottages of Walker's women artists are signs of the female body, whose uncolonized sexuality allows for artistic explosion. A lengthy passage, in which Fanny describes her love of spirits, establishes the house/body meta-

---

23. While this uncolonized maternal jungle roughly corresponds to the wilderness as a place of refuge and self-discovery in Melvin Dixon's *Ride Out the Wilderness: Geography and Identity in Afro-American Literature* (U of Illinois P, 1987), Walker operates outside Dixon's hierarchical framework, which from the underground sends the African American protagonist off to the mountaintop. With this gesture, Dixon convicts women novelists such as Hurston and Walker to difference for life by designating their "womanist spaces" a transitional function, paving the way for phallic heights.

phor, and, with its climactic organization, the connections between feminine self-invention and pleasure:

> "They open doors inside me. It's as if they're keys. To rooms inside myself. I find a door inside me and it's as if I hear a humming from behind it, and then I get inside somehow, with the keys the old ones give me, and are, and as I stumble about in the darkness of the room, I begin to feel the stirring in myself, the humming of the room, and my heart starts to expand with the absolute feeling of bravery, or love, or audacity, or commitment. It becomes a light, and the light enters me, by osmosis, and a part of me that was not clear before is clarified. I radiate this expanded light. Happiness." (185-86)

The libidinal-creative energy of women artists relates, in short, to the cosmic, unconscious and unappropriated female body. In the rather essentializing words of Cixous: "More so than men who are coaxed towards social success, toward sublimation, women are body. More body, hence more writing."[24] This celebration of femininity reverberates in Walker's descriptions of prehistoric women tribes, whose playful decorations of their anatomy with feathers, bark, sand, shells, and flowers constitute a bodily art that connects the women to the supernatural and inspires the envy of male tribes. Also Arveyda's mother expresses herself in a bodily discourse, when after years of "doing" for others she sits down to look out a window for three years: "She began to play with her makeup, painting her face, dyeing her hair, doing her nails as if she were creating a work of art with her body, and with her mind she appeared to roam great empty distances" (12-13). This cosmic, bodily art constitutes a sort of "anti-logos" weapon employed as well by Cixous's "admirable hysterics," who bombard masculine-Mosaic systems "with their carnal and passionate body words,... with their inaudible and thundering denunciations."[25] As Susan Willis notes in "Eruptions of Funk:

---

24. Cixous, "The Laugh of the Medusa," p. 257.
25. Cixous, "The Laugh of the Medusa," p. 257.

Historicizing Toni Morrison," on Morrison's eroticized descriptions, bodily representation explodes alienation and repression because "sensuality is embedded in a past which is inaccessible to sexual repression and bourgeois culture" and thus opens up for social and historical alternatives.[26] Interestingly, Fanny originally set up her massage shop to avoid marital and academic dominance. In a sensuously charged atmosphere of music and scent, Fanny inscribes as an artist her pain on the knotted body under her hands, and, at the end of a session, with both masseuse and client restored to themselves, "would look satisfied, as if she's achieved a sweet, if temporary, victory" (294).

However, while Fanny's satisfaction and the orgasmic structure of her house/body monologue indicate feminine (self)pleasure, the religious connotations of the passage introduce the female body as a temple, inhabited by spirit(s). In Walker's representation, women artists are vessels of spirituality, Goddesses of infinite power and wisdom. In the maternal jungle space, for example, the trees are "like cathedrals" (83); the African women who, through the generations, inhabit this space are angry "storehouses of energy" (267), worshippers of Medusa and Isis, "the Great Mother, Creator of All ... *The* Goddess" (268). Aware of her connections to African spirituality and creativity, Lissie tells Suwelo that his Uncle Rafe, "knowing me to contain everybody and everything, loved me wholeheartedly, as a goddess. Which I was" (372). The temple of Walker's title, which reappears in one of Lissie's dreams, is, in other words, a feminine text-body-space, occupied by a Goddess-Priestess and her interestingly phallic familiar or pet, a combination which suggests a Utopian dream of non-difference: an "in-between ... the ensemble of one and the other, not fixed in sequences of struggle and expulsion or some other form of death but infinitely dynamized by an incessant process of exchange from one subject to another."[27] In the postscript, Walker herself – as author or author-function – acknowledges her creative connec-

---

26. Susan Willis, "Eruptions of Funk: Historicizing Toni Morrison," in Gates, *Black Literature*, p. 268.
27. Cixous, "The Laugh of the Medusa," p. 254.

tion to process and infinity *a la* Lissie-as-Goddess: "I thank the universe for my participation in Existence. It is a pleasure to have always been present."

The spirituality of Walker's feminine artists is ultimately connected to their social/psychological function. While they are, as Arveyda speculates, messengers, whose modest task consists in "uniting the world" (123), they are, above all, allied with danger, with transformation. Their liminal sphere of activity becomes apparent, for example, in Zedé the Younger's tale of Ixtaphataphahex, whose name means the Goddess. Zedé describes this woman's role in female initiation rites as a feminine (non)center for liminal wetness, magic, and transition (46). On the socio-political level, Fanny unites with her African double, Nzingha, in writing plays in the tradition of their activist father, who comes to represent Fanny's discovery of roots and her escape from otherness. As in Carlotta's dream of being a cave-dweller, who fearlessly contemplates a "magnificently and scarily carved" wall decoration of a "strange beast with the head of a very ugly, big-nosed and long-lipped person," Walker's woman(ist) artist exists in a uteral zone of creativity and danger.

The red-slippered lion from Miss Lissie's last series of paintings marks this zone and presents itself as a sign of African American femininity. The self-portrait depicting a lion signals both the anonymity and marginality of the daring female I in relation to logocentric masculinity, and the multiplicity and difference of the feminine artist: the lion changes from painting to painting and is, moreover, unmistakably other, a depiction of concentrated energy and motion rather than a rational self. Its "dare-to-be-everything" lion's eyes nonetheless invites the reader/viewer to enter into its universe, where it has always existed, a knowing observer of natural and human life for generations and millenia. Associated with uncolonized African jungles, it communicates, moreover, the danger and wildness of its species, as well as its silent, prelinguistic modes of communication. It is, besides, a painting deconstructing the margin/center hierarchy, in that it invests significance in, above all, the detail: behind the lion's "tawny, luxuriant tail," itself a sign of the wasteful abundance of feminine art, is hidden the all-important "shiny red high-heeled slipper" (417). As argued in Siegfried Kracauer's work on ornamentation, the aesthetic detail satisfies the artist's subjective desire and, in a sense, prepares for new social formations by articulating repression. The ornamental detail accordingly links itself to flux, to transition, and to feminine expression.[28] The lion's wearing a shoe, in the first place, signifies in tricksterly fashion upon our preconceived expectations of good lion behavior and, furthermore, signals its unmistakable femininity.

The masculine I's studying this outrageous and powerful womanist text are ultimately changed by the experience. Suwelo, who has brought out the painting from under Hal's retirement home bed, has, through Lissie's paintings and stories, become able to experience the multiplicity and difference of Fanny (and Carlotta), and both Hal and Suwelo discover themselves to be in the presence of feminine magic. For in contemplating the red-slippered lion and listening to Lissie's tape-recorded tale of her prehistoric lion's life, Hal recovers his vision: "What's that reddish spot up in the corner?" (416). What Hal, without Lissie, sees somewhat imperfectly but Suwelo quite clearly is, of course, the feminine art through which they have both been transformed. Black or white, as Miss Lissie's many selves, this womanist art is above all red: daring, flamboyant, elegant, and dangerous.

---

28. See Siegfried Kracauer, *Orpheus in Paris: Offenbach and the Paris of His Time*, trans. Gwenda and Eric Mosbacher (New York: Vienna House, 1972).

Maya Angelou

CHAPTER ELEVEN

Bodies in Motion: Maya Angelou's *Wouldn't Take Nothing for My Journey Now*

In "A Journey through Life," a 1987 interview conducted by Valerie Webster of *The Yorkshire Post*, Maya Angelou promises her readers one more volume of autobiography, which would bring them up to the release of *I Know Why the Caged Bird Sings*, but no further. "After that," she tells the interviewer, "it would just be writing about writing which is something I don't want to do."[1] Angelou's collection of autobiographical essays, *Wouldn't Take Nothing for My Journey Now* (1993) nonetheless highlights the writing process, if only through its form. A series of expository prose segments – "Jealousy," for one, less than eight lines total – the collection offers Angelou's conclusions on a range of issues relating to (African American) women's lives, from pregnancy and charity to topics more explicitly related to speaking and writing: "Voices of Respect," "The Power of the Word," "Style." *Wouldn't Take Nothing* proposes, in fact, a theory of self-expression. It inserts into the text a procession of bodies that collectively narrate the story of African American lives. Its textual body points to the fragmentation and silences that characterize them, as well as to the kaleidoscopic perspectives that, like the title *Wouldn't Take Nothing*, gesture towards resistance and movement. Angelou accordingly passes on distillates of life wisdom to her audience through an autobiography that proposes the

---

1. Jeffrey M. Elliot, *Conversations with Maya Angelou* (Jackson: U P of Mississippi, 1989), p. 181.

body-in-motion, literal and textual, as a site of negotiation, and potentially, of change.

Historically, the African American body signifies enslavement and oppression; it is marked. "Marking," Carol Boyce Davies reminds us, "is the product of abuse and is linked to societal inscriptions on the body of the 'other.'"[2] The body functions, after all, as a "sorting mechanism" that assigns the dominant and the marginal their respective spaces in the body politic.[3] Female bodies and African color thus make for high visibility, never irrelevant, as Karla Holloway writes, "because of the specifically racist and sexist history of cultural politics in the United States."[4] Holloway's grandmother, in fact, warns her away from red, not a color for "nice" and, presumably, "dark" girls. To keep Karla Francesca out of trouble, her grandmother admonishes her to tone down her marked, public body: "dark skinned, daringly colored, and female."[5] Upon the African American woman's body, Karla learns, is inscribed "the history of gendered ethnic stereotype and abuse in U. S. history." It is "a site of public negotiation and private loss."[6] All too soon, the granddaughter enters the struggle to make this "common" body vaguely acceptable, what her grandmother calls "immaculate." In *The Alchemy of Race and Rights*, Patricia Williams describes the self-division and self-immolation among people of color that result in compulsive grooming:

> So we rub ointments on our skin and pull at our hair and wrap our bodies in silk and gold. We remake and redo and we sing and pray that the ugliness will be hidden and our beauty will shine through and be accepted. And we work

---

2. Carol Boyce Davies, *Black Women, Writing and Identity: Migrations of the Subject* (London: Routledge, 1994), p. 138.
3. Sidonie Smith, *Subjectivity, Identity, and the Body: Women's Autobiographical Practices in the Twentieth Century* (Bloomington: Indiana U P, 1993), p. 10.
4. Karla Holloway, *Codes of Conduct: Race, Ethics, and the Color of Our Character* (New Brunswick: Rutgers U P, 1995), p. 27.
5. Holloway, *Codes*, p. 17.
6. Holloway, *Codes*, p. 21.

and we work and we work at ourselves. Against ourselves, in spite of ourselves, and in subordination of ourselves.[7]

Karla Holloway regrets that Maya Angelou's performance at Bill Clinton's inauguration was uncharacteristically low key. She describes, in essence, the *absence* of Angelou's African American female body, which might have set in motion new readings and responses. By not insisting on ethnicity at the inauguration, Angelou inspired in Holloway a sense of cultural and racial loss. To Holloway, "Angelou's erasure of [African American] culture" thus reflects the Clinton Administration's "erasure of race as public policy."[8] Later, however, Holloway revises this reaction to Angelou's rendition: "I feel its words not 'merely spoken,' but deeply felt – the spirituals infusing their syllables with the dark and low tones that toll its story." By downplaying steps and gesture, Angelou reaches towards the others on the inaugural platform – as if, Holloway writes, "they too could share in the echoes of the song that resonate still for me."[9]

In both analyses of the inaugurational recital, Holloway stresses, however, the centrality of Angelou's body to interpretation, and, one might add, to writing. Tracing childhood, adolescence, courtship, and whatnot, autobiography constitutes "a script of female embodiment"[10]; it is a "fullbodied" genre, in which the bodies of writers participate in or become the text. By insisting upon the genre of autobiography, Angelou thus insists on the African American female body. She writes, in a sense, its history of private loss (and gain) into the public sphere, this time from a subject position.

Angelou's body – six feet tall and at the time six decades old – fills the pages of *Wouldn't Take Nothing for My Journey Now*. She describes, for example, her experience as an erotic dancer: "We were young and lithe. Our brown bodies shone with heavy applications

---

7. Patricia Williams, *The Alchemy of Race and Rights: Diary of a Law Professor* (Cambridge, Mass.: Harvard U P, 1991), p. 120.
8. Holloway, *Codes*, p. 81.
9. Holloway, *Codes*, p. 136.
10. Sidonie Smith, *Subjectivity*, p. 27.

of baby oil and Max Factor theatrical makeup."[11] Not only the ointments and the older women's hands readying her for the show by caressing her arms, her behind, and her back partake in Angelou's celebration of the African American/female body; in "Planned Pregnancy" she describes "the emergence of new and delightful sensualities" as the pregnant woman and her mate experience the changing female body moving towards parturition (133). By choosing clothes according to her own tastes and styles, Angelou further signals her enjoyment of body: "If I feel good inside my skin and clothes, I am thus free to allow my body its sway, its natural grace, its natural gesture" (56). With insistence on pleasure, Angelou rewrites the sexualized, marked body of the African American woman; as in Harriet Jacobs *Incidents in the Life of a Slave Woman*, freely chosen sexuality signifies humanity and pride. Other African American women, past and present, exist as powerful physical presences within Angelou's essays: the big-boned, cinnamon-colored Annie Henderson, Angelou's grandmother; Aunt Tee, who is "sinewy, strong, and the color of old lemons" (61).

Angelou represents as well the body as a site of depression and a spirituality that ultimate may suggest its dissolution. Sometimes, she writes, "it seems easier to lie prone than to press against the law of gravity and raise the body onto its feet and persist in remaining vertical" (79). The prone body signifies the giving in to the pressures of a racist society, just as the meeting with God that causes Angelou to fly may indicate more than liberation: "I am a big bird winging over high mountains, down into serene valleys. I am ripples of waves on silver seas. I'm a spring leaf trembling in anticipation" (76). The jubilant tone and vocabulary point towards change and potentiality, yet Angelou's dissolving body suggests as well what Lacan calls "fragilization," a reminder of the stressful and disrupted existence of the African American body.

Upon this background, writing functions as a gentle lover, whose caresses rescue this fragmented body, which even in "Sensual En-

---

11. Maya Angelou, *Wouldn't Take Nothing for My Journey Now* (1993, New York: Bantam, 1994), p. 95. Further references to this work will be given parenthetically in the text.

couragement," about Angelou's stint as a dancer, appears as "arms," "behind," and "back" (96). In various interviews, Angelou describes her writing routine much in the way one would an extra-marital romance, from renting a small motel room and going there at odd hours to the sipping of sherry and the rushed departure. To write autobiography has, moreover, as Susan Griffin reminds us, "an erotic edge," since the genre enters a private world and offers glimpses of what is usually veiled, "*private.*"[12] Not surprisingly, then, the textual body of *Wouldn't Take Nothing* is also a fragmented one, with short essays divided by blank pages, pages with merely a title, and texts beginning half-way down a page. This writing suggests, nonetheless, the pleasures of experimentation and, as in Mamie Garvin Fields's *Lemon Swamp,* the transformative power of the word.

The essay "Power of the Word" demonstrates not only the communicative but also the spiritual and ethical dimensions of language, as Angelou seeks to rescue words such as "purity," "goodness" and "worth" from oblivion and ridicule. Several essays in *Wouldn't Take Nothing* focus, indeed, on language as such, most eloquently in "Voices of Respect":

> When African Americans choose to speak sweetly to each other, not only do the voices fall in register, but there is an unconscious increase in music between the speakers. In fact, a conversation between friends can sound as melodic as a scripted song. (102)

African American voices may, like the bodies they inhabit, be marked, yet Angelou stresses the beauty, as well of the effectiveness, of their difference. Karla Holloway discusses in "The Body Politic" Lorene Cary's *Black Ice* in terms of African American women "turning it out," the decision to counter head-on racist stereotyping and behavioral patterns and moving race and sex to the center of the ensuing battle of words and wills.[13] Angelou herself

---

12. Susan Griffin, "Red Shoes," in Ruth-Ellen Joeres and Elizabeth Mittman, *The Politics of the Essay: Feminist Perspectives* (Bloomington: Indiana U P, 1993), p. 2.
13. Holloway, *Codes,* p. 30.

demonstrates mastery of such anti-authoritarian discourses not only in the title of *Wouldn't Take Nothing*. She stresses as well more subtle registers of resistance, as when in "Our Boys" she asks an acquaintance to repeat a racist phrase until he himself hears the insult. In a 1986 interview, she agrees with Russell Harris that linguistic skills are central to the fight for racial justice and emphasizes again the power of words: "A vocabulary is imperative. Imperative!"[14]

Implicitly, *Wouldn't Take Nothing* highlights the power of theory. Despite her declared unwillingness to write about writing, Angelou speaks with *Wouldn't Take Nothing* not only of dark female physicality but of and with the body of her text. Carol Boyce Davies contends in *Black Women, Writing and Identity* that theorizing does not necessarily limit itself to writing identifying itself as such.[15] As Barbara Christian points out in "The Race for Theory," African Americans theorize also in fiction, in folktales, in creative acts and arts.[16] The form of Angelou's text matters, in short, since it itself constitutes a theory of representing otherness. Moreover, Angelou's work demonstrates Edward Saïd's notion of "travelling theory," according to which a theory might move from its original position and function to other use(r)s. Also in various interviews does Angelou theorize about concepts such as identity, mobility, and place. "There is always movement ... nothing ceases," she states in discussing with Russell Harris the relation of African Americans to the dominant culture.[17]

Critics such as Deborah McDowell, Claudia Tate, Henry Louis Gates, Jr., Houston A. Baker and Ann DuCille have argued that African American literature does not simply depict experiental and social reality. Obviously, Angelou does not merely represent or distill her life in *Wouldn't Take Nothing*; she makes a series of formal choices, rewritten again by critical practices in its wake.

---

14. Elliot, p. 169.
15. Davies, p. 39.
16. Barbara Christian, "The Race for Theory," *Cultural Critique* 5 (Spring 1987), pp. 51-63.
17. Elliot, p. 167.

That Angelou chooses autobiography is hardly surprising; as she tells Jackie Kay in 1987, "I think I am the only serious writer who has chosen the autobiographical form as the main form to carry my work, my expression." Her feeling at this time of getting closer to "really manipulating and being manipulated" by the genre, to "pulling it open and stretching it"[18] points towards *Wouldn't Take Nothing*, in which she mixes autobiography and essay into a cocktail worthy of someone dedicated to the art of living well.

Though the essay is notoriously difficult to define,[19] the form shares with autobiography traits such as explicit authorial subjectivity, overlapping of subject and object, employment of experience as guiding principle, and, perhaps, a preference for non-fictional representation.[20] The self-relevation characteristic of at least the personal essay links the form with autobiography.

As the editors of *The Politics of the Essay* write in their introductory chapter, the origin of the essay is nonetheless entirely traditional, or, as they put it, "from a patriarchal European/white origin."[21] In this tradition, the essay serves a "clarifying" and "purifying" function by distilling, from the chaos of experience, pattern and form. The essay clears, for Montaigne and others, a space for reason and control.[22] Until very recently, it allies itself with mind, not with body. Susan Griffin explains: "As the essay moved further away from mediation and reflection, further from what we call 'confessions' and closer to science, with its claim of objectivity, it began to resemble more and more this celestially detached brain."[23] Both the brevity of Angelou's pieces and her prose reflect on occasion this tradition. She is given, for example, to sententiousness: "Living life as art requires a readiness to forgive" (65). It would

---

18. Elliot, p. 195.
19. Joeres and Mittman, p. 16; Tuzyline Jita Allan, "A Voice of One's Own: Implications of Impersonality in Essays of Virginia Woolf and Alice Walker," in Joeres and Mittman, p. 145.
20. Ruth-Ellen Joeres, "The Passionate Essay: Radical Feminist Essayists," in Joeres and Mittman, p. 156.
21. Joeres and Mittman, p. [12].
22. Joeres and Mittman, pp 13, 14.
23. Griffin, in Joeres and Mittman, p. 3.

seem that she approaches the double bind Katherine V. Snyder associates with Florence Nightingale: "masculine privilege is both the object of her social critique and the ultimate source from which she seeks discursive authority."[24] The perception of the essay as timeless, given to universal claims and truths, might clash with Angelou's womanist sympathies.[25]

Bettina Aptheker has claimed that the "legacy" of African American women is the responsibility to invent and inscribe the self historically withheld from them. From the Reconstruction novels preoccupied with marriage and domesticity to more recent literary productions such as Fields's *Lemon Swamp*, women of African descent have redefined the concept of womanhood while claiming "the right to participate in the American body politic and to control the politics of their own bodies."[26] Angelou's innumerable "I"s and "we"s, for example, disrupt essayistic objectivity and creates within a form still somewhat unaccustomed to such intimacy a site for what Allan calls "the aggressive recovery of self and race."[27] The essay's intersection of public and private space corresponds ideally to feminine experience and expression and dissolves, to a degree, the dilemma Ann DuCille describes in *The Coupling Convention*: "Can a critical practice claim *any* black experience without privileging it as *the* black experience, without valorizing it as the master narrative of the race?"[28] In *Wouldn't Take Nothing*, texts slide between the personal and the public, the individual and the representative, even between lines of color and gender. After all, African American writings intersect, as DuCille reminds us, with "so-called white cultural constructs and Western literary conventions."[29] The essay is a meeting point for self and world[30]; it com-

---

24. Katherine V. Snyder, "From Novel to Essay: Gender and Revision in Florence Nightingale's 'Cassandra,'" in Joeres and Mittman, p. 30.
25. Cp. Joeres, p. 164.
26. Bettina Aptheker, *Woman's Legacy: Essays on Race, Sex, and Class in American History* (Amherst: U of Massachusetts P, 1982), p. 30.
27. Allan, p. 136.
28. Ann DuCille, *The Coupling Convention: Sex, Text and Tradition in Black Women's Fiction* (New York: Oxford U P, 1993), pp. 6-7.
29. DuCille, p. 9.
30. Allan, p. 145.

bines form and forum and instigates the dialogue often identified with the genre.³¹

Angelou's mixture of essay and autobiography creates a hybrid form, which itself allows for the mixture of discursive fields characteristic of *Wouldn't Take Nothing*. Her shifts from quasifictional techniques to expository prose and back express the complexity of (African American) woman/ism. Like Hélène Cixous in "The Laugh of the Medusa," Angelou stresses and complicates the writing subject, which alternates between dominant presence and sudden absence. In "Further New Directions," Angelou seemingly vacates the scene through an impersonal, general mode of expression: "In order to survive, the ample soul needs refreshments and reminders daily of its right to be and to be wherever it finds itself." Immediately afterwards, however, she is fully present: "I was fired from a job when I was sixteen years old and was devastated" (79). Within the same segment, she communicates the dialogue between Maya and her flamboyant mother, Vivian Baxter, and ends the text with a poem written in her honor. Angelou stretches, in short, the traditional forms of essay and autobiography in order to articulate an African American/feminine perspective. Susan Griffin grapples with similar issues as she browses though a recent *Paris Review* and finds Natalie Sarraute is being interviewed: "'...it seemed impossible to me,' [Sarraute] said, 'to write in the traditional forms. They seemed to have no access to what we experienced.'"³² Like Griffin, Angelou reinvents, so to speak, the essay. She takes the elements of the genre suited to the self-expression of an African American woman – the personal emphasis, the basis in specific experiences, the process orientation and, not least, the elasticity and flexibility of the essay³³ – and discards the rest.

Angelou correlates her African American and her textual body in *Wouldn't Take Nothing* through a marking of self and of origins. With a specificity that undercuts the universalizing thrust of the

---

31. Joeres, pp. 155f.
32. Griffin, in Joeres and Mittman, p. 9.
33. Pamela Klass Mittlefehldt, "'A Weaponry of Choice': Black American Women Writers and the Essay," in Joeres and Mittman, p. 198.

essay, she discusses, say, her resistance to phrases such as "Don't mind me, I'm brutally frank" and "I hope you won't take this the wrong way" (117-118), or her decision to give herself a day away every year or so. Unlike the generalizing subject of traditional essays, she marks her difference first thing: "In All Ways a Woman," she titles the first chapter of *Wouldn't Take Nothing*. Like Karla Holloway, and like her own grandmother, Angelou thus refuses to tone down her marked body in the body of her text, which stands out female, and, to be sure, "daringly colored." In the process, Angelou manages not only to establish her own position and thus to insert herself into the body politic but also to reach out to her audience. By insisting on otherness, she allows non-dominant groups to identify with her and dominant groups to follow her – textually, if not literally.[34]

Angelou stresses in a 1986 interview the fluidity of the self,[35] a view she inscribes in *Wouldn't Take Nothing* by presenting herself from multiple angles and in multiple postures. The performativity of Angelou's body and voice is well documented, but within the confines of her text she manages as well to cover the range. She splits up her voice into an experiencing I, a commenting I and an I who presents the distilled life wisdoms gained on the way, and crosses as well identity lines separating genders, races and generations.

This "mobility of voice"[36] articulates perfectly the "beyond" or *au-delà* in which Homi K. Bhabha locates "border lives."[37] It allows, moreover, for the repetition variously associated with pleasure and with the problems of self-inscription.[38] Sidonie Smith notes in *Subjectivity, Identity and the Body* that autobiography has given the culturally marginalized a chance to enter into language rather than resign themselves to the "inauthentic voices" assigned to them by the dominant culture.[39] If, as Carol Boyce Davies suggests with the subtitle to *Black Women, Writing and Identity: Migrations of the Subject*,

---

34. Joeres, p. 159.
35. Elliot, p. 163.
36. Sidonie Smith, *Subjectivity*, p. 120.
37. Homi K. Bhabha, *The Location of Culture* (London: Routledge, 1994), p. 1.
38. Bhabha, pp. 56-57.
39. Sidonie Smith, *Subjectivity*, p. 61.

the literary productions of African American women are always already boundary-crossing, the essay might equally well give form to their transgressions. It does not, after all, fit classical lyric-epic-dramatic paradigms; it lacks the neat packaging of poetry and the "narrative completion" of novels and short fiction.[40] Its "elusiveness" and "fringe nature" might indeed suit it particularly to the needs of writers "themselves on the fringe." Moreover, as Joeres argues, the essay resembles the political tract or speech and thus lends itself to arguments for change.[41] What Mittlefehldt calls the genre's "own internal tensions" makes it a useful weapon for women of African descent.[42] In a conversation with Rosa Guy in 1988, Angelou refers to her decision to enter a literature dominated in the West by white men as "the canvas of contradiction"; she recognizes, besides, that as an African American (writer) she is always already politicized.[43] The author of "Our Boys," for example, is also an instructor in the politics of race: "We all should know that diversity makes for a rich tapestry, and we must understand that all the threads of the tapestry are equal in value no matter their color; equal in importance no matter their texture" (124).

As the "we-ness"[44] of her narrating voice suggests, Angelou dramatizes the dialogic pattern characteristic of African American women writers. Even within the genre of autobiography, associated with individual experience and achievement, she calls out to other selves, other experiences, and other spaces than those she herself has occupied. Angelou's communal approach to writing and living represents a theoretical and political choice. For one thing, by elasticizing self-other schisms, Angelou provides women of African descent, historically "the other of the other," with a chance to speak.[45] She joins, moreover, a narrative circle of women writers who, as Sidonie Smith notes about Harriet Jacobs, "eschews the representation of herself as the isolato, self-contained in her rebellion, figur-

---

40. Mittlefehldt, p. 208.
41. Joeres, p. 152.
42. Mittlefehldt, p. 197.
43. Elliot, pp. 219, 196.
44. Sidonie Smith, *Subjectivity*, p. 68.
45. Sidonie Smith, *Subjectivity*, p. 34.

ing herself instead as dependent always on the support of family and friends...."[46] Angelou stresses the *inter* of interactive and international, an "in-between space" that, in Homi K. Bhabha's phrase, "may elude the politics of polarity" and allow us "to emerge as the others of our selves."[47]

This traveling, elusive, yet ever-present "diasporan subject," to use Sidonie Smith's term for Hurston, travels in- and outside identities, simultaneously critical and appreciative. This body-in-motion is also, as Smith writes, "intimately tied to community as the other tongue crosses over its tongue endlessly and the other of the tongue speaks."[48] Angelou's language of mobility takes a good deal of courage, for a woman (writer/traveler). In "On the Road Again: Metaphors of Travel in Cultural Criticism," Janet Wolf proposes a relationship between masculinity and travel metaphors, not simply because access to the road is gender-specific and unproblematic mobility accordingly a deception.[49] The "already-gendered language of mobility," she argues, pushes aside women participating in cultural theory, or any other theoretical project. The metaphors of travel and movement, frequently employed in efforts to destabilize dicourses of power, thus work conservatively in terms of gender.

Fearlessly, Angelou nonetheless employs an imagery of movement throughout *Wouldn't Take Nothing for My Journey Now*. In "Passport to Understanding," she extends the title metaphor of the life journey; travel becomes a vehicle for appreciating cultural and national difference: "I encourage travel to as many destinations as possible for the sake of education as well as pleasure" (11). Travel functions, in short, as a metaphor of affinity and tolerance: "perhaps travel cannot prevent bigotry, but by demonstrating that all peoples cry, laugh, eat, worry, and die, it can introduce the idea that if we try to understand each other, we may even become friends" (12). Another chapter heading, "Extending the Bounda-

---

46. Sidonie Smith, *Subjectivity*, p. 50.
47. Bhabha, p. 38.
48. Sidonie Smith, *Subjectivity*, p. 124.
49. Janet Wolf, "On the Road Again: Metaphors of Travel in Cultural Criticism," *Cultural Studies* 7.2 (May 1993), p. 235.

ries," carries the language of travel into the realm of body, sexuality and race. In "Voices of Respect," the language of movement serves to communicate Angelou's views on child-rearing in the African American community: "If we persist in self-disrespect and then ask our children to respect themselves, it is as if we break all their bones and then insist that they win Olympic gold medals for the hundred-yard dash" (103).

By depicting herself and others in motion, Angelou reappropriates, as Wolf recommends,[50] the metaphors of travel for her own purposes. She rearranges, for example, the concept of home, the site that frames the concept of travel. To her, home involves a series of locations, much as bell hooks describes what has traditionally been a place of conflict and repression for women (of color):

> The very meaning of home changes with the experience of decolonization, of radicalization. At times home is nowhere. At times one knows only extreme estrangement and alienation. Then home is no longer just one place. It is locations. Home is that place which enables and promotes varied ever-changing perspectives, a place where one discovers new ways of seeing reality, frontiers of difference.[51]

Home, in other words, can be a site of beginnings, of unpredictability.[52]

Angelou further usurps travel as metaphor and mode of existence by relating ideas of identity and motion to Africa. Though she stresses the importance of reading Aristotle, Plato, Pascal, she emphasizes especially what the African folk tale may teach us about movement:

> One must worry over ideas that if I come forward how far do we have to go before we meet? And when we meet will I go through you and you go through me and continue till we

---

50. Wolf, p. 235.
51. Qtd. Davies, p. 49.
52. Cp. Bhabha, p. 62.

meet someone else? This is an African concept. Do we stay once we meet or do I actually go right through you and pass through you and continue on that road.[53]

Furthermore, like the editors of collections such as *Charting the Journey: Writings by Black and Third World Women*,[54] Angelou uses the frameworks of home and exile to map where she is going and where she has been.

The African American female body traveling across the pages of Angelou's works is not, however, the nomad of postmodern feminist theory but rather what Davies labels a migratory subject, "moving to specific places and for specific reasons."[55] Angelou as author-function shares the flexibility and fluidity of the nomadic subject, as when she argues for life as adventure, even art. We must, she writes, "remember that we are created creative and can invent new scenarios as frequently as they are needed" (66). In shifting between the local and the global, between Winston-Salem, say, and the diaspora, Angelou further links up to postmodern subjectivity. Yet Angelou remains firmly in control of her journey, at least discursively. Her somewhat sententious style indicates her sense of purpose and locates her simultaneously "elsewhere" and "somewhere."

What constitutes a journey in Angelou's usage further removes her from the travellers Janet Wolf identifies. In *Wouldn't Take Nothing*, Angelou describes what Deleuze calls "trips in intensity" or journeys *in situ*.[56] Typical of the genre of autobiography, she charts the distance travelled from a younger version of the self to the moment of writing. At forty-one, for example, she began, as she

---

53. Elliot, p. 172.
54. Shabna Grewal, Jackie Kay, *et al.*, *Charting the Journey: Writings by Black and Third World Women* (London: Sheba Feminist Publishers, 1988).
55. Davies, p. 37. See also Helen Taylor's discussion of Angelou and the diaspora in "'A Black Ocean, Leaping and Wide': The Ambition of Maya Angelou," Chapter 6 in *Circling Dixie: Contemporary Southern Culture Through a Transatlantic Lens* (New Brunswick, N.J.: Rutgers U P, 2001).
56. Giles Deleuze, "Nomad Thought," in *The New Nietzche*, ed. David B. Allison (New York: Dell, 1977), p. 149.

writes, "a performance which now, more than twenty years later, can cause me to seriously consider changing my name and my country of residence" (110). Moreover, she distinguishes herself from her communities by subscribing to what Davies calls the "visitor theory" approach, "a kind of *critical relationality* in which various theoretical positions are interrogated for their specific applicability to Black women's experiences and textualities and negotiated within a particular inquiry with a necessary eclecticism." In other words, Angelou goes "a piece of the way" with the characters and positions she introduces in her writings, but ultimately chooses her individual path. The result is, in Smith's phrase, a "mobility of voice," a "self-multiplication"[57] that places Angelou in an intriguing relation to the communities she identifies.

The definition of community is in itself elusive. Variously defined as "an appeal to a collective praxis," "the commonality of our differences,"[58] it depends, as Homi Bhabha reminds us, on "what's being said and who's saying what, who's representing who?" "I have trouble," he admits in *The Location of Culture*, "with thinking all these things as monolithic fixed categories."[59] Angelou, however, gets around the problems of usurping other voices and perspectives by locating herself in a variety of contexts. Like Karla Holloway in *Codes of Conduct*, she abandons the division between private and public domains and insists on the perspective of an African American woman.[60] "Her history," Holloway argues, "overwhelmingly [encourages] her to hold in tandem all of the components of her identity."[61] Angelou's writings, then, remain centered in the history, lives and bodies of African Americans. After all, she inscribes the usage of many of her people in the title of her collection. "Wouldn't take nothing," she says, signaling with the

---

57. Sidonie Smith, *Subjectivity*, pp. 120-21.
58. Joan Wallach Scott, "The Campaign against Political Correctness, in *PC Wars: Politics and Theory in the Academy*, ed. Jeffrey Williams (New York: Routledge, 1995), p. 42.
59. Bhabha, p. 3.
60. Cp. Brita Lindberg-Seyersted, *Black and Female: Essays on Writings by Black Women in the Diaspora* (Oslo: Scandinavian U P, 1994), p. 75.
61. Holloway, *Codes*, pp. 10-11.

double negative from where and to whom she is primarily traveling. Though Angelou explicitly addresses herself to an international readership, the superaddressee of her life story, to use Bakhtin's term, remains the people of African descent for whom her experiences may have a special resonance. Most explicitly, Angelou as narrator communicates her membership of the African American community through the first and second person plural pronoun. "We have used these terms [of kinship]," she writes in "Voices of Respect," "to help us survive slavery, its aftermath, and today's crisis of revived racism." In other statements, however, Angelou discreetly withdraws into third person and preliminary subjects to allow for other readers and experiences to join in: "When African Americans choose to speak sweetly to each other, not only do the voices fall in register, but there is an unconscious increase in music between the speakers" (102).

With this gesture, Angelou establishes a community of writer and audience that contributes to the wide circulation of her works. She includes, for example, a series of anecdotes in *Wouldn't Take Nothing* that minimizes the distance between writers and readers,[62] among them her martini-based attempts at getting and holding the attention of a group of male journalists of African descent, who remain oblivious to her accomplishments in a variety of areas: house-keeping, publishing, sex, clothing, and more. Explaining her determination to disregard race and nationality in choosing future partners, this incident in "Extending the Boundaries" illustrates as well the performative dimension of Angelou's prose. As we have seen, her career as a performer spills into the pages of *Wouldn't Take Nothing*, for example in "Sensual Encouragement," but also in the self-dramatization of the work. Angelou fills the text with bodies, who enact the life lessons she shares with her readership. As Paul Gilroy explains, the performance of "expressive cultures" seeks to connect performer and audience through "dialogic rituals" that encourage the symbols or formations of community."[63]

---

62. Allan, p. 137.
63. Bhabha, p. 30.

Angelou identifies as well with a community of writers, predominantly but not exclusively of African American women. "I'm impressed," she states in *Conversations*, "by Toni Morrison a great deal... I'm impressed by the growth of Rosa Guy. I'm impressed by Ann Petry. I'm impressed by the work of Joan Didion.... I would walk fifty blocks in high heels to buy the works of any of these writers" (156). Also William Shakespeare, Paul Laurence Dunbar, James Weldon Johnson, and James Baldwin belong to this community, which, however rooted in African American experiences and cultures, transcends gender, time, and race.

The courage Angelou stresses as the unifying characteristic of these writers would apply as well to her community of women. She places first in *Wouldn't Take Nothing* the essay "In All Ways a Woman" to signal the importance of this community, and the many calls for courage it faces. "Being a woman is hard work," she states. "Not without joy or even ecstasy, but still relentless, unending work" (6). At times she sounds like a feminist, as when she notes that "in a time and world where males hold sway and control, the pressure upon women to yield their rights-of-way is tremendous" (6). She encourages women to cultivate a sense of humor and an eye for absurdity, qualities that might come in handy in what she considers a gender war: "Women should be tough, tender, laugh as much as possible, and live long lives. The struggle for equality continues unabated, and the woman warrior who is armed with wit and courage will be among the first to celebrate victory" (7). Angelou moves, however, from this oppositional positioning of women into a more womanist realm, where playfulness and abandonment might liberate women from "becoming a mirror image of those men who value power above life" (7).

Though Angelou goes out of her way to include others, for example by addressing directly her (female) readers, she avoids the first person plural in discussing the feminine. She remains an "I," and readers "you," and she thus asserts the individual within the communal, as in her advice on style. Writing simultaneously inside and outside the group, she escapes the fixity she finds claustrophobic. Her oscillations between sameness and difference create "a multiple *dialogic of differences*," which, in Sidonie Smith's formulation, "operates to both accommodate and diffuse identification between narrator and reader."[64] In her discussion of community bonds, Angelou as author/body simultaneously rests and flies.

From this traveling perspective, Angelou stresses the importance of alliances. She worries about divisions within the African American community and in her writings lavishes first/second person plural pronouns upon discussions of this issue. Their divisions healed, African Americans would challenge the current definition of nation and establish instead a diasporic community across traditional political borders. In discussing with Rosa Guy the "casual indifference" of young African Americans to their history, Angelou emphasizes that their future is linked with, say, Nicaragua or the Middle East.[65] Immediately afterwards in this 1988 interview, Angelou turns to the topic of women of color, thus implicitly supporting the contention of feminist scholars that the concept of "nation" originates in masculine, Eurocentric thought. Angelou returns, in fact, to the shared, often painful history of various ethnic groups out of her belief that human bodies and experiences are more alike than unalike. As she puts it in *Conversations*, "black Americans have been here since the year 1619, and this is as much our country as anybody else's, save the Native Americans. We will all live together or not at all."[66] To all human beings, she argues, community functions as a support system that helps us survive and endure.

Motion and writing help Angelou establish the community bonds that make possible this survival. These activities become reconnection, a literal and symbolic way of healing differences in the process of acknowledging them. Carol Boyce Davies explains:

> Because we were/are products of separations and dislocations and dis-memberings, people of African descent in the Americas historically have sought reconnection. From the "flying back" stories which originated in slavery ... this need to reconnect and re-member ... has been a central impulse in the structuring of Black thought.[67]

---

64. Sidonie Smith, *Subjectivity*, p. 52.
65. Elliot, p. 234.
66. Elliot, p. 158.
67. Davies, p. 17.

By crossing boundaries, *Wouldn't Take Nothing* shifts the categories and the canons that have traditionally defined African American women's writings. Body, movement, and writing thus bring about a new, more fluid identity, much like Angelou describes herself in "A Day Away": "If I am living in a city, I wander streets, window-shop, or gaze at buildings. I enter and leave public parks, libraries, the lobbies of skyscrapers, and movie houses. I stay in no place for very long" (138). The subjectivity of *Wouldn't Take Nothing* accordingly moves towards the "affinity" politics Donna Haraway associates with the cyborg and Sidonie Smith with late-twentieth-century autobiography.[68] Individual/communal, grounded/in motion, the narrator of *Wouldn't Take Nothing* resists, escapes, and writes.

Wouldn't Take Nothing for My Journey Now thus constitutes a rejection not only of established racial and generic but also narrative paradigms. Its textual body speaks of the fragmentation characteristic of twentieth century writings and lives, yet manages, at the same time, to present a vision of difference. Like the radical essayists Joeres explores, Angelou has elasticized a previously elitist form not only by mixing it with autobiography but also by bridging within the essayistic space the individual and the communal, male and female, European American and African American, conservatism and radicalism. If, as some critics argue, the essayist resembles a traveller due to the aura of "containment," "detachment," and distance that characterize both,[69] Angelou takes herself and her readership into territories where involvement and tolerance are mandatory, and where bodies of all colors and genders intermingle.

---

68. Sidonie Smith, *Subjectivity*, pp. 181f.
69. Mittlefehldt, p. 197.

Ruth Moose

CHAPTER TWELVE

Southern Dreams: Ruth Moose's Fiction

The opening lines of "Cows, Coathangers, and the K-Mart Kid," a title in Ruth Moose's second collection of short stories, *Dreaming in Color* (1989), hint beneath a caption, "The Voice," at the author's aesthetics:

> Each neighborhood must have a single voice. One nobody would claim. A sound you'd hear if you put your ear to the ground in the middle of the night. A chatty, busybody, gossipy, snippy sort of barnyard voice that is heard when people live too close and pick, pick, pick into each other's lives.[1]

Belonging simultaneously to somebody and nobody, Moose's neighborhood voice enjoys the mimetic, bodiless freedom that to Joyce Carol Oates characterizes the craft of writing. "Consisting solely of words," she writes in *(Woman) Writer: Occasions and Opportunities* (1988), "it demands no displacement or intrusion in the world; it exults in its own being."[2] The adjectives of the Moose passage suggest, however – if only ironically – that her exuberant no-body is somehow gendered. Chatty, gossippy, communal and contextual, the voice of Moose's southern neighborhood implies femininity and domesticity, as well as a reliance on audience alien to Oates's

---

1. Ruth Moose, *Dreaming in Color* (Little Rock: August House, 1988), p. 145. References to Moose's fiction will appear parenthetically in the text, with the abbreviation *DC* for *Dreaming in Color* and *WR* for *The Wreath Ribbon Quilt and Other Stories* (Laurinburg, NC: St. Andrew's P, 1987).
2. Joyce Carol Oates, *(Woman) Writer: Occasions and Opportunities* (New York: E.P. Dutton, 1988), p. 26.

celebration of the uniquely individual. Moose's reader must, it seems, be willing to put an ear to the ground at uncomfortable hours in order to help shape her stories. In other words, the author invites her audience to inhabit the southern community of her fiction and help bring to life the female dreams and nightmares characteristic of her work. Both *Dreaming in Color* and *The Wreath Ribbon Quilt*, her first collection of stories published in 1987, demonstrate that what Oates labels "the primitive force fields that generate 'theme' (or obsession)"[3] for Ruth Moose, as for other writers in this volume, is southern female life, with language an important means of self-definition and -invention. As in the quoted paragraph, language overflows, repeats, and creates the feminine South that also engages this North Carolina writer, in whose work theme becomes technique; obsession, metaphor. Or, as Daphne Athas writes in "Why There Are No Southern Writers," "if Southernness was once an obvious characteristic of writers, it is now mere evidence, detectable in style, waiting perhaps to be recognized."[4]

While Joyce Carol Oates complains that readers abroad interpret American writings as "allegorical" and "self-consciously 'American'" ... ("what is idiosyncratic becomes symbolic"),[5] Ruth Moose flaunts the regionalism that critics – northern, transatlantic or whatever – invariably identify in contemporary southern writings. In fact, she establishes in her stories a chorus of southern literary voices that, unlike anxiety-ridden misprisioners, forms a harmonious polyphony of primarily feminine influences. Faulkner, of course, looms simultaneously as absence and presence in Aunt Lillian's discussion in "Judas at the Table" of her family heritage of neurosis, paranoia, and depression (*DC* 174), just as the "bad house" in the suburban Ashwood Heights of another *Dreaming in Color* story is veiled in disease imagery. Like the mansion in "A Rose for Emily" it seems to the surrounding community an eyesore (*DC* 146).

Almost rendering inaudible the inevitable paternal voice, however, echoes of literary mothers and daughters resound in Moose's

---

3. Oates, p. 4.
4. Daphne Athas, "Why There Are No Southern Writers," in *Women Writers of the Contemporary South*, ed. Peggy Prenshaw (Jackson: U P of Mississippi, 1984), p. 306.
5. Oates, p. 335.

fiction. The small town teeming with a mixture of eccentricity and normalcy evokes Eudora Welty, while the Bible Belt (anti)Christs, and Betta'lain of "Sisters Under the Skin" (cheerfully retarded with a string of teabags round her neck) hint at Flannery O'Connor. Moose's predilection for the adolescent point of view, as during the fast wedding of "Green Lightning and the Tablecloth Bride," might stem from Carson McCullers. Parallels to Bobbie Anne Mason suggest themselves in Moose's ironic pleasure in New South icons such as K-Marts, Pepsi trucks, and flowered plastic placemats, as well as in her women characters' fatigue with their ineffectual, frequently unemployed and emotionally sterile husbands. Moose shares with Mamie Fields, Alice Walker and Maya Angelou the generational emphasis, in addition to a metaphorical preoccupation with gardens and kitchens as feminine artistic territory. These domestic settings, and a repeated focus on so-called "contact points" involving family and community members and strangers, are typical also of Anne Tyler.[6] With these and other gestures towards the inescapable southern tradition, Moose makes it her own. And, as with the wreath ribbon quilt of her title, she simultaneously commemorates her heritage and reshapes it to unexpected purposes.

Moose's narration relies, to be sure, on techniques by which short stories condense entire lives into significant moments: memory and association. Her method of juxtaposing two narrative levels, frequently interweaving past and present time to suggest the texture of southern life, moves her plots towards increased complication and deeper narrative layers, with characters' ellipses and evasions providing suspense as events and patterns unfold. Her preference for linear chronology in stories such as "Biography in 7 Lives," which follows the protagonist through life from fifteen to forty, further links Moose with traditional short story methodology, as do her various "wallpaper stories," defined by Kay Boyle as a text in which an often eccentric character enters the lives of others, has a significant impact, and exits.[7]

---

6. See Mary F. Robertson, "Anne Tyler: Medusa Points and Contact Points," in *Contemporary American Women Writers: Narrative Strategies,* ed. Catherine Rainwater and William J. Scheick (Lexington: U P of Kentucky, 1985).
7. Doris Betts, "The Fiction of Anne Tyler," in Prenshaw, p. 34.

Even Moose's established short story devices, however, show traces of experimentation. Verbal associative links may be humorously subversive, as when metaphorical wolves at the door in "Who Cooks for You?" (embodied in "the food market woolf," "the utility company woolf," or "the mortgage woolf") turn into a woolf of the male persuasion, with an appetite for microwave demonstrators (*DC* 105). Moreover, Moose's extensive use of dialogue for exposition and characterization suggests what Ronald Schleifer labels the "maieutic" function of discourse. As a sort of midwife, the author transmits the play of voices with the aim of creating an occasion for listening, perhaps indeed for collaboration. Moose's storytelling depends, like motherhood in Julia Kristeva's analysis, on a heterogeneous otherness outside authorial control that might induce a "permanent calling into question."[8] Indeed, the author-narrator's voices blend with characters' voices, a *style indirect libre* making for overlapping idioms and phrases. This technique results in a suggestive balance of empathy and ironic distance between the author and the lives portrayed, a simultaneous confirmation and calling into question of southern society.

Moose achieves a similar ambiguity on the paragraph and sentence levels. In "Biography in 7 Lives," the opening story of *The Wreath Ribbon Quilt*, short, terse sentences or sentence fragments create an effect of tight-lipped rage, as in the segment "At Forty": "I find my son in the closet kissing the Avon lady. She is fifteen, dressed in blue. Her hat and satchel match. Her legs in fringed short jeans match. It's our latest shade, she says. Would you care for a sample?" (*WR* 11). Not only the vignette form of the text itself, which freezes the protagonist into seven shots and inscribes narrative silences into her life story, but also the insistence on verbal economy within individual sentences suggests a character practically muted by repressed resentment. At the same time, however, Moose's ever-present humor undercuts her heroine's anger, frequently, as in Alice Walker's fiction, through irreverent details that unbalance the overall narrative. When the son leaves with the

---

8. Ronald Schleifer, "Grace Paley: Chaste Compactness," in Rainwater and Scheick, pp. 42, 43.

Southern Dreams: Ruth Moose's Fiction

Avon lady in a van, his mother reads on the rear bumpersticker "Preserve Wildlife. Kill Hunters." And though Savannah of "The Women's Club" resents the ladling out of guilt that compels her to join the club, she notices at her installment ceremony with a mixture of rage and humor that she now reeks "of Estee Lauder in all twenty-eight flavors" (*DC* 25). As Naomi Schor argues, the feminine detail disturbs the dominant discourse,[9] which in both *The Wreath Ribbon Quilt* and *Dreaming in Color* is decidedly feminist. Moose accordingly tempers anger with humor; feminism, with femininity. Or, to use a term from "Moon Over Magnolias" meaning anyone teasingly put down, she "magnolias" her audience (*WR* 15).

As the title "Moon Over Magnolias" implies, Moose's discursive strategies include as well the sentimental model, which simultaneously legitimizes and comments upon the quotidian women's lives of her fiction. The minister in "Moon over Magnolias" looks to Annabelle, the protagonist, like Robert Redford, a detail suggestive of the interpretative framework of Moose's characters. In "Green Lightning and the Tablecloth Bride," Moose employs the structure of courtship, wedding, honeymoon, and motherhood to tell the story of the lush Frances Anne Gurley from the point of view of May Kay, an admiring adolescent girl up the street. Yet the story draws its energy from departures from the sentimental plot, present as well in the girls' addiction to magazines like "True Heart" and "Intimate Romances." Neighbors procure Frankie's wedding dress, cake, bouquet, and other ceremonial paraphernalia, including a preacher, within less than three hours, and the shotgun wedding becomes a shotgun separation as during the first night of the honeymoon policemen arrest and imprison the groom. In "King of the Comics" the Superman collector living next door lures the preteen Frances Bolt with magazines like "Love Secrets" and "Five Exciting Romances in One Big Issue," only to violate her youthful naiveté in going to his room with dirty hands grabbing her halter and sharp teeth hurting her lips. The merging of popular culture and female life in the contemporary South informs as well "The Green Car,"

---

9. Naomi Schor, *Reading in Detail: Aesthetics and the Feminine* (New York: Routledge, Chapman and Hall, 1987).

in which the narrator within two sentences compares herself to a pioneer wife and to the women of *Gunsmoke* (*DC* 86).

By engaging popular cultural forms on the level of narrative technique, Moose portrays a female culture rooted in dailiness and repetition, while the discrepancies between popular ideals and everyday realities make for a humorous blend of critique and endorsement. Like any model Adonis, one beau of "Green Lightning ..." sports hair "so wavy it made you dizzy to look long" and even plays the guitar; unlike his magazine or movie counterparts he has learned this romantic skill "in twelve easy lessons" (*WR* 106). To imagine him a romantic hero points both, Ruth Moose implies, towards triviality and imagination.

Moose's narrative technique thus engages popular fiction, soaps, and, as the title *Dreaming in Color* hints, photography and film. Stories such as "The Women's Club" and "Happy Birthday, Billy Boy" both invest climactic energy in the taking of photographs, with final passages pointing towards the author's visual sensibility. Take Savannah facing the club women:

> The ladies blink. It is as if she has taken their photograph. This is the moment later. They move from the ranks and back to their lives. Savannah takes the photograph home and for a long time finds it hard to flip past the images lodged like a slide caught crosswise in a projector, light cutting off the corners and edges until the whole thing rounds like an eye. The projector fan hums in her head and the dust motes of all time dance, dance like things alive in the air. (*DC* 30)

While the photographic or cinematic representation here functions primarily metaphorically and thematically in the merging of past and present time, the passage experiments as well with the invention of a female gaze. The slide is, after all, "caught crosswise" to suggest an-other perspective blocking linear movement. As Savannah attempts to look, the slide itself turns into an eye, thus obliterating the difference between subject and object in a sort of double vision characteristic of Moose's own representational strategies. The four-generation photograph closing "Happy Birthday, Billy Boy" also implies a different feminine vision. Though "everybody" applauds the picture in the *Horsepoint Herald*, seemingly illustrating familial and social stability, the protagonist, Evanelle, knows that D.R. the D.J. and not her husband has fathered Billy Boy, a detail that certainly widens the symbolic possibilities of the photographed generations. With Evanelle looking at Evanelle looking, the female gaze makes for a cross-eyed interpretation that substitutes the title's celebration of masculinity with the ending's imaging of femininity.

The cinematic influences on Moose's narration surface most obviously in her use of montage in texts such as "Biography in 7 Lives," "He Holds a Black Umbrella," and "Friends and Oranges," in which the juxtaposition of scenes and fragments increases dramatic and symbolic effects. Even in more seamless stories, however, her dialogues suggest a scenic imagination, as do her interruptions of narrative sequences with shots of poignant details. In "The Vinegar Jug," for example, which depicts a marital battle between Sharon and her unemployed husband, Rob, Sharon's thoughts and actions are truncated with close-ups of the couple's old cat, Rob's brush-cutting axe, and the copperhead swinging on a beech tree, "like a warning" (*WR* 37).

Other elements of classic Hollywood cinema address more directly Moose's preoccupation with the construction of womanhood. As in traditional film narration, she interrupts plot movement to dwell on a female figure, a technique that, as Laura Mulvey has shown, makes for visual pleasure and the alignment of Woman with (narrative) trouble.[10] But Moose consistently teases the pleasure invited through lingering close-ups of women characters by disappointing the erotic expectations of the (male) gaze, as in "The Eyes of Argus": "Mrs. Holly was thin as a post with long stilt-like legs, dangling arms and large hands. She had quick black eyes that didn't miss a trick and knew everything in the neighborhood before it happened" (*WR* 67-68). Moose confronts the audience's gaze not only with Mrs. Holly's own "quick black eyes" but also by depriving her of erotic potential. And, when such erotic possibility seems omni-

---

10. See Laura Mulvey's classic essay "Visual Pleasure and Narrative Cinema," *Screen* 16.3 (1975), pp. 6-18.

present, as in "Even the Bees in Denmark," Moose's female protagonist goes all out to protect the erotic object from the gaze of the male spectator.

The American husband of "Even the Bees...," which deals with a couple's vacation in Denmark, identifies himself with looking by frequenting museums, carrying a camera, and, most significantly, by diverting himself (and later Baptist and Methodist friends back home) with Danish beach nudity. His wife resents his eroticizing what she considers natural and holds to herself "a scene he missed, he'd never know because she'd never tell him" (*DC* 177). While the husband is busily staring at paintings, his wife watches the lawn outside the art museum:

> In the center of the lawn lay a woman on a blanket. She wore a straw hat tied under her chin with a purple scarf, sunglasses and sandals. Otherwise she was nude. Completely naked. She had narrow hips, long legs, and very large breasts. She too was reading and looked completely comfortable where she was, as she was. No one paid any attention to her. (*DC* 186)

The female spectator here observes the naked woman in context and protects her from erotic objectification by blocking her husband's view. Significantly, his camera is broken throughout their stay in Denmark, a reminder of the limitations of his vision. In the words of his wife, aligning herself with Woman in/as trouble, "all he did was fuss about the good photos he missed, the great shots" (*DC* 187). With similar cunning, Moose herself draws on photographic and cinematic techniques to deconstruct Woman as spectacle and invent a feminine point of view.

Ultimately, Moose's narrative devices activate the linguistic struggle permeating "Even the Bees...." By denying her husband's visual pleasure, the wife has, in a sense, rewritten the story he would like to tell: "'The best-looking one I saw was in downtown Copenhagen, broad daylight,' [then he would] laugh at his pun, describe the scene, embellish all of it. Destroy it for her." Against his outpourings she proposes a knowledgeable and victorious silence: "Later when he talked on and on of the nude beaches, she smiled, said nothing" (*DC* 187). By keeping her mouth shut, the wife expresses, with other of Moose's women (not to mention Jaques Lacan), that language constitutes masculine territory, yet she experiments, like Moose and other writers discussed, with techniques articulating feminine positions.

Several stories further explore the southern geography of language that to Moose privileges the male speaker. "At Twenty-One," a vignette of "Biography in 7 Lives," describes the female protagonist's alienation from the corporate world in which "the numbers are a language all their own." "I cannot speak it...," she acknowledges. During lunch breaks she seeks out a fruit vendor who "speaks no English" but represents the possibility of other communicational modes. His perfect fruit is, she notices, "shiny enough for a painting." When the vendor eventually speaks, however, his words express the masculine desire that marginalizes feminine experience: "We mekka beautiful baby, no?" (*WR* 8-9). Other men in Moose's fiction linguistically ally themselves with institutions such as the university and the church, thus censoring feminine discourses. The truth about Rob's novel in "The Vinegar Jug" is, Sharon observes, "that academia had stilted his style, locked in his vocabulary," but when she tries to suggest re-visions, "he couldn't see them, argued, became loud" (*WR* 36). The voice of the preacher who in "The Swing" addresses "Our Father" seems to his wife "like an old motor grinding, yet running forever" (*WR* 56). Patsy's father of "The Silver Crescent" occupies both metaphorically and linguistically the driver's seat and, over her mother's objections, silences the daughter returning from a New Jersey vacation: "'My flesh and blood don't talk Yankee.' Daddy slammed on brakes for a stop sign. I didn't say anything else, except in whispers..." (*DC* 136). Among women, however, silence might articulate understanding and closeness beyond words. The daughter parting with her mother in "King of the Comics" kisses the older woman's cheek: "It's all right, I want to say. I love you. She waves as I start down the stairs. She knows" (*DC* 121).

Most of Moose's middle-class women nonetheless seek access to linguistic grounds, which they attempt to mold according to their needs. The adolescent May Kay of "Green Lightning and the Tablecloth Bride" acknowledges the power of words during her initiation into womanhood one hot summer in North Carolina: "I read a lot, walked downtown to the library and carried home armloads of books. When I wasn't reading, I pretended to be. Held a book in front of my face and listened..." (*WR* 104). Recognizing the power of language as well, the preacher's wife of "The Swing" attempts, if only non-verbally, to rewrite her husband's condolences to the Worseley family: "Thou has seen fit to take their youngest from them." Margaret thinks to herself, "he's better off than in that squalor" and proceeds to interrupt the patriarchal sermon with a cough and a wink to her granddaughter Laura (*WR* 56). In the course of the story, Laura learns to distinguish between her grandfather's and her grandmother's use of language, exemplified by their different Bible editions. She fails her grandfather's linguistic test when she recites Bible verses without the selahs, as in Margaret's text, but is initiated into feminine discourse when her grandmother substitutes for the five-dollar prize denied by the preacher a red-painted swing. With its joyous color, generational heritage and rhythmic repetitions, the swing represents a feminine expressive mode unrecognized by Margaret's husband: "He's never sat in it to this day, acts like it's not even here. I've seen him bump into it many a time" (*WR* 54).

Language serves, in short, as both battleground and weapon in the war between the sexes permeating many Moose stories. Her women characters take up linguistic arms with reluctance, like Sharon of "The Vinegar Jug," who responds to Rob's "I'll get a job" with silence: "When? She wanted to say, but didn't. There was so much she didn't say lately." Once engaged in battle, however, words may cut and hurt: "'A job, that's what. J-O-B,' she spelled the letters loud, distinct, final, sharp as broken glass" (*WR* 31-32). Sharon nonetheless feels uneasy about verbal warfare, which might transform a southern woman into an American bitch, or witch: "All the things she'd told herself she wouldn't ever say she'd said. And the ugly creature her words had made hopped around the empty room, made faces at her; green, purple, black Halloween witch faces" (*WR* 32). An unholy linguistic encounter creates, it seems, a monster.

Sharon accordingly invents a different language. In a haze after the quarrel, she spins around and knocks over a jar of pickles, spilling a yellow brine on the kitchen floor as her good-bye note to Rob: "When she thought of him finding the puddle of brine, she laughed. She hoped he'd think it was urine" (*WR* 40). With this unconscious if artificial writing of the body, Sharon drives away, yet she is intentionally composing letters steeped in conventional discourse: "Dear Dr. Ornsby, Due to unforeseen circumstances ... Dear Marvin and Frances, Thank you for the use of the cabin ..." (*WR* 40). A (southern) woman is, perhaps, a signifying schiz, forever at the edge of language.

On the traditional map of southern discourse, Moose's heroines inhabit a blank. The girl who has managed to photograph Christ lives, according to Ellis of "Peanut Dreams and the Blue-Eyed Jesus," in Locust Link, a site unreachable by means of conventional logic: "'What's it close to?' Shelby would ask. 'I mean what's the largest city?' 'Nothing,' Ellis would say. 'It's between nothing and close to nothing.' Then she would laugh big, as if she'd made a joke" (*DC* 10). The youthful Medusa's explosive mirth characterizes also the jelly-making Marie of "The Summer Kitchen," who here speaks a language of her own. Stirring her broth, she "wishes she knew words or chants to make her jelly magic, full of health and vitamins and summer. But she does not know chants or charms, so she hums and stirs, does small dance steps with her old woodstove partner" (*WR* 42-43). Significantly, Marie's aesthetics include a talent for listening and seeing. While her husband works in the city, Marie overhears an owl convention in her trees. She is "the only one to see the herd of deer move silently through their back yard" (*WR* 43). A different feminine language might even grow from disaster. As Lov and Mary Em of "The Girl Who Looked Like Irma Budd's Little Sister" bend over the title figure lying crushed by a delivery truck, the shrill scream from their teakettle expresses their anguish. Lov's habit of finishing Mary Em's sentences develops into a communal language of comfort, as she rewrites her old sister's self-accusations: "'It's – ' Mary Em put her hands over her face. ' – not your fault.' Lov came up behind her, laid her arm across Mary Em's shoulders, drew her close" (*DC* 36).

As the girl photographer's picture of Jesus, Marie's stove gleaming "like a genie's lamp" (*WR* 43) and Lov's long skirts and "fringed things" (*DC* 34) might hint, these women are artists, intent, like Moose herself, on creating a southern languagescape. Moose's working-class women employ, like the pregnant Ellis, their considerable talents in directions leading towards more conventional products, but most middle-class women of her fiction create their South through art. Sharon thinks of herself writing as she leaves Rob behind, while other characters knit, bake, cook, or sew their feminine (re)visions. The protagonist of "Biography in 7 Lives," muted through most of her existence, ends the segment "At Forty" by shouting her own name, the hotblooded game warden having defrosted her capacity for metaphor. The narrator of "Friends and Oranges," the story closing *Dreaming in Color*, loses a husband but becomes a successful potter, able to "dance by myself in all the places I never knew before" (*DC* 198).

Like her characters, Moose intends with her fiction to enter all these places, accessible, as echoed in her titles, through quilting or dreaming (or writing or reading or living). She writes, like the authors filling these pages, the female South she lives. "That writers should ... write so directly from life; that they should 'cannibalize' and even 'vampirize' their own experiences," notes Joyce Carol Oates in *(Woman) Writer*, remains, perhaps, "a surprising (and disturbing) fact to many literary observers." But, she continues, "the artist is driven by passion; and passion most powerfully derives from our own experiences and memories."[11] The narrative and linguistic strategies of both *The Wreath Ribbon Quilt* and *Dreaming in Color* consequently point the way not only towards what Gayatri Spivak calls a "feminization" of reading[12] or, one might add, of writing, but towards an-other South altogether. To dream this South, in color even, is certainly to help (re)shape it.

---

11. Oates, p. 6.
12. Gayatri Spivak, "Displacement and the Discourse of Woman," in *Displacement: Derrida and After*, ed. Mark Krupnick (Bloomington: Indiana U P, 1983), p. 173.

CONCLUSION

The women writers of this volume wriggled themselves in, and, hungry for audiences, they refuse to depart in a timely fashion. Collectively a bunch of shrewd negotiators, they insist on finishing their stories. Like women all over the South, they condemn us to that third helping of butter beans, to extra hours on the porch, and to kissing other plans goodbye.

Their stories must, of course, be told and read, because they insist on difference. From Fanny Kemble's criss-crossings of Georgia properties and ideologies, to Gertrude Thomas's view of aggressive creditors from curtained carriage windows, to Andrew Sheffield's muffled protestations behind Bryce Hospital walls, the narratives the women collectively write remain not only dramatic, intriguing, even endless, but also distinctly different from what we now, fondly even, designate master narratives. Whether we are inside Mary Chesnut's crowded drawingroom, heavy with political intrigues and scandals, or we have escaped to Alice Walker's California herb gardens, the voices we hear come across as feminine, even feminist. They tell us of women's lives across two centuries and, opinionated, genteel, rusty, but never dull, they complement the southern traditions and tales we already know and might even (hate to) love.

Autobiography, in its more informal forms, lends itself most readily to the lives these women push towards representation. The intimacy of the genre alleviates what feminine hesitation these writers might secretly nurse. Autobiography, diaries and letters further remain conveniently "interruptious," to use Mary Chesnut's Lincoln term. Besides, the genre allows for the silences that dot these women writers' texts, and prevent them from running their mouths on sensitive issues. From Kemble and Thomas, who struggled to hold their tongues on marital irregularities, to Andrews and Angelou, not above "turning it out" as well as (re)creating their spaces through muteness and silence, these women writers speak the unspoken, between the lines and between chapters. The performativity of autobiography also appeals to this group of high-profile and, to be sure, high-maintenance women. Whether professional actresses like Kemble and Angelou, given to high drama like Chesnut and Andrews, or everyday performers like Thomas and Fields, the various roles they act out suggest possibilities and change and invite their readers to help write new scripts.

Identifying themselves with silences, masks, and roles, the women here rely in their performances on language, which they elasticize, bite into, lick, and sometimes explode. Within the language of their fathers, editors, husbands and mentors, the women enact their struggle for self-representation by creating a feminine, coded, even subterranean voice. Fanny Kemble and Frances Leigh invented new sentences and new selves to go with Butler morasses, both drawing as well on the maternal discourse that helped Fields push through the racial and social reforms in Charleston she wanted. Lyrical, excessive, melodramatic, energetic, tricksterly, the words of the women here spill onto their manuscript pages in new formations. Alice Walker's red lion's shoe and the feminine detail it represents thus combines with Moose's maieutic dialogues and cross-eyed gazes, or Sarah Morgan's hair-entwined bouquets, into a feminine mode of expression that allows for or, indeed, constitutes *différance*. Across the space/time continuum Alice Walker de/constructs, the women writers gang up with Hélène Cixous and other unruly poststructuralist daughters in advocating linguistic activism.

Like Cixous, who in *Livre de Promethea* emerges from her text sticky with the Atlantic and covered in spots of crystal, the women writers here remain a slippery group. They resist, it seems, professorial attempts to hold them to their words, and they thrive on constant ambiguities. Fanny Kemble and Frances Leigh share, if nothing else, pendulous descriptions of Butler plantation life, while Kate Stone, Sarah Morgan and Ruth Moose simultaneously celebrate and condemn the Souths they know. As the women write tensions into their texts, they claim for themselves a space within as well as without the discourses they inhabit. Mamie Fields, for example, claims both a bourgeois, traditionalist language as well as a tricksterly signifying, thus carving an African American space for herself in pre-civil rights Charleston. Also Andrew Sheffield, the unfortunate woman of prominence, simultaneously employs the language of her controllers and that of her own design in order to escape from Bryce Hospital to the penitentiary. The ideological and discursive oscillations of the women in this volume implicitly comment on work by historians and critics such as Elizabeth Fox-Genovese and Minrose C. Gwin, who debate whether or not southern white women endorsed the systems that produced them and discuss relations between black and white women in terms of hostility or nurture. Like Kemble and Leigh, the women write themselves as outsiders looking in and insiders looking out, sometimes, if not always, alert to their own inconsistencies and complexities. In the mode of Virginia Woolf's Mary Beton or Mary Seton, the women here insist on multiple subjectivities so as to escape patriarchal pens and escape into texts of their own.

Unlike Cixous, these women may not invite readers to lick the salt off Atlantic-drenched shoulders, yet their writings celebrate, in content and form, a certain physicality. Autobiography becomes "fullbodied" simply because it delineates some/body's birth, maturation, and decline. Since the female body constitutes contested space, so to speak, and obviously signifies differences of gender and race, the writers of this volume produce a writing of the body. Like Promethea, they have done their best, as Cixous explains: "She has taken from her organs, her desires, from her memory; we can say that the text, for the most part, is made of her."[1]

Fanny Kemble, for example, focuses throughout her life and journal entries on physical exercise, hygiene, as well as obviously corporal activities such as acting. She fills, as we have seen, her Georgia account with all sorts of female bodies: pregnant, ailing, abused, provocative, insistent. Her own passionate and energetic physicality repeatedly disrupts her plots and her syntax, and would in later life result not just in horseback-riding and fishing, but in mountain climbing in the Alps every summer. Gertrude Thomas

---

1. Hélène Cixous, *Le Livre de Promethea* (Paris: Gallimard, 1983), p. 11. Quotations from this text translated by Beth Baptist.

might hide her physical ills and pleasures, not to mention those of Jefferson Thomas, behind the elaborate veils of which she was more than fond, but her own body subtly breaks through her social and textual frames. Mary Chesnut and Sarah Morgan, to mention just a few more Confederate ladies, articulate themselves through hysterical fits and fainting spells, and both Grace King and Andrew Sheffield recount, much differently, the stories of southern women's bodies at the close of the nineteenth century. The perfectly groomed Mamie Fields embodies through manners and morals the bourgeois activism that shook up racial arrangements in Charleston, as do other of the African American bodies that the Confederate ladies had failed to decipher. Maya Angelou's daringly colored one looms large in late-twentieth-century feminine autobiography, where textually, sexually and globally she sets in motion established notions of race and gender. Through a discursive corporeity, the women writers gathered here inscribe their identities and their differences. They have indeed used their organs, their desires – in Cixous's phrase "physically, morally, nervously."[2]

Their nervousness originates, among other things, in the monstrosity of autobiography. Despite the authors' attempt at control, their life writings might reveal the face of the other woman, the one behind the mirror or displayed without feminine tampering. Fanny Kemble never learned to veil her criticism of marriage and slavery and paid the price of a woman *impropre*, while Mary Chesnut took to scratching out whatever troubles and faces she wished to hide. Sarah Morgan did not quite hold herself to prescribed dicourses either, while Andrew Sheffield inside Bryce Hospital slowly turned into the monster her male relatives found her to be. As the years passed within asylum wards, her grey locks and wrinkled face testified to her unwillingness and inability to "come under" and to the weight she ultimately placed on her brain. Even the dainty Miss King of New Orleans invented in representing the woman artist a sort of monster, who crosses discursive and racial boundaries in order to become herself. Much later, Alice Walker celebrates monstrosity by inventing an artist figure who transcends

---

2. Cixous, *Promethea*, p. 11.

Conclusion

all sorts of binaries, among them death/life, human/animal, and time/space. Barbara Johnson's "filthy creation" has in twentieth-century women's autobiography moved in with the nineteenth-century domestic angel.

They obviously enjoy each other's company, which provides a measure of security. The women writing the South live precariously, after all, within their defining categories. Since Roland Barthes, authors can no longer count on permanent positions, stolen nowadays by language that speaks and readers who interpret their texts. "I am not at all of the Creator's species," writes the voice of Cixous's *Promethea*. "I am just an author. This is a very slight character."[3] The author-function spoken here promises humbly to give each sentence not belonging to her back to whoever owns it, and attempts an introduction only because nobody else wants to perform the task. The women writers in this volume respond with equal modesty and ingenuity to the author's death. Before as well as after Roland Barthes's orbituary, they admit each other into life texts that, as doors open and close, become conversations across time, space and race. Fanny Kemble merges her voice with those of Butler Island slaves and even makes her way into the reluctant Frances Leigh's account of Reconstruction Georgia. Mary Chesnut writes friends and enemies into every line, and Grace King of New Orleans inhabits in life and fiction communities of women. Mamie Fields speaks in the first person plural with and for the African American Charlestonians who inhabit *Lemon Swamp*, while Maya Angelou through travel sets up alliances with everybody. Ruth Moose allows in her works the neighborhood an independent existence. She invites the gossipy, communal and intertextual voice of the South into her life stories and in the process merges writer and reader.

Also the category of "woman" seems less than stable, the storytellers' female persuasions notwithstanding. Unless policed, "woman" disappears into a social construction, a linguistic position, an injection of negativity, a cyborg, or, indeed, a man. Everybody in this volume has helped along such gender trouble. Fanny Kemble donned men's clothes on horseback rides and set the stage for

---

3. *Promethea*, p. 12.

transvestite fantasies among the Confederate ladies following her. Sarah Morgan and Frances Leigh both wrote themselves as phallic women, and even Miss King contributed with feminine men and masculine women to the general confusion, which Andrew Sheffield intensified not just with her name. Despite flirtations with literary theorists, the writers here adress their audience in feminine voices and head towards female lives. They ask us to listen to dialogues between biography and text, where sexual difference and modes of resistance intertwine and perform. With Judith Butler's view of gender as performative, the writers here engage in constant reinscriptions of female identity. In short, they come and go as women and "woman."

The South that defines them remains undefinable, but the landscapes the writers move across make up their identities and their texts. The rice fields of coastal Georgia, the cities of Louisiana, or the institutions of Alabama sustain the stories and inform the aesthetics of these women writing the South, whether or not they live their lives and write their texts within southern boundaries. In the words of Eudora Welty, "A place that ever was lived in is like a fire that never goes out."[4] Maybe, as Peter Applebome and Helen Taylor argue, the South has spread to everywhere and turned as global as it first began. All over, then, women write the Souths that certainly exist in the cadences, the silences and the self-representations of their pages. As they open doors leading nowhere and everywhere, their voices linger on, nervously, randomly, finally.

---

4. See Jan Gretlund, *Eudora Welty and the Aesthetics of Place* (Odense, Denmark: Odense U P, 1994); the Welty quote appears on p. 358.

BIBLIOGRAPHY

Abel, Elizabeth, ed. *Writing and Sexual Difference.* Brighton: Harvester, 1982.

Akward, Michael. *Inspiriting Influences: Tradition, Revision, and Afro-American Women's Novels.* New York: Columbia U P, 1989.

Allan, Tuzyline Jita. "A Voice of One's Own: Implications of Impersonality in Essays of Virginia Woolf and Alice Walker." In Joeres and Mittman. [131]-47.

Anderson, John Q., ed. *Brokenburn: The Journal of Kate Stone, 1861-1868.* 1955. Baton Rouge: LSU P, 1972.

Andrews, William L., ed. *African American Autobiography: A Collection of Critical Essays.* Englewood Cliffs, NJ: Prentice-Hall, 1993.

Andrews, William L., "The First Fifty Years of the Slave Narrative, 1760-1810." In Sekora and Turner. 6-35.

Andrews, William L., ed. *Journeys in New Worlds: Early American Women's Narratives.* Madison, Wis.: U of Wisconsin P, 1990.

Andrews, William L., *Sisters of the Spirit: Three Black Women's Autobiographies in the Nineteenth Century.* Bloomington: Indiana U P, 1986.

Andrews, William L., *To Tell a Free Story: The First Century of Afro-American Autobiography, 1760-1865.* Chicago: U of Illinois P, 1986.

Andrews, William L., et al., ed. *The Literature of the American South.* New York: W. W. Norton, 1998.

Angelou, Maya. *Wouldn't Take Nothing for My Journey Now.* 1993. New York: Bantam, 1994.

Applebome, Peter. *Dixie Rising: How the South Is Shaping American Values, Politics, and Culture.* New York: Random House, 1996.

Aptheker, Bettina. *Woman's Legacy: Essays on Race, Sex, and Class in American History.* Amherst: U of Massachusetts P, 1982.

Armstrong, Margaret. *Fanny Kemble: A Passionate Victorian.* New York: Macmillan, 1938.

Athas, Daphne. "Why There Are No Southern Writers." In Prenshaw. 295-306.

Bair, Deidre. "'My life ... This Curious Object': Simone de Beauvoir on Autobiography." In Stanton. 237-45.

Baker, Jr., Houston A. *Blues, Ideology, and Afro-American Literature.* Chicago: U of Chicago P, 1984.

Bartley, Numan V. *The New South, 1945-1980.* Baton Rouge: LSU P, 1995.

Bartley, Numan V. "Social Change and Sectional Identity." *The Journal of Southern History* 61.1 (February 1995): [3]-16.

Bartram, William. *Travels through North and South Carolina, Georgia, East and West Florida.* Charlottesville: U P of Virginia, 1980.
Bell, Jr., Malcolm. *Major Butler's Legacy: Five Generations of a Slaveholding Family.* Athens: U of Georgia P, 1987.
Berry, Mary Frances. "Judging Morality: Sexual Behavior and Legal Consequences in the Late Nineteenth-Century South." *The Journal of American History* 78 (December 1991): 835-56.
Betts, Doris. "The Fiction of Anne Tyler." In Prenshaw. 23-37.
Bhabha, Homi K. *The Location of Culture.* London: Routledge, 1994.
Billson, Marcus K. and Sidonie A. Smith. "Lillian Hellman and the Strategy of the 'Other.'" In Jelinek, *Women's Autobiography: Essays.* 163-79.
Blackwelder, Julia Kirk. "Ladies, Belles, Working Women, and Civil Rights." In *The New South for Southerners.* Ed. Paul D. Escott and David R. Goldfield. Chapel Hill: U of N Carolina P, 1991. 94-113.
Blanchard, Mary W. "Boundaries and the Victorian Body: Aesthetic Fashion in Gilded Age America." *American Historical Review* 100 (February 1995): 21-50.
Bleser, Carol, ed. *In Joy and Sorrow: Women, Family and Marriage in the Victorian South, 1830-1900.* New York: Oxford U P, 1991.
Bordo, Susan. *Unbearable Weight: Feminism, Western Culture, and the Body.* Los Angeles: U of California P, 1993.
Braxton, Joanne M. *Black Women Writing Autobiography: A Tradition Within a Tradition.* Philadelphia: Temple U P, 1989.
Braxton, Joanne M. and Andrée Nicola McLaughlin, ed. *Wild Women in the Whirlwind: Afra-American Culture and the Contemporary Literary Renaissance.* London: Serpent's Tail, 1990.
Brée, Germaine. "Autogynography." *Southern Review* 22 (Spring 1986): 223-30.
Brodzki, Bella and Celeste Schenck, ed. *Life/Lines: Theorizing Women's Autobiography.* Ithaca: Cornell U P, 1988.
Bruss, Elizabeth W. *Autobiographical Acts: The Changing Situation of a Literary Genre.* Baltimore: Johns Hopkins U P, 1976.
Bush, Robert. "Charles Gayarré and Grace King." *Southern Literary Journal* (Fall 1974): 100-31.
Bush, Robert. "Grace King: The Emergence of a Southern Intellectual Woman." *Southern Review* 13 (Spring 1977): 272-88.
Bush, Robert. "Grace King and Mark Twain." *American Literature* 44 (March 1972): 31-51.
Bush, Robert. ed. *Grace King of New Orleans: A Selection of Her Works.* Baton Rouge: LSU P, 1973.
Bush, Robert. *Grace King: A Southern Destiny.* Baton Rouge: LSU P, 1983.
Butler, Judith. *Bodies That Matter: On the Discursive Limits of "Sex."* New York: Routledge, 1993.
Butler, Judith. *Gender Trouble: Feminism and the Subversion of Identity.* New York: Routledge, 1990.
Butterfield, Stephen. *Black Autobiography in America.* Amherst: U of Mass. P, 1974.

Bibliography

Byerman, Keith. *Fingering the Jagged Grain: Tradition and Form in Recent Black Fiction*. Athens: U of Georgia P, 1985.

Byerman, Keith. "We Wear the Mask: Deceit as Theme and Style in Slave Narratives." In Sekora and Turner. 70-82.

Callahan, John F. *In the African-American Grain: The Pursuit of Voice in Twentieth-Century Black Fiction*. Chicago: U of Illinois P, 1988.

Chandler, Zala. "Voices Beyond the Veil: An Interview with Toni Cade Bambara and Sonia Sanchez." In Braxton and McLaughlin. [342]-62.

Chinosole. "Audre Lorde and Matrilinear Diaspora: Moving History beyond Nightmare into Structures for the Future." In Braxton and McLaughlin. [379]-94.

Chesler, Phyllis. *Women and Madness*. Garden City, NY: Doubleday, 1972.

Christian, Barbara. "The Race for Theory." *Cultural Critique* 6 (Spring 1987): 51-63.

Cixous, Hélène. "The Laugh of the Medusa." In Marks and de Courtivron. 245-64.

Cixous, Hélène. *Le Livre de Promethea*. Paris: Gallimard, 1983.

Cixous, Hélène and Catherine Clement. *The Newly Born Woman*. Minneapolis: U of Minnesota P, 1986.

Clinton, Catherine. *Fanny Kemble's Civil Wars*. NY: Simon & Schuster, 2000.

Clinton, Catherine. *The Other Civil War*. New York: Hill and Wang, 1984.

Clinton, Catherine. *The Plantation Mistress: Woman's World in The Old South*. New York: Pantheon, 1982.

Clinton, Catherine. *Southern Families at War: Loyalty and Conflict in the Civil War South*. New York: Oxford U P, 2000.

Clinton, Catherine and Nina Silber, ed. *Divided Houses: Gender and the Civil War*. New York: Oxford U P, 1992.

Courtwright, David T. "The Female Opiate Addict in Nineteenth-Century America." *Essays in Arts and Sciences* 10.2 (March 1982): 161-71.

Courtwright, David T. "The Hidden Epidemic: Opiate Addiction and Cocaine Use in the South, 1860-1920." *Journal of Southern History* 49 (Feb. 1983): 57-72.

Crow, Terrell Armistad. "'As Thy Days, So Shall Thy Strength Be': North Carolina Planter Women in War and Peace." *Carolina Comments* 28.1 (Jan. 1980): 24-31.

Dainotto, Roberto Maria. "'All the Regions Do Smilingly Revolt': The Literature of Place and Region." *Critical Inquiry* 22 (Spring 1996): [486]-505.

Dart, Henry P. "Miss King's Historical Works." *Louisiana Historical Quarterly* 6.3 (July 1923): 347-53.

Davies, Carol Boyce. *Black Women, Writing and Identity: Migrations of the Subject*. London: Routledge, 1994.

Davis, Natalie Z. "Women on Top." *Society and Culture in Early Modern France*. Stanford: Stanford U P, 1975. [124]-51.

Dawson, Sarah Morgan. *A Confederate Girl's Diary*. 1913. Ed. James I. Robertson, Jr. Bloomington: Indiana U P, 1960.

Dawson, Warrington. "Introduction." In Dawson. xxvii-[xxxvii].
Deleuze, Giles. "Nomad Thought." In *The New Nietzche*. Ed. David B. Allison. New York: Dell, 1977. 142-49.
Delphy, Christine. "Protofeminism and Antifeminism." In Moi. 80-109.
Diffley, Kathleen. *Where My Heart Is Turning Ever: Civil War Stories and Constitutional Reform, 1861-1876*. U of Georgia P, 1992.
Dixon, Melvin. *Ride Out the Wilderness: Geography and Identity in Afro-American Literature*. Carbondale: U of Illinois P, 1987.
Du Bois, W. E. B. *The Souls of Black Folk*. 1903. New York: Signet, 1969.
DuCille, Ann. *The Coupling Convention: Sex, Text and Tradition in Black Women's Fiction*. New York: Oxford U P, 1993.
Dwyer, Ellen. "A Historical Perspective." In *Sex Roles and Psychopathology*. Ed. Cathy S. Widom. New York: Plenum, 1984. 19-48.
Dwyer, Ellen. *Homes for the Mad: Life inside Two Nineteenth-Century Asylums*. New Brunswick, NJ: Rutgers U P, 1987.
Eagleton, Mary. *Feminist Literary Theory*. Oxford: Basil Blackwell, 1986.
East, Charles, ed. *The Civil War Diary of Sarah Morgan*. Athens: U of Georgia P, 1991.
Elliot, Jeffrey M. *Conversations with Maya Angelou*. Jackson: U P of Mississippi, 1989.
Ellison, Ralph. *Shadow and Act*. New York: Signet, 1966.
Faust, Drew Gilpin. "Altars of Sacrifice: Confederate Women and the Narratives of War." *The Journal of American History* 76 (March 1990): 1200-28.
Faust, Drew Gilpin. *Mothers of Invention: Women of the Slaveholding South in the American Civil War*. Chapel Hill: U of North Carolina P, 1996.
Faust, Drew Gilpin. "'A Riddle of Death': Mortality and Meaning in the American Civil War," 34th Annual Fortenbaugh Memorial Lecture, Gettysburg College, 1995. 7-30.
Fields, Mamie Garvin, with Karen E. Fields. *Lemon Swamp and Other Places: A Carolina Memoir*. New York: Free P, 1983.
Fleishman, Avon. *Figures of Autobiography: The Language of Self-Writing in Victorian and Modern England*. Berkeley: U of California P, 1983.
Fletcher, Marie. "Grace Elizabeth King: Her Delineation of the Southern Heroine." *Louisiana Studies* 5 (Spring 1966): 50-60.
Fox-Genovese, Elizabeth. "Family and Female Identity in the Antebellum South: Sarah Gayle and Her Family." In Bleser. 15-31.
Friedman, Jean E. *The Enclosed Garden: Women and Community in the Evangelical South, 1830-1900*. Chapel Hill: U of North Carolina P, 1985.
Furnas, J. C. *Fanny Kemble: Leading Lady of the Nineteenth-Century Stage*. New York: Dial, 1982.
Gallop, Jane. *The Daughter's Seduction: Feminism and Psychoanalysis*. Ithaca: Cornell U P, 1982.
Gardiner, Judith Kegan. "On Female Identity and Writing by Women." In Abel. 177-91.
Gates, Jr., Henry Louis, ed. *Black Literature and Literary Theory*. New York: Methuen, 1984.

Bibliography

Gates, Jr., Henry Louis. *Figures in Black: Words, Signs, and the "Racial" Self.* New York: Oxford U P, 1987.

Gay, Mary. A. H. *Life in Dixie During the War.* Ed. J. H. Segars. Macon, Ga.: Mercer U P, 2001.

Gilbert, Sandra M. "Costumes of the Mind: Transvestism as Metaphor in Modern Literature." In Abel. 177-91.

Gilbert, Sandra M. and Susan Gubar. "Ceremonies of the Alphabet: Female Grandmatologies and the Female Authorgraph." In Stanton. 23-52.

Gilbert, Sandra M. *The Madwoman in the Attic: The Woman Writer and the Nineteenth-Century Literary Imagination.* New Haven: Yale U P, 1979.

Grewal, Shabna, Jackie E. Kay, *et al. Charting the Journey: Writings by Black and Third World Women.* London: Sheba Feminist Publishers, 1988.

Griffin, Susan. "Red Shoes." In Joeres and Mittman. [1]-11.

Gretlund, Jan Nordby. *Eudora Welty's Aesthetics of Place.* Odense, Denmark: Odense U P, 1994.

Grosz, Elizabeth. *Volatile Bodies: Toward a Corporeal Feminism.* Bloomington: Indiana U P, 1994.

Gubar, Susan. "'The Blank Page' and the Issues of Female Creativity." In Showalter, *Feminist Criticism.* 292-313.

Hagler, D. Harland. "The Ideal Woman in the Antebellum South: Lady or Farmwife?" *The Journal of Southern History* 46.3 (Aug. 1980): [405]-18.

Hall, Stuart. "Metaphors of Transformation." In White. [1]-25.

Hedin, Raymond. "Strategies of Form in the American Slave Narrative." In Sekora and Turner. 25-34.

Higonnet, Margaret Randolph, *et al.*, ed. *Behind the Wars: Gender and the Two World Wars.* New Haven: Yale U P, 1987.

Himelhoch, Myra Samuels and Arthur H. Schaffer. "Elizabeth Packard: Nineteenth-Century Crusader for the Rights of Mental Patients." *Journal of American Studies* 13.3 (1979): 343-76.

Holloway, Karla F. C. *Codes of Conduct: Race, Ethics, and the Color of Our Character.* New Brunswick: Rutgers U P, 1995.

Holloway, Karla F. C. *Moorings and Metaphors: Figures of Culture and Gender in Black Women's Literature.* New Brunswick, N. J.: Rutgers U P, 1992.

Horwitz, Allan V. *The Social Control of Mental Illness.* New York: Academic P, 1982.

Hughes, John S. "Introduction." In Hughes, *Letters.* 1-45.

Hughes, John S., ed. *The Letters of a Victorian Madwoman.* Columbia: U of South Carolina P, 1993.

Hughes, John S. "The Madness of Separate Spheres: Insanity and Masculinity in Victorian Alabama." In Mark Carnes and Clyde Griffen, ed. *Meanings for Manhood: Constructions of Masculinity in Victorian America.* Chicago: U of Chicago P, 1990. 67-78.

Irigaray, Luce. "When the Goods Get Together." In Marks and de Courtivron. 107-10.

Iser, Wolfgang. *The Act of Reading: A Theory of Aesthetic Response.* Baltimore: Johns Hopkins U P, 1978.

Jacobus, Mary. *Reading Woman (Reading): Essays in Feminist Criticism.* New York: Columbia U P, 1986.

James, Henry. "Frances Anne Kemble." *Essays in London and Elsewhere.* London: James R. Osgood et al., 1893. [86]-127.

Jardine, Alice. *Gynesis: Configurations of Woman and Modernity.* Ithaca: Cornell U P, 1985.

Jelinek, Estelle J. *The Tradition of Woman's Autobiography: From Antiquity to the Present.* Boston: Twayne, 1986.

Jelinek, Estelle J., ed. *Women's Autobiography: Essays in Criticism.* Bloomington: Indiana U P, 1980.

Joeres, Ruth-Ellen. "The Passionate Essay: Radical Feminist Essayists." In Joeres and Mittman. [151]-71.

Joeres, Ruth-Ellen and Elizabeth Mittman. *The Politics of the Essay: Feminist Perspectives.* Bloomington: Indiana U P, 1993.

Johnson, Barbara. "My Monster/My Self." *Diacritics* 12 (1982): 2-10.

Jones, Ann Rosalind. "Surprising Fame: Renaissance Gender Ideologies and Women's Lyric." In *The Poetics of Gender.* Ed. Nancy K. Miller. New York: Columbia U P, 1986. 74-95.

Jones, Anne Goodwin. *Tomorrow Is Another Day: The Woman Writer in the South, 1859-1936.* Baton Rouge: LSU P, 1981.

Jones, Gayl. *Liberating Voices: Oral Traditions in African American Literature.* Cambridge, Mass.: Harvard U P, 1991.

Joyner, Charles. "Introduction." In Pringle. xiii-xlvii.

Jugurtha, Lillie Butler. "Point of View in the Afro-American Slave Narratives: A Study of Narratives by Douglass and Pennington." In Sekora and Turner. 110-19.

Juhasz, Suzanne. "Towards a Theory of Form in Feminist Autobiography: Kate Millett's *Flying* and *Sita*; Maxine Hong Kingston's *The Woman Warrior.*" In Jelinek, *Women's Autobiography: Essays.* 221-37.

Kemble, Frances Anne. *Journal of a Residence on a Georgian Plantation in 1838-39.* 1863. Ed. John A. Scott. Athens: U of Georgia P, 1984.

Kemble, Frances Anne. *Records of a Girlhood.* 3 vols. London: Richard Bentley and Son, 1878-79.

Kemble, Frances Anne. *Records of Later Life.* 3 vols. London: Richard Bentley and Son, 1882.

Kendall, John S. "A New Orleans Lady of Letters." *Louisiana Historical Quarterly* 19.2 (April 1936): 436-65.

King, Grace. "Annette: A Story of the Street." *New Orleanian* 1.3 (20 Sept. 1930): 16-17, 36-37.

King, Grace. "At Chenière Caminada." *Harper's* 88 (May 1894): 871-74.

King, Grace. *Balcony Stories.* New York: Century, 1893.

King, Grace. "Bonne Maman." *Harper's* 73 (June-Nov. 1886): 293-308.

King, Grace. "Le Chevalier Alain de Triton." *Chautauquan* 13 (July 1891): 409-64.

King, Grace. "The Clodhopper." *McClure* 28 (March 1907): 487-91.

King, Grace. *La Dame de Saint Hermine.* New York: Macmillan, 1898.

King, Grace. *De Soto and His Men in the Land of Florida.* New York: Macmillan, 1898.
King, Grace. "A Domestic Interior." *Harper's* 90 (Feb. 1895): 407-11.
King, Grace. "Earthlings." *Lippincott's Monthly Magazine* 42 (Nov. 1888): 601-79.
King, Grace. "The Flitting of 'Sister.'" *Youth's Companion* 77 (25 June 1903): 305-6.
King, Grace. "An Interlude." *Harper's* 89 (Nov. 1894): 918-20.
King, Grace. *Jean Baptiste Le Moyne, Sieur de Bienville.* New York: Dodd, 1893.
King, Grace. "Madrilène; Or, The Festival of the Dead." *Harper's* 81 (June-Nov. 1890): [869]-86.
King, Grace. *Memories of a Southern Woman of Letters.* New York: Macmillan, 1932.
King, Grace. *Monsieur Motte.* New York: Armstrong, 1888.
King, Grace. "Old New Orleans." *The Bookman* 63 (March 1926): 74-78.
King, Grace. "One Woman's Story." *Harper's Bazar* 14 (21 March 1891): 218-19.
King, Grace. *The Pleasant Ways of St. Médard.* New York: Holt, 1916.
King, Grace. "The Self-Made Man: An Impression." *Harper's Bazaar* 13 (5 April 1890): 258-59.
King, Grace. "A Splendid Offer: A Comedy for Women." *Drama* 16 (March 1926): 213-15, 235-37.
Kirby, David. *Grace King.* Boston: Twayne, 1980.
Kracauer, Siegfried. *Orpheus in Paris: Offenbach and the Paris of His Time.* Trans. Gwenda and Eric Mosbacher. New York: Vienna House, 1972.
Kreyling, Michael. *Inventing Southern Literature.* Jackson: U P of Mississippi, 1998.
Kristeva, Julia. *The Kristeva Reader.* Ed. Toril Moi. New York: Columbia U P, 1986.
Kristeva, Julia. "Oscillation Between Power and Denial." In Marks and de Courtivron. [165]-67.
Kristeva, Julia. *Tales of Love.* New York: Columbia U P, 1987.
Kristeva, Julia. "Talking about *Polylogue.*" In Moi, *French Feminist Thought.* 110-17.
Kristeva, Julia. "Woman Can Never Be Defined." In Marks and de Courtivron. [137]f.
Lawson-Peebles, Robert. *Landscape and Written Expression in Revolutionary America.* Cambridge: Cambridge U P, 1988.
Leigh, Frances Butler. *Ten Years on a Georgia Plantation Since the War.* 1883. Savannah: Beehive, 1992.
Leigh, J. W. *Other Days.* New York: Macmillan, 1921.
Leonard, Elizabeth D. *Yankee Women: Gender Battles in the Civil War.* New York: W. W. Norton, 1994.
Lindberg-Seyersted, Brita. *Black and Female: Essays on Writings by Black Women in the Diaspora.* Oslo: Scandinavian U P, 1994.
Lionnet, Francoise. *Autobiographical Voices: Race, Gender, Self-Portraiture.* Ithaca: Cornell U P, 1989.
Marks, Elaine and Isabelle de Courtivron, ed. *New French Feminisms.* New York: Schocken, 1981.
McCandless, Peter. "'A House of Cure': The Antebellum South Carolina Lunatic Asylum." *Bulletin of the History of Medicine* 64 (Summer 1990): 220-42.
McCurry, Stephanie. "The Two Faces of Republicanism: Gender and Proslavery

Politics in Antebellum South Carolina." *The Journal of American History* 79 (March 1992): 1245-64.

McDowell, Deborah. "'The Changing Same': Generational Connections and Black Women Novelists." *New Literary History* 18.2 (Winter 1987): [281]-302.

McDowell, Deborah. "In the First Place: Making Frederick Douglass and the Afro-American Narrative Tradition." In Andrews, *African American Autobiography*. 36-58.

McKinley, Emilie Riley. *From the Pen of a She-Rebel: The Civil War Diary of Emilie Riley McKinley.* U of South Carolina P, 2001.

McSherry, Jr., Frank, Charles G. Waugh and Martin Greenberg, ed. *Civil War Women.* New York: Touchstone, 1990.

Miles, Agnes. *Women and Mental Illness: The Social Context of Female Neurosis.* Brighton: Wheatsheaf, 1988.

Miller, David. *Dark Eden: The Swamp in Nineteenth-Century American Literature.* Cambridge: Cambridge U P, 1990.

Miller, Nancy. "Emphasis Added: Plots and Plausibilities in Women's Fiction." *PMLA* 96 (January 1981): 36-48.

Mills, Sara. *Discourses of Difference: An Analysis of Women's Travel Writing and Colonialism.* London: Routledge, 1991.

Milroy, Beth Moore and Susan Wismer. "Communities, Work, and Public/Private Sphere Models." *Gender, Place and Culture* 1.1 (1994): 71-90.

Miner, Earl. "Literary Diaries and the Boundaries of Literature." *Yearbook of Comparative and General Literature* 21 (1972): 46-51.

Mitchie, Helen. *The Flesh Made Word: Female Figures and Women's Bodies.* New York: Oxford U P, 1987.

Mittlefehldt, Pamela Klass. "'A Weaponry of Choice': Black American Women Writers and the Essay." In Joeres and Mittman. [196]-208.

Moi, Toril, ed. *French Feminist Thought.* Oxford: Basil Blackwell, 1987.

Moose, Ruth. *Dreaming in Color.* Little Rock: August House, 1988.

Moose, Ruth. *The Wreath Ribbon Quilt and Other Stories.* Laurinburg, NC: St. Andrew's P, 1987.

Morrison, Toni. *Playing in the Dark: Whiteness and the Literary Imagination.* Cambridge: Harvard U P, 1992.

Muhlenfeld, Elisabeth. *Mary Chesnut: A Biography.* Baton Rouge: LSU P, 1981.

Mulvey, Laura. "Visual Pleasure and Narrative Cinema." *Screen* 16.3 (1975): 6-18.

Nicolson, Nigel, ed. *A Reflection of the Other Person: The Letters of Virginia Woolf IV, 1929-31.* London: Hogarth P, 1978.

Niemtzow, Annette. "The Problematic of Self in Autobiography: The Example of the Slave Narrative." In Sekora and Turner. 96-109.

Oates, Joyce Carol. *(Woman) Writer: Occasions and Opportunities.* New York: E. P. Dutton, 1988.

Painter, Nell Irvin. "Introduction: The Journal of Ella Gertrude Clanton Thomas: An Educated White Woman in the Eras of Slavery, War, and Reconstruction." In Thomas. 1- 67.

Bibliography

Pattee, Fred Lewis. *American Literature Since 1870.* 1915. New York: Cooper Square, 1968.

Pember, Phoebe Yates. *A Southern Woman's Story.* U of South Carolina P, 2001.

Perkins, Linda. "The Impact of the 'Cult of True Womanhood' on the Education of Black Women." *Journal of Social Issues* 39.3 (1983): 17-28.

Pfister, Joel and Nancy Schnog, ed. *Inventing the Psychological: Toward a Cultural History of Emotional Life in America.* New Haven: Yale U P, 1997.

Pratt, Mary Louise. *Imperial Eyes: Travel Writing and Transculturation.* London: Routledge, 1992.

Prenshaw, Peggy, ed. *Woman Writers of the Contemporary South.* Jackson: U P of Mississippi, 1984.

Pringle, Elizabeth Allston. *A Woman Rice Planter.* Ed. Charles Joyner. Columbia: U of South Carolina P, 1992.

Rable, George C. *Civil Wars: Women and the Crisis of Southern Nationalism.* Urbana: U of Illinois P, 1991.

Rainwater, Catherine and William J. Scheick, ed. *Contemporary American Women Writers: Narrative Strategies.* Lexington: U P of Kentucky, 1985.

Reidy, Joseph P. "Calliope and Clio: The Style and Substance of Recent Historical Writing on the South." *Southern Review* 32.2 (April 1996): 373-89.

Reimer, Gail Twersky. "Revisions of Labor in Margaret Oliphant's Autobiography." In Brodzski and Schenck. 203-20.

Ripa, Yannick. *Women and Madness: The Incarceration of Women in Nineteenth-Century France.* Cambridge, UK: Polity P and Basil Blackwell, 1990.

Robertson, Mary F. "Anne Tyler: Medusa Points and Contact Points." In Rainwater and Scheick. 119-42.

Robertson, Jr., James I. "Foreword." In Dawson. xi-xxvi.

Rosenblum, Dolores. "Christina Rosetti: The Inward Pose." In *Shakespeare's Sisters: Feminist Essays on Women Poets.* Ed. Sandra M. Gilbert and Susan Gubar. Bloomington: Indiana U P, 1979. 82-98.

Salvatori, Maria. "Reading and Writing a Text: Correlations Between Reading and Writing Patterns." *College English* 45 (1983): 657-66.

Schleifer, Ronald. "Grace Paley: Chaste Compactness." In Rainwater and Scheick. 31-48.

Schor, Naomi. *Reading in Detail: Aesthetics and the Feminine.* New York: Routledge, Chapman and Hall, 1987.

Scott, Ann Firor. *The Southern Lady: From Pedestal to Politics, 1830-1930.* Chicago: U of Chicago P, 1970.

Scott, Ann Firor. "The 'New Woman' in the New South." *South Atlantic Quarterly* 61 (Autumn 1962): 473-83.

Scott, Ann Firor. "Women's Perspective on the Patriarchy in the 1850s." *Journal of American History* 61 (June 1974): 52-64.

Scott, Joan Wallach. "The Campaign against Political Correctness." In *PC Wars: Politics and Theory in the Academy.* Ed. Jeffrey Williams. New York: Routledge, 1995. 22-43.

Scott, John A. "Introduction." In Kemble, *Journal.* [ix]-lxi.

Sedgwick, Eve K. *Between Men: English Literature and Male Homosocial Desire.* New York: Columbia U P, 1985.

Sekora, John and Darwin T. Turner, ed. *The Art of Slave Narrative: Original Essays in Criticism and Theory.* N.p.: Western Illinois U P, 1982.

Sharpe, Patricia, F. E. Mascia-Lees and C. B. Cohen. "White Women and Black Men: Differential Responses to Reading Black Women's Texts." *College English* 52.2 (February 1990): 142-53.

Showalter, Elaine. *The Female Malady: Women, Madness and English Culture, 1830-1980.* New York: Pantheon, 1985.

Showalter, Elaine., ed. *Feminist Criticism: Essays on Women, Literature and Theory.* New York: Pantheon, 1985.

Showalter, Elaine. "Feminist Criticism in the Wilderness." *Critical Inquiry* 8 (Winter 1981): 179-205.

Showalter, Elaine. "Victorian Women and Insanity." *Victorian Studies* 23.2 (Winter 1980): [157]-81.

Smiley, David. "The Quest for a Central Theme in Southern History." *South Atlantic Quarterly* 71 (Summer 1972): 307-25.

Smith, Sidonie. *A Poetics of Women's Autobiography: Marginality and the Fictions of Self-Representation.* Bloomington: Indiana U P, 1987.

Smith, Sidonie. "Self, Subject, and Resistance: Marginalities and Twentieth-Century Autobiographical Practice." *Tulsa Studies in Women's Literature* 9 (Spring 1990): 11-24.

Smith, Sidonie. *Subjectivity, Identity, and the Body: Women's Autobiographical Practices in the Twentieth Century.* Bloomington: Indiana U P, 1993.

Smith, Valerie. *Self-Discovery and Authority in Afro-American Narrative.* Cambridge, Mass.: Harvard U P, 1987.

Smith-Rosenberg, Carroll. *Disorderly Conduct: Visions of Gender in Victorian America.* New York: Alfred A. Knopf, 1985.

Smith-Rosenberg, Carroll. "The Female World of Love and Ritual: Relations Between Women in Nineteenth-Century America." *Signs* 1.1 (1975): 1-29.

Smith-Rosenberg, Carroll. "The Hysterical Woman: Sex Roles and Role Conflict in 19th-Century America." *Social Research* 39.4 (Winter 1972): [652]-78.

Smith-Rosenberg, Carroll and Charles Rosenberg. "The Female Animal: Medical and Biological Views of Woman and Her Role in Nineteenth-Century America." *Journal of American History* 60.1 (June-Sept. 1973): 332-56.

Snyder, Katherine V. "From Novel to Essay: Gender and Revision in Florence Nightingale's 'Cassandra.'" In Joeres and Mittman. [23]-40.

Sobel, Mechal. *The World They Made Together: Black and White Values in Eighteenth-Century Virginia.* Princeton: Princeton U P, 1987.

Spacks, Patricia M. "Selves in Hiding." In Jelinek, *Women's Autobiography: Essays.* 112-32.

Spacks, Patricia M. "Women's Stories, Women's Selves." *The Hudson Review* 30.1 (Spring 1977): 29-46.

Spengemann, William C. *The Forms of Autobiography: Episodes in the History of a Literary Genre.* New Haven: Yale U P, 1980.

Bibliography

Spivak, Gayatri. "Displacement and the Discourse of Woman." In *Displacement: Derrida and After*. Ed. Mark Krupnick. Bloomington: Indiana U P, 1983.

Stanton, Domna E., ed. *The Female Autograph*. New York: New York Literary Forum, 1984.

Stearns, Peter. "Liberty and Lunacy: The Victorians and Wrongful Confinement." *Journal of Social History* 11.3 (Spring 1978): [361]-86.

Stepto, Robert. *From Behind the Veil: A Study of Afro-American Narrative*. Urbana: U of Illinois P, 1979.

Stimpson, Catherine R. "The Female Sociograph: The Theater of Virginia Woolf's Letters." In Stanton. 193-203.

Stone, Albert E. "After *Black Boy* and *Dusk of Dawn*: Patterns in Recent Black Autobiography." 1978. Rpt. in Andrews, *African American Autobiography*. 171-86.

Stone, Albert E. "Postscript: Looking Back in 1992." In Andrews, *African American Autobiography*. 186-95.

Sullivan, Buddy. *Early Days on the Georgia Tidewater: The Story of McIntosh County and Sapelo*. Darien, Ga.: McIntosh County Board of Commissioners, 1990.

Sutherland, Daniel E., ed. *A Very Violent Rebel: The Civil War Diary of Ellen Renshaw House*. Knoxville: U of Tennessee P, 1996.

Tate, Claudia. *Domestic Allegories of Political Desire*. Cambridge: Oxford U P, 1993.

Taylor, Gordon D. "Voices from the Veil: Black American Autobiography." *Georgia Review* 35 (Summer 1981): 341-61.

Taylor, Helen. "The Case of Grace King." *Southern Review* 18 (Fall 1982): 685-702.

Taylor, Helen. *Circling Dixie: Contemporary Southern Culture through a Transatlantic Lens*. New Brunswick, N.J.: Rutgers U P, 2001.

Thomas, Ella Gertrude Clanton. *The Secret Eye: The Journal of Ella Gertrude Clanton Thomas, 1848-1889*. Ed. Virginia Ingraham Burr. Chapel Hill: U of North Carolina P, 1990.

Vann Woodward, C., ed. *Mary Chesnut's Civil War*. New Haven: Yale U P, 1981.

Vann Woodward, C. and Elizabeth Muhlenfeld, ed. *The Private Mary Chesnut: The Unpublished Civil War Diaries*. New York: Oxford U P, 1984.

Walker, Alice. *In Search of Our Mothers' Gardens: Womanist Prose*. New York: Harcourt Brace Jovanovitch, 1984.

Walker, Alice. *The Temple of My Familiar*. New York: Pocket, 1989.

Walter, Roland. "The Dialectics Between the Act of Writing and the Act of Reading in Alice Walker's *The Temple of My Familiar*, Gloria Naylor's *Mama Day* and Toni Morrison's *Jazz*." *The Southern Quarterly* 35.3 (Spring 1997), pp. 55-66.

Warhol, Robyn R. and Diane Price Herndl, ed. *Feminisms: An Anthology of Literary Theory and Criticism*. Rev. Ed. Houndmills, UK: Macmillan, 1997.

Warren, Robert Penn. *The Legacy of the Civil War: Meditations on the Centennial*. New York: Random, 1961.

Weaks, Mary Louise. "Three Women of Letters in the South: 1863-1913." *Mississippi Quarterly* 46.4 (Fall 1993): [617]-624.

White, Allon. *Carnival, Hysteria, Writing: Collected Essays and Autobiography*. Oxford: Clarendon P, 1993.

Whites, LeeAnn. "The Civil War as a Crisis in Gender." In Clinton and Silber. 3-21.
Whites, LeeAnn. *The Civil War as a Crisis in Gender: Augusta, Georgia, 1860-1890.* 1995. U of Georgia P, 2000.
Wiley, Bell Irvin. *Confederate Women.* New York: Barnes & Noble, 1975.
Williams, Patricia J. *The Alchemy of Race and Rights: Diary of a Law Professor.* Cambridge, Mass.: Harvard U P, 1991.
Willis, Susan. *Specifying: Black Women Writing the American Experience.* Madison: U of Wisconsin P, 1986.
Wilson, Edmund. *Patriotic Gore: Studies in the Literature of the American Civil War.* New York: Oxford U P, 1962.
Wisker, Gina, ed. *Black Women's Writing.* New York: St. Martin's, 1993.
Wolf, Janet. "On the Road Again: Metaphors of Travel in Cultural Criticism." *Cultural Studies* 7.2 (May 1993): 224-39.
Wolff, Sally. "Some Talk about Autobiography: An Interview with Eudora Welty." *The Southern Reader* 2.2 (Summer 1990): 58-62.
Woolf, Virginia. "Professions for Women." In Eagleton. 51-53.
Wright, Constance. *Fanny Kemble and the Lovely Land.* New York: Dodd, Mead, 1972.
Yaeger, Patricia. *Dirt and Desire: Reconstructing Southern Women's Writing, 1930-1990.* Chicago: U of Chicago P, 2000.

Photo Credits

Frances Anne Kemble: Library of Congress
Ella Gertrude Clanton Thomas: F. Michael Despeaux; photography A. James Lyday, Jr.
Sarah Katherine Stone: Department of Archives and Manuscripts, LSU
Mary Boykin Chesnut: Mrs. Hendrik B. van Rensslaer
Sarah Morgan Dawson: *A Confederate Girl's Diary*
Frances Butler Leigh: The Historical Society of Pennsylvania
Grace Elizabeth King: The Historic New Orleans Collection
Mamie Garvin Fields: *The Post and Courier*, Charleston
Alice Walker: Nan E. Park
Maya Angelou: Library of Congress
Ruth Moose: Ruth Moose